TEXAS WOMAN'S UNIVERSITY LIBRARY

D0849876

Date Due

287800

 Printed in U.S.A.

MODERN NOVEL WRITING and AZEMIA

Modern Novel Writing
(1796)

AND

Azemia
(1797)

BY

William Beckford

FACSIMILE REPRODUCTIONS

WITH AN INTRODUCTION

BY

Herman Mittle Levy, Jr.

Four Volumes in One

GAINESVILLE, FLORIDA

SCHOLARS' FACSIMILES & REPRINTS

1970

SCHOLARS' FACSIMILES & REPRINTS

1605 N.W. 14TH AVENUE

GAINESVILLE, FLORIDA, 32601, U.S.A.

HARRY R. WARFEL, GENERAL EDITOR

Modern Novel Writing is reproduced from a copy in and with the permission of The Houghton Library, Harvard University.

Azemia is reproduced from a copy in and with the permission of The Library of the Boston Athenaeum.

L. C. CATALOG CARD NUMBER: 74-81366

SBN 8201-1063-9

Manufactured in the U.S.A.

CONTENTS

TEXAS WOMAN'S UNIVERSITY
LIBRARY

INTRODUCTION

In 1796 and 1797 William Beckford published two anti-sentiment novels. These pseudonymous works, *Modern Novel Writing* and *Azemia,* express his antagonism for his step-sister, Mrs. Elizabeth Hervey, nee Marsh. There is no doubt that he came to dislike Mrs. Hervey and that she is a part of his target. Her novels, *Lousia* and *Melissa and Marcia,* are typical of the sentimental school and were published anonymously, as was the custom. If it were not for Beckford, these works would be justly forgotten. They are full of distressed maidens in "beautiful" landscapes, as are nearly all the sentimental works of the end of the Eighteenth century. It is the typicality of *Louisa* and not Mrs. Hervey's authorship of it which is important.

Had her novels been good, Beckford would certainly not have attacked her through them. However, Mrs. Hervey compares herself with Fanny Burney, modestly, and a little more favorably with Charlotte Smith, mentioning the *Recluse of the Lake.* Both these writers are superior to Mrs. Hervey, but this is not the point. It is the decline of the novel which these names signify that is the point. Beckford knew the novels of Defoe, Sterne, Fielding, and Richardson, and as the irony of his title *Modern Novel Writing* would indicate, he is pointing to the decline of the genre and warning the then moderns away from the school of sentiment, as well as the Gothic, because of its extensive use of overblown emotions.

vii

An omnivorous reader and collector of books, Beckford is here writing as an artist-critic who has recognized the novel as an art form. The end of the Eighteenth century produced no drama, and even narrative poetry was a contributor to the taste for novels. However, there were not enough Byrons to supply the readers. Furthermore, seeing that women like Mrs. Smith and Lady Hervey could gain audiences must have frightened Beckford into the belief that the novel would be much harmed, if not destroyed, by the growth of an audience with a taste for sentiment in the novel.

Modern Novel Writing demonstrates how shallow and stupid the sentimental vision of the world is, and most especially so when it is nothing but the hackneyed repetition of conventionalized plotlessness and conventionalized responses. In these terms *Modern Novel Writing* shows itself to be a writer's handbook of errors. Beckford was giving a list of don'ts for his contemporaries; and the work is still instructive today for the student of romantic and sentimental fiction, because it contains all the conventions of these kinds of writing. Today even the good practitioners of this kind of fiction are illuminated by Beckford's work. Jane Austen's manners and Emily Bronte's Gothicism derive from the school of sentiment. Fortunately, they guard against the excesses which were so offensive to Beckford: these include plots that have no purpose but the stringing of pearls of sentiment and the interpolating of pretty poetry, as well as the presentation of characters with no reality whatsoever, and all presented on stilts of dead language. *Modern Novel Writing* turns these weaknesses to good fun while castigating them, as the following example will show. A report tells Arabella, the heroine, of course, that her love, Henry Lambert, has been lost on the coast of Guinea and: "Arabella suffered a new and more terrible shock, which the lenient hand of time could hope to mollify. The original breaking of his collar bone, by the fall from his famous hunter, which had so alarmed the ladies in the park was no longer an object of material magnitude, but the execrable idea of those barbaric savages, and innumerable difficulties he might labor under, was indeed a stroke which required the utmost fortitude, and every religious consideration to combat and sustain. Neither the Colonel, nor Lady Maria, nor even the languishing Arabella herself had received any intelligence for many weeks, so that his gout not returning at its accustomed period, the old couple repaired to Bath, where a great number of distinguished foreigners were already assembled" (pp. 6-7). The diction of the school is present and scored in both books. *Azemia* has much the same tone as *Modern Novel Writing* and adds the plot of the damsel in distress to show the lack of originality at every level of sentimental fiction.

The theme of *Azemia* is the procrastinated rape of Richardson's *Pamela,* which is directly referred to as a possible protection for Azemia, "if she had only read it." Beckford's description of *Pamela* fits precisely the terms of the plot of *Azemia.* He says that *Pamela* is a book "shewing how damsels have been spirited off, and shut up by sundry evil-disposed gentlemen," and leaving nothing to conjecture, he goes on to add "-a circumstance which is hardly omitted in any novel since the confinement of Pamela at Mr. B-----'s house in Lincolnshire."

Modern Novel Writing and *Azemia* demonstrate that Beckford was aware of the flaws of the romantic and sentimental school of fiction and that it is his purpose to guide the writers of his time away from them in order to benefit the genre, and by no means merely to take revenge on Lady Hervey. She is a mere image of the amateurish lack of skill which was near to being accepted as art, to the great detriment of the novel — the only important new growth in literary history in his time.

HERMAN MITTLE LEVY, JR.

Loyola University
New Orleans, Louisiana

NOTES TO *AZEMIA*

In the copy of *Azemia* at the Boston Athenaeum are longhand notes indicating that the novel is a Roman à clef and identifying certain characters with known persons. The page number is followed by the line number; then the character and the identification in italics.

VOLUME I

21: 5   Swan of Lichfield: *Miss Seward*(?), *Miss Samson*(?).
141: 4   Mrs. Herbert: *afterwards called Chesterton.*
203:10   her: *Rebecca.*

VOLUME II

23: 4   lady: *Mrs. Piozzi.*
24: 7   Mr. Gallstone: *Dr. Johnson.*
26:13   Dr. Prose: *Q. if meant for Moore.*
33: 2   Quackly: *Montague.*
39:17   Duke: *of Leeds.*
40: 4   Blow-up: *Andrews.*
43:10   All in: *Vide Miss Historia's Sir Glidad* (?) *of the Bower.*
61: 2   Mrs. Chiverly: *Q. if meant for Mrs. Crispigni of Camberwale.*
83 fn.   Lady H. . .: *Hawke.*
90:16   *Vide Mrs. Barbauld's Sir Bertram.*
128: 1   figure: *Pratt.*

Modern Novel Writing,

OR THE

ELEGANT ENTHUSIAST;

AND

Interesting Emotions

OF

Arabella Bloomville.

A RHAPSODICAL ROMANCE;

INTERSPERSED WITH

Poetry.

IN TWO VOLUMES.

Vol. I.

BY THE RIGHT HON.

LADY HARRIET MARLOW.

I nod in company, I wake at night,
Fools rush into my head, and so I write.

Pope.

London:

PRINTED FOR G. G. AND J. ROBINSON.

MDCCXCVI.

DEDICATION.

To her Grace the Duchess of——,

MADAM,

ALTHOUGH the captivating diffidence of your Grace's noble mind forbids me to prefix your name to this dedication, yet when I affirm that to all the exterior charms of person, and a loveliness beyond compare, you add the most engaging and condescending manners, joined to the extreme of every human virtue, it will be impossible that you should remain concealed:—no, Madam, the observant and adoring public will instantly discover my enchanting Friend and Patroness, whose greatness of soul cannot brook even the idea of flattery, but whose characteristic it is to

' Do good by stealth, and blush to find it fame.'

As it has been entirely owing to the fostering smiles of your Grace's approbation,

ii

that this little work presumes to shew itself to the world, so I am emboldened to hope that the enlightened reader will not find it totally destitute of merit. I have, indeed, endeavoured to unite correct, delicate, and vivid imagery to an animated moral sensibility, and at the same time to enrich it by various incident, lively sallies, fashionable intrigue, picturesque description, and, in fine, to mark it with the striking features of a bold originality, without which, no daughter of the Muses can ever expect to produce that phœnix of literary zoology—a perfect novel.

I have the honor and happiness to be,

Madam,

Your Grace's most obliged,

Most obedient, most devoted

And most affectionate humble servant,

HARRIET MARLOW.

HYACINTH LODGE,
March 31, 1796.

CONTENTS.

Vol. 1.

CONTENTS.

ERRATA.

Vol. 1.

ELEGANT ENTHUSIAST.

Chapter 1.

A RURAL PICTURE.

AT the foot of a verdant declivity overshadowed by woodbine, jesfamine and myrtle, and softly inundated by a sapphire rivulet that wandered through the neighbouring woods in serpentine simplicity, stood the sweet and elegant retired cottage of Arabella Bloomville. A majestic grove of aged oaks nodded in awful and

B　　　　　　sublime

2

sublime splendor on one side, while abrupt and fantastic rocks added dignity to the scene on the other. Here in spring was heard the mellifluous chorus of the goldfinch, the throstle, the linnet, the blackbird, the cuckoo, and the woodlark, nor was the melancholy bird of evening silent when the sun hid himself behind the western horizon. It was then that the pensive and matchless Arabella indulged her tender grief, and softly answered with her sighs to the pathetic melody of the feathered songstress. O enviable state of retired competence, how widely different from the turbulent occupations of exalted life, where vanity and factitious joys corrode the heart, and robbing it of its

native

3

native captivation, leave us nothing but a blank !

Here the lovely girl would sit for hours with her blushing cheek pressed upon her lily hand, ruminating on the various disasters of her undirected youth, so young, and so unhappy! and here also the cherished miniature of her beloved absent Henry would prey upon her feelings.

   ' She sat, like patience on a monument
   ' Smiling at grief.'*

Her dear and valuable parents in the grave, alas! the amiable orphan thus left to her own sad reflection in the very blossom of her days, without a

   * Shakespeare.

B 2　　　　　　friend

friend into whofe bofom fhe could pour her defolating woe; except the faithful Margaret Grimes, who had been the companion of her earlieft infancy, and who had attended her through every viciffitude of her un-common deftiny. Arabella was but in the firft fpring of life, feventeen fummers only had bleached her fnowy bofom, yet the fatal experience of evil had more than doubled her years; what breaft but muft fympathize with fuch fuffering excellence?

Let thofe feel now, who never felt before,
Let thofe who always felt, now feel the more.

Here for a moment let us drop the veil of oblivion on fo deeply interreft-ing a contemplation.

Chapter

Chapter 2.

A STORM AT SEA.

HENRY Lambert, was the only fon of Colonel and Lady Maria Lambert, his Father had fat feveral feffions in the Britifh Parliament with the moft exemplary and noble incorruptibility. Now though a rich grandmother on the maternal fide was but juft returned from Canada when the Newmarket races began, yet the ancient country feat had been completely repaired upon the occafion, and the captivating diverfion of the chafe frequently af-forded them the happieft relaxation.

Henry was now in the twenty-fourth

B 3   year

year of his age, and had already ferved three campaigns with unfufpected honor, when it fo fell out, that the fhip meeting with a moft tremendous gale on the coaft of Guinea about two months after his firft journey to Ma-drid, the finer feelings of the celef-tial Arabella fuffered a new and more terrible fhock, which the lenient hand of time could alone hope to mollify. The original breaking of his collar bone, by the fall from his famous hunter, which had once fo cruelly alarmed the ladies in the park, was no longer an object of material mag-nitude, but the execrable idea of thofe barbarous favages, and the in-numerable difficulties he might labor under, was indeed a ftroke which required

required the utmoft fortitude, and every religious confideration to com-bat and fuftain. Neither the Colonel, nor Lady Maria, nor even the lan-guifhing Arabella herfelf had received any intelligence for many weeks, fo that his gout not returning at its ac-cuftomed period, the old couple re-paired to Bath, where a great number of diftinguifhed foreigners were al-ready affembled.

The houfe however they had hired on the foreft was fo completely out of repair, that the diftant bells from the village had a peculiar pathos, when the benighted traveller repofed himfelf in the hawthorn grove. This could not be prevented, by the ufual

B 4   operation

8

operation of forefight, nor did the howling of the yard dog, during the tempeft, in any manner decreafe the general perturbation. Lady Maria indeed who flept in the attic ftory firft caught the alarm, and rufhing through the flames, defcended by a back ftair-cafe into the garden. The clock ftruck ONE at the moment, and the awful folemnity of the fcene was horribly impreffive. Yet but a little while before fhe might have collected herfelf with propriety, even though the danger had been ten times more imminent, for in all active emergency, nature is prone to fubfide, and yield the palm to the confiftency of power. The expected vifitors not coming the next day, rendered the fituation of Lady

9

Lady Maria ftill more perplexing, becaufe fhe had promifed the Duchefs and the Mifs Pebleys to meet them at the rooms that very evening.

There is no rank in life exempt from misfortunes, and even the happieft of mortals have but too much reafon to complain: from his internal refources Man can alone hope to triumph in the hour of trial.

Well, all intercourfe for the time was neceffarily broken off, and Arabella's picture, painted by the immortal Weft, which hung in the grand faloon, having fuffered the moft material injury, it was thought advifeable to wait the refult of their

B 5 laft

10

laft difpatches, and not further improve the grounds till the enfuing fpring; for as the colonel was far advanced in years, and Henry's tafte had not been confulted in the affair, it was difficult to afcertain how long it might be before the wifhed-for union of the young people could take place. This reflection too often embittered the vernal hours of the blooming Arabella, and thus impreffed with melancholy ideas, her active mind would frequently call aid from the tender mufe to diffipate her chagrin. The following fweet lines may give a fpecimen of her exquifite poetical powers.

11

Sonnet.

WHEN forrow's humbleft haunts reflect the beam
That patient virtue fcatters o'er the plain,
No wanton zephyr curls the languid ftream,
No melting woodlark wakes the warbled ftrain.

For me, alas! befet with ftorms of woe,
Where plaintive ecchoes die upon the gale,
May the ftill voice of agony beftow,
The fofteft requiem to the ruftic vale.

O! my lov'd Henry! fhouldft thou ever hear
How feebly flows the meditated lay,
While the pale moonfhine gilds the checquer'd
        fphere;
Thou might'ft again the diftant theme difplay,
Might'ft drop th' appropriate plaudit of a tear,
And whifper fweetnefs to the charms of May.

12

By amufements fuch as thefe, would the divine Arabella beguile the threatning difficulties, for the youthful mind is almoft always amiable, while hoary time hardens the heart, alas! two often with the mufcular anatomy. As there was great reafon to fuppofe that the fyftem of ethics they had ftrenuoufly adopted was in faft defeftive, fo, Lady Maria, by the advice of the Duchefs, prevailed upon the Colonel to leave London without lofs of time, for no veffel could arrive after the monfoons were 'fet in. Having paffed a week in their paffage with Sir George Darlington, and gone through the vexatious ceremony of a regular prefentation, they fortunately arrived at

13

at the afylum of their hopes, when the fragrant dews of evening were on every fide arifing from the furrounding lakes.

Chapter

15

Chapter 3.

A TERRIBLE ENCOUNTER.

DURING the fiege, Henry Lambert particularly diftinguifhed himfelf by that prevailing fuavity which operates beyond the fhafts of courage, or even the prevalence of defpair. Now the commanding Officer's horfe having been killed under him, the whole plan of the attack was immediately changed. and indeed it became every hour more neceffary, for vegetables were uncommonly fcarce, and what was ftill worfe, no letters had arrived from England. It was therefore properly decided by the

the military council, that the theatres ſhould be cloſed during the remainder of the week; nor need this be much wondered at, for the commoneſt candles were three and ſixpence each, and there really was not a ſingle wheelwright to be found in the whole vicinity.

Henry, therefore, whoſe mind was half diſtracted by a variety of occurrences, leaped haſtily into his phaeton and four, and purſued his journey with the higheſt animation. The Old Woman, whoſe early influence might have demanded a more permanent attention in the preſent inſtance, had conjured him to ſtay, with tears in her eyes, but his military duty

duty got the better of all ſelfiſh conſiderations, while the fond remembrance of his adorable Arabella preſſed cloſely to his heart, and occupied all his ſenſes.

The moon now ſcattered her virgin tints over an unclouded hemiſphere, when he reached the ſea ſhore, but the baggage waggon had been gone above an hour, and as the mountain was inacceſſible in conſequence of the immenſe fall of ſnow, he determined to poſtpone his project till the morrow, when he might look for the arrival of his friends Ferguſſon, and Jennings to aſſiſt him in the undertaking.

It

It was not however eaſy under ſuch circumſtances, to approach the farm houſe, for the walls were covered with ivy, and many of the elms had been blown down at the preceding aſſizes; beſides, the Biſhop and Sir George Walker had abſolutely forbidden any perſon to kill game in that neighbourhood. The gallant Henry was entirely at a loſs what to do in ſo critical an emergency, when calling to mind his early attachment, and ſubſequent promiſe to the divine Arabella, at the ſame time recollecting all the diſaſters he had ſuffered on her account, he heaved a gentle but heart-rending ſigh, and beckoning to his ſervant, who was half petrified with fear, haſtily ſeized his piſtols.

The

The Bear was within ten yards of him, when the ſhot miſſed, ſo that if his foot had not ſtruck againſt the jutting root of an old oak which in ſome degree broke his fall, he, in all probability, would have periſhed. There was now no alternative, for the ſhepherd's boy who had been preſent at the outſet of the conflict, was unable to get round the garden in time, and the ice ſuddenly gave way, therefore had not Henry at the ſame moment ſprung forward, with the utmoſt activity, the Bear muſt inevitably have eſcaped.

The farmer, whoſe gratitude knew no bounds for the ſignal ſervice which Henry had thus rendered him, entreated

entreated the young foldier to partake of his frugal board, and the beautiful Marianne who gazed upon him with ineffable delight, added infinitely to his delicate embarraffment. Now it happened that an owl had deftroyed all the pigeons, and there was no market on a Saturday, notwithftanding which, Henry flept more ferenely on his humble pallet, than perhaps the moft luxurious nobleman on his bed of down. The vifionary image of his celeftial Arabella enriched his flumbers with fancy's fairy train. O! had the miftrefs of his foul been witnefs to all thofe mental agitations, which originate in true love, yet which her own tender fenfations had fufficiently inculcated, the reftlefs doubts that

that harrafs the fubjugated fpirit, would have given way to the moft unbounded confidence; but the real event of things is never known till, perhaps, the remedy is inapplicable, as Mr. Chapman would often tell Henry in their moments of relaxation. But then the latter feldom failed to exclaim — " You cannot ' conceive the perfection of my Ara- ' bella, fhe is the Paphian queen ' in all her glory,'

' Grace is in all her fleps, Heav'n in her eye,
' In all her geftures dignity and love.'

MILTON.

Chapter

Chapter 4.

A POLITE CIRCLE.

THE fudden appearance of the Bear had produced great anxiety in the minds of the three women in the cart, but the Curate was by no means to blame, for he had not been a fifhing before for fix months, and was totally ignorant of the matter. Lord Giblet had indeed promifed him a pointer if the parliament fhould be diffolved before the froft fet in, but the light dragoons who were quartered in the next village, had abfolutely fold their library by public auction. This naturally occafioned much deep inveftigation, investigation, in the polite circle which the Colonel and Lady Maria Lambert joined, at the magnificent castle of Sir George Darlington. This castle was situated on a rising eminence, with a beautiful command of the adjacent prospect, where verdant meadows and fallow lands, upon either bank of a rapid navigable river delighted the roving eye. Cattle of every kind there cropped their green delicious banquet, and there the placid sheep by their innocent bleatings gently aroused the plaintive ecchoes of the circumambient groves. ‘ My ‘ charming Lucinda,’ said the Countess of Fairville, as she lightly took up a bit of muffin with her taper fingers, ‘ My dear girl I fear there is some ‘ latent

‘ latent cause that preys upon your ‘ vernal prime, and casts this fatal ‘ gloom over your naturally gay ‘ spirits.’ A lucid drop quivered upon the eyelid of Lucinda, she could not speak, but letting fall her teacup upon the floor, tenderly exclaimed, ‘ O madam, your ladyship's atten- ‘ tion and affecting kindness oppress ‘ me still more than even the seve- ‘ rity of my fate, alas! your ladyship ‘ is too good, indeed you are all per- ‘ fection.’ Having uttered these words, she fainted, but Miss Perkins running with a bottle of salts, and Dr. Philbert softly chafing her temples, she by degrees recovered her wonted serenity of aspect, and cast a languishing look of pathetic meaning towards the

C   Countess

Countess, whose charming cheeks were already bathed in tears. To the amazement of all present, at this instant, upstarted Lord Mahogany, and with a frown declared, that the prevalence of sedition was become abominable, especially in this happy country where the poor are equally protected with the rich, and which enjoys the most perfect constitution that the wisdom of man could invent, which is as incorruptible in its principle as generally beneficial in its practice. Having uttered this with an indignant tone of rage, he overturned the silver tea urn on Lucy Melville's favorite lapdog, which Major Pemberton had brought her from the East Indies, and

and to which she was attached with perhaps an improper, yet enthusiastic fondness.

The maid servant who had been sent up stairs for the Castle of Otranto, met Matthew the butler on the landing place, and being in the secret of Lucinda's perturbation, asked him rather petulantly, whether Jim the groom had sent the parson the potatoes. As lady Di Martin came out of the parlour, she eagerly enquired if the Letters were come in, which very much tended to confirm Matthew's suspicion, for as Captain Warley and his three sisters were expected to dinner, it gave a scope to the discussion. In the mean time Lord

C 2   Mahogany

Mahogany, though one of the best chefs players in Europe could not find his *spencer*, and as the key of the hall door had been left in the green-house, by Peggy Tomlinson the housemaid, so it was absolutely impossible to get the chaise ready in time. The confusion therefore was great in every part of that venerable mansion, yet the hapless Lucinda, profiting of the occasion, suffered herself to be led quietly to her chamber by the compassionating Countess; then throwing herself upon a chintz sopha she gave vent to the most lamentable accents of anguish and despair. Had the sentinel kept his word, perhaps nothing of the kind would have happened, for Lord Mahogany's first

first wife was a cheesemonger's daughter, and his eldest child had been born with a hare lip; this therefore was the only circumstance that could so materially have offended him. A vindictive mind, it must be owned, is a scourge to the possessor, for one of the greatest virtues is, that a man should learn to subdue his passions.

At dinner the Earl gave way to his usual merriment, and rallied Sukey Sanders upon her mistaken attachment, but unfortunately the venison was over roasted, and the youngest Miss Warley having swallowed a pin, Henry's letter which that moment arrived, was thrown into the fire by mistake. Now as the Mayor's ball

C 3   had

had been the night before, and as the High Sheriff was gone to London, so the absence of Colonel Lambert and his Lady was doubly unfortunate.

How to remedy this inconvenience occupied the thoughts of Lord Mahogany during the whole night, though he had sent to Arabella but the week before, for a pot of tamarinds, and who, but for this fatal catastrophe, might have gained some intelligence of her valuable and beloved Henry. But alas! in the pesent instance, poor Margaret Grimes was obliged to return home without the shadow of a consolation, and to acquaint her agitated lady, that her every hope was abortive in the extreme.

Chapter

Chapter 5.

DESCRIPTION OF A BEAUTY.

ARABELLA, as has been observed, had now attained her seventeenth year : her form was the animated portrait of her mind; truth, benignity, pure and unstudied delicacy, the meekness of sensibility, and the dignity of innate virtue, claimed the esteem, while the exquisite beauty of her bewitching countenance captivated the heart of every beholder! She was tall, and finely proportioned; her complexion was neither the insipid whiteness of the lily-bosomed Circassian, nor the

C 4   the

32

the mafculine fhade of the Gallic
brunette; the frefhnefs of health
glowed upon her cheek, while the
luftre of her dark blue eyes borrowed
its fplendor from the unfullied flame,
that gave her mind the perfection of
intellect! Her hair which fell over
her fhoulders in copious ringlets,
was of the moft beautiful brown,
rather inclining to the auburn, and
her teeth and lips,

    ' Were pearls within a ruby cafe.'

Her bofom was the throne of love,
full, firm, and fairer than the pureft
ivory; her voice was mild as the
cooings of the ring-dove; and her
fmile the gentle harbinger of tendernefs

33

dernefs and complacency! She had
alfo acquired confiderable eminence
in the fcience of harmony: her finging was the feraphic eccho of her
lute, whofe chords fpoke to the
foul, under the magic touch of her
fkilful fingers. She had all that animation which is more ufually found
among the natives of the South of
Europe; yet this fpirited expreffion
often melted into foftnefs fo infinuating, that it was difficult to fay
whether penfive tendernefs or fparkling vivacity was the moft predo-
minant: in fhort fhe was every thing
that fancy could picture or con-
viction adore! Perfection could go
no further. Her arms were of a
delicate fnowy whitenefs, and caft in

C 5   the

34

the moft exquifite mould of tapering
formation, and her little feet were
fo enchantingly pretty, that they
ravifhed all beholders. Such was
Arabella.

Henry Lambert, the dear object
of her unalterable affections, was
equally engaging in his perfon for
a man, as fhe was for a female. He
was fix feet two inches in height,
and his form was the moft elegant
that can be conceived, but his face
furpaffed all defcription, fuch fenfibility marked every feature! his
eyes fparkling with native vivacity,
were of a bright hazle, his nofe was
inclined to the Grecian, he had the
moft beautiful mouth and teeth ever
beheld,

35

beheld, with uncommonly fine dark
hair, and beautifully fpreading whifkers, the whole heightened by a
complexion fair as alabafter;

    ' Ah! fure a pair was never feen,
      ' So juftly form'd to meet, by nature,
    ' The youth excelling fo in mien,
      ' The maid in ev'ry grace of feature.'

Chapter

Chapter 6.

FRESH EMBARRASSMENTS.

FATE seemed to have interwove in the same loom the destinies of Arabella Bloomville and Lucinda Howard, and the touching sensibilities were equally appropriate to either. The wanderings of fancy and the ebullitions of the imagination may indeed awhile mislead the most amiable, but consistent virtue can neither be shaken nor controuled. The gay flowers of hope cannot long stem the current of adversity, which in its rapid endeavours spreads a dragon wing over every ray of human

human comfort. Arabella thus separated from her Lucinda, had no resource but in the soothing melodies of her piano forte, on which she played with bewitching delicacy,

    ' Her flying fingers touch'd the keys,
    ' And heavenly joys inspired.'

Nor did the worthy Mr. Bangrove, curate of the little flock amongst which she lived, ever deviate from those principles which reconcile us to the losses of this life, and lead us throught a dreary wilderness of earthly turmoil, to a flowery paradise of hope.

It was in one of those delicious nights,

nights, when the heavens are bespangled with stars, and tranquil silence sits brooding over the autumnal plain, that Sir Peter Simpson's elegant gig drove by her open window ; the lonely owl sung a horrid dirge to the murmuring stream that meandered by the side of the road over which it passed, though the worthy Baronet himself seemed deeply absorbed in the propriety of a general inclosure of waste lands. Now Margaret Grimes, having but just gathered the misletoe, could not give the wondering Arabella any further means of unravelling the clue, for the patient villagers were for the most part retired to their placid rest, and unfortunately the mail coach had neither brought

brought the oyfters, nor the French dictionary.

This occafioned a more material embarraffment, and threw a new light upon the fubject, for if Lieutenant Jenkinfon had really quitted his lodgings in Dover Street, and the muflins had not arrived, it was abfolutely impoffible for either of them by the utmoft ftretch of their ingenuity to folve the enigma. It was certain that the county juftices had dined together the preceding Friday, and that the militia was fpeedily to be embodied; but in the interim the right wing of the old manfion might be taken down, and the profpect from the high ground rendered much more interefting,

interefting: now in that cafe it muft be difficult for the beauteous Arabella to divine how far her fondeft wifhes could expect ever to be realized. Under this impreffion of fufpence and anxiety, Arabella flew for refuge to her harp, which had the power of confolation in all emergencies. She then fweetly fung the following delicious air, accompanied by the filver melody of the inftrument:

Song.

Love is a foft, involuntary flame,
   Beyond the pow'r of language to exprefs;
That throws refiftlefs magic o'er the frame,
   And leads to boundlefs pleafure or diftrefs.

From

From love misfortune takes her earlieft date,
   Or rapt'rous blifs prepares the flow'ry way;
Wak'd at our birth, they mingle with our fate,
   And cling to life, till vanquifh'd by decay.

E'en when in youth we feel the hand of death
Obfcure the profpect of a cloudlefs fky.
All conqu'ring love attends the fleeting breath,
   And Nature's fond, laft effort, is a figh.

Then tell me, Henry! what avail the cares
   That taint our joys with bitternefs and pain?
If to our aid the god of love repairs,
   And Henry fmiles, misfortunes frown in vain.

Having finifhed her fong, fhe wiped a cryftal tear from her glittering eye, and again betook herfelf to reflection. Perfons, alas! can eafily judge the conduct of others, where themfelves are not compromifed, but to preferve the

the true medium under every difadvantage, is, and muft ever be, a moft difficult endeavour. Not but that there are diftinguifhed perfonages in high life who draw different conclufions, and form their mode of conduct on a more extenfive fyftem: but the greateft allowance muft furely be made for an unfortunate young woman launched into life without a compafs or a guide. Nothing peculiarly interefting happened the fucceeding day, but about eleven at night, the belfry took fire, and nobody could pafs the ferry on account of Mrs. Pendigrafs's lying in, for the London Doctor had gone by miftake to Banbury, and bought all the beft pictures before

before Lord Damplin's agent could get there.

The hunting season being now pretty generally at an end, except upon the lakes, which were innavigable, and amongst the smaller hamlets, so the best part of Sir George Mumford's grounds were entirely overflowed. The gardiner certainly was not to blame in the affair, for his wife had absolutely consented to the marriage of her youngest daughter, and had the carpenter himself acted an honourable part, every article might have been happily arranged; but Miss Sanders's intrigue coming to light at the very moment, not a human being in the neighbourhood thought

thought proper to interfere. In consequence of this succession of untoward circumstances, the probability of Henry's speedy return was fainter than heretofore, and the charming Arabella found no longer any comfort in tending her little family of flowers, but renouncing every species of active amusement, entirely devoted herself to the study of the *Belles Lettres*. In this, by degrees she succeeded wonderfully, and gave some light productions to the public, that discovered an animated genius and a liberal mind, and being totally free from vanity, prejudice or affectation, were particularly admired by the celebrated Miss Maria Helen, who is so justly celebrated throughout Europe

rope for the impartiality of her writings, and her *rational* love of liberty. As for the melancholy Arabella she embraced the only opportunity that offered itself to obtain a momentary tranquility, or occasionally to dissipate her chagrin.

Chapter

Chapter 7.

THE DISCOVERY OF A STRANGER.

GENERAL Barton had a noble mansion at but a little distance from the humble abode of the mellifluous Arabella: and being rather of a choleric disposition, would oftentimes indulge himself in a free use of wine. As he was an excellent player at billiards, and had in the early part of life visited most of the courts upon the Continent, he could never be brought to adopt the fashionable mode of improving his extensive premises. Not however being particularly fond of field sports, but in fact almost

48

almoſt a martyr to a violent bilious-diſorder, his houſe was conſtantly frequented by a number of rakiſh companions. As ſitting penſively under a weeping willow by the ſide of a purling ſtream was a favorite occupation of the amiable Lucinda Howard as well as of Arabella, ſo General Barton would ſometimes ſaunter in the hayfields during the Turtle ſeaſon, and amuſe himſelf by ſinging the following lively air, which had in conſequence become extremely popular in the country :

Air.

Ye Gods diſperſe
This painful verſe,
By ſome wild whirlwind thro' the ſkies !

Left

49

Left in amaze-
Ment at my lays,
The folks my folly ſhould deſpiſe.

Then chip the bread, and lay the cloth,
Nor will we differ while we dine ;
Dear Phillis! I have got ſome broth,
Some parſley, bacon, beans, and wine.

Nay ſtart no, ſweet maiden! at what I require,
The gridiron is hiſſing e'en now on the fire,
And whatever you fancy for filling your belly,
You ſhall have, tho' a Griffin, in ſavory jelly.

The General indeed did not ſo much indulge his comic vein in this manner, with a view to promote his intereſt in the county, as to learn what merchants ſettled in that quarter were moſt famous for their breed of horſes.

D   Now

50

Now had he but poſſeſſed a mule of his own, or had lived in any intimacy with a biſcuit baker, he would probably have eſcaped many inconveniencies, to which his natural impetuoſity rendered him liable. Be this as it may, Arabella abſolutely deſpaired of ever again ſeeing her Henry, whom ſhe was now but too fatally convinced that ſhe loved with an ardent and unalterable affection. And ſurely he well merited this faithful teſtimony at her hands, for it muſt be owned, that the arrows of true paſſion, when ſharpened by the ſceptre of diſappointment, envelope the heart with a weight of woe, and forcibly obumbrate the fineſt feelings of the ſoul. Animated

by

51

by theſe obſervations which flowed naturally from her peculiarly intereſting ſituation, Arabella wandered beyond the uſual boundaries of her little domain, till near a ſmall copſe of Aſpin and Poplar trees, ſhe met at the cloſe of day a moſt ſtrikingly beauteous Lady, who ſeemed a victim to the utmoſt deſolation and deſpair, and who ſoon made the melting Arabella forget her own proper ſorrows in the tenderer emotions of a ſympathetic nervous ſenſibility. As ſhe gazed on the melancholy Lady, ſhe was charmed by hearing her ſing in a pathetic tone the ſubſequent faſcinating ſonnet,

D 2   O gentle

O gentle gale ! could I thy flight arreſt,
Thou ſoft companion of the midnight hour !
I'd bid thee cheer with thy refreſhing pow'r,
My abſent love, and die upon his breaſt.

Sweet plaintive bird that now forſak'ſt thy neſt !
Mild Queen of Night that now aloft doſt tow'r !
His be the ſong, and his the moonlight bow'r,
No more, alas ! can I with thoſe be bleſt.

Ah ! once-loved objeſts which to joy invite !
For me you ſhed your ſoothing charms in vain,
While that fine form no more enchants my ſight,
My lyre I tune, but mournful is the ſtrain :
All that to other breaſts imparts delight
Can only bring to me increaſe of pain !

As the fair ſtranger cloſed her
melody, the village clock ſtruck
nine, and the ſolitary bat began his
veſpers ; Arabella therefore flew to
her

her aſſiſtance, and though Margaret
Grimes had ſcarcely time to put on
a ſilk gown, before the Conſtable
had actually apprehended three
poachers, and diſcovered Betſy
Blanket and her Sweet-heart in the
lane, yet Arabella ſeizing time by
the forelock, led her new acquaintance to the woodbine bower, which
amorous innocence had wove for
contemplation and repoſe.

The London waggon had but juſt
gone by, and the accuſtomed for-
malities paſſed between this exquiſite
pair of enchanting beauties, when
Arabella prepared to liſten with an
engaging and compaſſionate attention
to the ſweet Lady's narrative, who,

D 3   animated

animated by the generous pity of her
friend, took out a red Morocco
pocket book, filled with vine leaves
and violets ; then collecting all her
fortitude, and throwing away her ink-
horn, ſhe began as follows in the next
chapter.

Chapter

Chapter 8.

THE FAIR STRANGER'S STORY.

' MY father was the youngeſt ſon
of Lord Danton an Iriſh Baron, and
happening to fall in love with the
only daughter of Viſcount Roſebud,
he married her againſt the inclination
of the friends of both parties. As
Lucy my valuable mother was in conſequence rejected by her family, and
as my father's pecuniary reſources
were at a low ebb, ſo they thought it
adviſeable to retire to Liſbon with the
little modicum they could now call
their own. There my honoured father entered into the wine trade, but

D 4   meeting

meeting with confiderable loffes in bufinefs, he died in lefs than four years of a broken heart, leaving his difconfolate widow, with the little Amelia, which is myfelf, the only remaining pledge of their affection. My excellent mamma now formed a plan of life conformable to her narrow circumftances, devoting all her time to my education, and to the improvement of my perfonal charms. The numberlefs flatterers with whom my inexperienced youth was furrounded, have told me that fhe fucceeded in both endeavours even beyond her moft ardent expectations.

' However this might have been, I grew taller and more blooming every

every day, till the fame of my beauty excited the attention of the principal nobility at Lifbon. I fpeak only of the male part, for it muft be owned our fex is very envious, and the Portuguefe ladies do certainly not afford an exception to the general rule.

' Don Pedro de Gonzales, a young Spanifh grandee of the firft clafs, and who was as eftimable for the virtues of his heart, as he was diftinguifhed by the incomparable elegance of his perfon, foon profeffed himfelf my moft vehement adorer. His refidence at Lifbon being at the hotel of a Dutch merchant, Mynheer Van Woolengen, which was near

D 5   our

our habitation, and as the faid merchant had married an Englifh lady at the Brazils, Don Pedro had but too frequent opportunities to plead his tender pain to me; I, who was young, lively, handfome, animated and ingenuous, being then only in my fixteenth year, liftened perhaps too willingly to his amorous tale, but on fuch occafions, furely a proper inveftigation of caufes and effects might tend to do away thofe harfh impreffions which malice, and hard-heartednefs too readily imbibe.

' Now there was a Duchefs de Guides who had contracted a clofe intimacy with my mamma, and who had been married much againft her inclination

inclination to a man old enough to be her grandfather. The Duchefs had a daughter Adeline de Guides, whom fhe cherifhed with true maternal care, but whofe difpofition was rather too violent, and indeed I may fay ferocious.

' This young lady had been brought up in a convent, and was, as you may fuppofe, completely bigotted to the ignorant fuperftition of her country, yet having encouraged a fatal paffion for the young Count Velafquez, who was alfo amongft the number of my lovers, it gave birth to many cruel dangers which afterwards threatened me, as you will fee by the fequel.

D 6   ' Don

' Don Pedro had formed a strict friendship with the Baron de Plombal, who, you must know, was a near relation of Count Velasquez, had resided in England for several years, and spoke the language of the country in its greatest purity. He had also much distinguished himself in the Republic of Letters. I should however previously have mentioned, that an English woman of distinction, Lady Anna Maria Delville arrived at Lisbon from Falmouth, after a very bad passage of fourteen days. Her ladyship had been sent thither by order of the faculty, as her malady was supposed to be a decline or rather a galloping consumption. In the same packet that brought her ladyship, came

came Captain O'Donnel, an Irish officer, of most extraordinary beauty, and whose mind was eminently honourable and enlightened. He had distinguished himself in several duels by his bravery and moderation, which very much interested us all in his favor, for we women, you know my dear madam, are always strenuous admirers of courage in a man; nor is this to be wondered at when we consider that woman, being the weaker vessel, stands in need of protection.

' It should seem, by the bye, that Captain O'Donnel's mother had been a Portuguese lady of some rank, on which account the charming fellow found no difficulty in introducing himself

self to the Marquis de Suza, a minister of state, and who was his distant relation. All the best company of Lisbon resorted to the house of this Marquis, and amongst other persons of high fashion, the much admired Donna Isabella Cordova, a young widow of infinite attraction, but rather more famed for her gallantries than either for her virtue or benevolence.

' But I should have told you beforehand, that for sometime past my dear mother's health had been very precarious, and seemed to threaten her with approaching dissolution, so that she determined at all events to return home to her native land,

land, that she might resign her existence amongst the few friends, of whom the withering blasts of adversity had not totally deprived her."

As the fair Stranger now perceived Arabella's liquid sorrows to flow apace down her lovely cheeks, she paused---and as the evening mists were rolling gradually over the side of the neighbouring hills, and thick damps were arising from the adjoining lake, Arabella led her melancholy associate to her neat but humble cottage, where the attentive Margaret Grimes soon presented them with toast and butter, eggs, tea, cake, and other elegant refreshments.

Chapter

65

Chapter 9.

CONTINUATION OF THE FAIR
STRANGER'S STORY.

WHEN the two ladies had finished their temperate repast, the unfortunate Amelia thus proceeded: ' I informed you, Madam, that my only parent was from sickness gradually descending to the tomb, and that in consequence we were hastening our departure from Lisbon. This fatal conjuncture, which in all probability, would separate me for ever from the sole master of my heart, the excellent Don Pedro, overwhelmed him also with despair, and forced us to adopt

66

adopt the rash measure of a private marriage. You must know that one of Don Pedro's family was a Benedictine Friar, and resided in a convent at a small distance from the metropolis, in perhaps one of the most delicious situations upon earth, for it stood immediately upon the banks of the Tagus. The name of this venerable Monk, was Father Laurence, yet he had in the spring of life been an officer of established bravery, and was now equally celebrated for meek resignation and unaffected piety. The superior however of this religious society, it must be observed, was an inquisitor of the holy office, and generally reputed a man of a most sanguinary disposition. I should

67

I should not have touched upon his character, but that he had a nephew who was a major in the Portuguese service, who had travelled into China a few years before, and had since married a Spanish Lady, who was desperately in love with my Don Pedro. Now Don Pedro was himself of a frank and open nature, but rather too apt to place confidence in such persons as, under the hypocritical veil of sanctity, hide vices of a scarlet dye. Suffice it to say, that the nuptial ceremony was performed in the chapel belonging to the aforementioned convent, in presence of Mrs. Jemina Johnson an English shopkeeper, Mr. George Adamson, cornfactor, and Don Lopez de Ximenes.

menes. I cannot here pafs over a circumstance of the moft extraordinary import, for about two hours after the ceremony was performed, and I had returned home to my mother, to prevent whofe fufpicions, I was forced to trump up fome ftory or other, which I have now forgot; it fo happened that a famous Englifh phyfician, a Doctor Lambton, arrived in the city, and had brought with him the moft beautiful Newfoundland dog that ever I fet eyes on in the whole courfe of my life. This worthy man hearing of my mother's ill ftate of health, thought it in fome degree his duty to pay a vifit to her, and offer her his advice. Now he was a very grofs fat man in his perfon, and had a way

a way of fquinting which rendered him highly ridiculous in my eyes, fo that I had much difficulty to keep my countenance while he was prefent, notwithftanding the perplexing predicament in which I ftood. It came out from fome part of his converfation that he was a Chefhire man, and an intimate friend of Sir Simon Delves, with whom my poor father had fought a duel in his early youth. The particulars my beloved mamma did not think proper to explain, though I have fince difcovered that a Lord Newton had been the chief inftigator of the affair. But not to digrefs, or trefpafs, my dear Madam, upon your patience, the next morning at fix o'clock, and without my having had

had any previous notice, we embarked on board the Minerva packet, Captain Peter Smith, and failed with a fair wind for Falmouth.

‘ I had only been able to fee my adored Don Pedro for five minutes, fince we were united at the altar; but you may judge from the following verfes which he flipped into my hand at our laft interview, how cruel and heart-rending were the pangs of our feparation. The lines were originally written in Spanifh, but I have tranflated them at my leifure, being perfect miftrefs of that enchanting language.'

VERSES WRITTEN BY DON PEDRO

How foft are the notes of the fpring !
   What fragrance exhales from the grove !
Ye birds, taught by you, I would fing,
   And here I for ever could rove.

Tho' its bottom is clear, yet the rill
   Delights from the rock to defcend ;
So I, from Ambition's fteep hill,
   My days in the valley would end.

The waves that, fo ruffled awhile,
   Were, glittering, dafh'd in the fun,
On the bordering violets fmile,
   And kifs them, and murmuring run.

Thus let me the fplendor and ftrife
   Of the rich and exalted forego ;
With beauty ftill fweeten my life,
   And love's gentle ftorm only know !

VERSES

What

What joy the Bee-murmurs impart!
 The zephyrs that curl the blue waves!
Soft whifpers that fteal to the heart!
 And echo that talks in the caves!

Peace, Babblers, or only repeat
 The filver defcent of the fprings;
Fond fhepherds frame here no deceit,
 But fcandal has numerous wings.

I call'd you to witnefs, tis true,
 The vows to Amelia I fwore,
Methinks ftill her blufhes I view,
 And, trembling, forgivenefs implore.

Her charms I will grave on my heart,
 Her name upon every tree;
And fooner fhall love want a dart,
 Than fickelnefs harbour with me.

' You may judge from this flight fpecimen what an excellently fine poet my Don Pedro was; but, alas! I fhall never behold him more, O Heavens! Here the amiable Amelia fell into a ftrong hyfteric fit, from which it was with the utmoft difficulty that the celeftial Arabella, with the affiftance of Margaret Grimes, could recover her.'

' You

E

Chapter

75

Chapter 10.

THE FAIR STRANGER'S STORY CONTINUED.

WHEN the divine Amelia had in fome degree recovered her fpirits, with an eye of expreffive languor caft upon Arabella, fhe thus continued her moft interefting narrative. ' My mind, dear madam, as you may well fuppofe, was perplexed by a thoufand alarming apprehenfions; I trembled left the tale fhould tranfpire, yet my wounded pride would fcarcely fuffer me to conceal it. The idea of being in the power of a man, though in faft my hufband; the indelicacy, if

E 2

not

not difgrace, that would attach itfelf to my name, for having ventured fo far, and fo imprudently towards the precipice of deftruction, the contempt I muft inevitably excite in the mind of Don Pedro, and the idea of practifing fo unworthy a deception towards my adored mamma, fo preyed upon my fpirits, that my delicate frame yielded to anxiety, which in a few hours, brought on an alarming and delirious fever.

' There happened fortunately to be a phyfician on board, who at my mother's inftigation, kindly offered his falutary aid, though his humane attention has proved in the end, moft fatal to my repofe. From the firft moment

moment he beheld me, the captivating graces of my perfon and demeanour fafcinated the heart of Don Gomez d'Aldova, for that was his name. The natural fiercenefs of his character foftened before the irrefiftible attractions of virtue and benignity. An unufual fenfation of exquifite delight penetrated his mind, and the engaging anxiety I evinced for the fuccefs of his prefcriptions, ferved only to augment the admiration I had infpired.

' Love has that fweet, that undefcribable power, which gives mildnefs to ferocity, and refolution to inftability ; it humbles the proudeft, and exalts the meekeft ; the libertine is

E 3   awed

awed by its influence, and the man of feeling adds dignity to his being, by following its dictates. The tendernefs of refined fympathy, the rapture of conferring happinefs, the confcious delight of expunging from the foul every vicious propenfity, by the difpaffionate councils of reafon and penetration, are the peculiar attributes of a beloved object. The moft dulcet tones, the moft fublime efforts of perfuafive eloquence, and the tinfel blandifhments of empty fophiftry, vanifh before the refiftlefs influence of the voice we love ! It has the power to harmonife the feelings with undefcribable magic, leading the fenfes captive, till every idea is fafcinated with the fpells of admiration

ration and efteem.' As the matchlefs Amelia uttered the foregoing enthufiaftic rhapfody with almoft fuperhuman energy, fo it fuddenly overpowered her weak nerves, and fhe again fell fenfelefs to the floor, while the fympathifing Arabella wiped a lambent tear from her finely fuffufed eye, with a clean cambric handkerchief, and then again adminiftered her benign relief to the fair evanefcent ftranger.

E 4   Chapter

Chapter 11.

THE FAIR STRANGER CONTINUES HER STORY.

BEING come to herself, the captivating Amelia thus proceeded in her clear and extraordinary narrative, having firſt begged pardon, of the languiſhing Arabella for the alarm and trouble ſhe had occaſioned: ' After a tedious voyage, in which our veſſel encountered many dreadful ſtorms, we arrived in ſafety at Falmouth, when my ever honored mamma and myſelf were received by Mr. Oldfield, a couſin of my father's, with all the kindneſs and hoſpitality

E 5   which

which ſo eminently charaƈterize the Engliſh nation.

' There was in the houſe a Miſs Ford who was rather approaching to that period when old maidiſhneſs begins; ſhe, obſerving my dejeƈtion in conſequence of Don Pedro's neglect, which now alas! became too well aſcertained, thought proper to introduce to my acquaintance a Captain Beville, a nephew of hers, and who was a young man of moſt elegant manners. Indeed, my dear, he was uncommonly handſome, ſenſible, and engaging. Yet the firſt introduƈtion was in ſome degree owing to an accident, for he was thrown from his horſe at our door, and having fainted

away,

away, was in conſequence brought into the parlour, and laid upon a blue damaſk ſopha, when I unfortunately entered. The crimſon fountain of life had ſcarcely ſpread its ſoft tints upon his pallid lips, when his languid eyes were fixed in ſpeechleſs extaſy on the countenance of your poor Amelia, whoſe cheek met his gaze as the meek roſe encounters the burning glances of the meridian ſun! Overpowered by his admiration, I was preparing to depart, when the Captain fearful of loſing the ſight of ſo charming an objeƈt, in a feeble voice accompanied by the moſt impreſſive manner entreated me to ſtay, ' beauteous Lady' ſaid he ' if thou art indeed a mortal, for thy

E 6   outward

outward form bears the strong resemblance of divinity, suffer me for a moment to enjoy the Elysium that presents itself before me: surely I am in the castle of inchantment, and thou art the fair mistress of the air-built habitation! if my returning faculties do not deceive me, I awake from the shades of death to taste the supreme felicities of a terrestial paradise!'

'Miss Ford who witnessed this eloquent harrange, cast a look of soft sympathy upon my heaving bosom, and seemed anxiously to expect my reply, but supper was just bringing in, and the two Miss Maddox's joined our party, who with their usual

usual good nature wished to give a more lively turn to the conversation. I, however, was too much affected by the scene before me, and hastily retired to my mamma's chamber, where I found her in a very languishing condition, the gout which had first seized all her limbs, having now settled in her head, and occasioned the most excruciating tortures. But O! they did not long afflict her, for on the third day, she grew much worse, and towards evening expired, leaving me alone and unprotected in a cruel world, to struggle with my fate.'

Here Amelia's tears began to flow afresh, and the gentle Arabella answered

swered them by her sighs, while Margaret Grimes with louder and more piercing notes, joined the melancholy concert of Affliction.

Chapter 12.

THE FAIR STRANGER'S STORY CONCLUDED.

AFTER a short pause the mild Amelia thus continued her narrative. 'I confess with some degree of shame, my dear lady, that Captain Beville occupied my thoughts more than perhaps I ought to acknowledge, all circumstances considered, but Don Pedro's conduct had in a great degree alienated my affection, for the blossoms of true love spread their full sails before the gales of prosperity, but cannot resist the tempestuous ocean of adversity. It happened that on on a fine summer's evening *I* went to pay a visit without my mamma to a Mr. Gifford, a gentleman somewhat known in the literary world, and who has written a satirical poem called the Baviad. This terrible writer who modestly stiles himself the modern Perseus, is a little sour looking fellow but prodigiously powerful with his pen, for he is desperately severe, and though he cannot write a line of genuine poetry himself, yet he is extremely alert in abusing those who can. He was formerly a metaphorical bear-leader to my Lord Belgrave, and after his return from the Continent, became literally the tutor of a real bear which his lordship had brought home with him, and which was

was one of the valuable acquisitions he had made on his travels. Now you must know that one day Mr. Gifford, being negligent of his charge, suffered the bear to eat a whole basket of butter, which the butter-man had left in the passage: this threw his lordship into a great passion, and he immediately discharged the tutor for his carelessness, and placed the hopeful pupil under a more attentive master. It was at this period I paid my visit, and the poor man was quite in a fury at his disgrace, in having his bear taken from him, and consequently he devoted himself to satire, by way of revenge. In this man's society I passed several pleasant hours, and almost forgot the dangers that surrounded

surrounded me, when unfortunately Captain Beville arrived: at sight of him, my agonies were renewed, and we agreed to meet the week after, at the house of a Mrs. Martin, in Hertfordshire. This you will allow was imprudent, but who can be wise at all times? Let me now hasten to the conclusion of my melancholy tale, and endeavour to describe in proper colours the awful catastrophe that awaited the destiny of the too wretched Amelia. On this very day I was induced to call at Mrs. Martin's aforesaid, at Daisy Place, when wandering through her improvements, which by the bye, discover her to possess the most refined taste; whom should I meet in the hermitage but Captain

Captain Beville. O my friend! think on my situation. He caught me in his arms and vowing eternal love imprinted a thousand amorous kisses on my lips. Just heavens! the crisis of my fate was at had.—The dog barked, I looked up, and saw the enraged Don Pedro with a countenance flashing with fire and indignation, and with a drawn sword in his hand. In a moment Captain Beville lay weltering in his blood, I fled, as you may naturally suppose, till I reached the spot where I had the supreme felicity to meet the mellifluous Arabella; I had been just exclaiming before you appeared, from the divine Milton

‘ O where

‘ O where elfe
Shall I *deform* my *unattainted* feet,
In the blind *maffes* of this *dangled* wood ?
For I am wearied out
With the long way *refolving* here to lodge
Under the fpreading *flavour* of thefe pines.’

The virtuous and much injured
Amelia having brought her forlorn
hiftory to a conclufion, began again
to weep, and the fufceptible Arabella
haftened to pour a healing balm into
her recent wounds, then kindly led
her to her chamber, and wifhing her
a good night, retired herfelf alfo to
enjoy the refrefhing flumbers of innocence. At the fame time Margaret Grimes afcended to her little
garret, and the cat flept in the kitchen.

Chapter

friend was no longer her immediate
tafk, fhe fhould dwell with more
painful and more fteady folicitude
on her own fingular and unfortunate
fituation.

Margaret Grimes, warmly attached
as fhe was to both, from gratitude
and from affeftion, had no power to
fpeak comfort to either. Early in
the morning fhe had met the chim-
ney fweeper, and had gone through
Lucinda Howard's letter: but though
her mind fometimes ftrongly refifted
the idea of hafty marriages, fhe had
nothing to offer againft it, and could
only figh over the incurable unhappinefs with which fhe faw the future

days

Chapter 13.

THE PARTING.

THE morning at length arrived,
and the friends who had found all
the confolation their circumftances
admitted of in being together, were
now to part; uncertain when or if
ever they were to meet again. Amelia finking as fhe was under oppreffion of many prefent forrows and
future apprehenfions, yet found them
all deepened by the lofs of Arabella,
who had fo generoufly affifted her
in fupporting them, and Arabella
felt, that when to foothe the fpirits
and ftrengthen the refolution of her

friend

days of friends fhe fo much loved
would be clouded.

Silently they all affembled round
the breakfaft table ; but nobody
could eat. Alderman Barlow tried
to talk of his Maria, of his houfe,
of his farm, of his fortunate prof-
pefts, and of his fifter's two little
girls, whom he had taken home ;
but there was not one topic on which
he could fpeak, that did not remind
him of the obligations he owed to
General Barton, and the Howard
family, nor one idea which arofe
unimbittered with the reflefion, that
they, to whom he was indebted for
all *his* happinefs, were themfelves
miferable.

About

About twelve o'clock Mr. Peter Perkins came into the room in his usual way; and enquired eagerly of Arabella whether she intended going to the races, and whether he could see her there; and without waiting for an answer to his enquiry, told her that he had that morning met Colonel Symes, a particular friend of Henry Lambert, and that Lady Susan Harris had been in the country about a week. Every body who was acquainted with her dear Henry could not fail to be interesting to Arabella, and from Lady Susan she had always supposed more might be collected than from any other person: but now her mind was too much oppressed and too much confused

fused to allow her to distinguish her sensations, or to arrange any settled plan for her future conduct towards Lady Susan. She received Mr. Peter Perkins's information, therefore, with coldness, and indeed her manners towards him were very constrained and distant, which he either did not or would not notice; rattling on in his usual wild way, though he saw the dejection and concern of the party; a circumstance that more than ever disgusted Arabella, who began some time before to doubt whether the credit which 'Mr. Peter Perkins had for good nature, was not given him on very slender foundations: for to be so entirely occupied by his own pleasures and pur-

F   suits,

suits, as to be incapable of the least sympathy towards others, to be unable or unwilling to check for one moment his vivacity in compliment to their despondence, seemed to Arabella such a want of sensibility, as gave her a very indifferent opinion of his heart.

Amelia quitted the room to make the last preparations for her departure: but Margaret Grimes who had settled every thing before, remained with Arabella and Mr. Peter Perkins. He would have given the world to have passed these moments in conversation with her, but the presence of a third person, and especially of Margaret Grimes, put an end to all hope

hope he had of an opportunity of explaining to her with that tenderness and caution, which the subject required, some circumstances relative to Henry Lambert's fortune, which had lately come to his knowledge. New embarrassments seemed threatening him, and a law suit, involving part of the property which belonged to the Devonshire estate, appeared likely to increase these embarrassments.

All this Mr. Peter Perkins thought Arabella ought to know, yet in their first interview that morning, he had not courage to tell her of it, and now General Barton had left him no chance of doing it, for while he yet

F 2   deliberated,

deliberated, the coach fent by the Marchionefs of Oakley ftopped at the door, and the moment was come in which he was to take his leave of her.

He took her hand, and kiffed it with an air of grateful refpect; but he could only fay, ' I fhall write to you in a few days, and I hope, give you a good account of my grandmother, and of little Peggy.

' I hope you will,' returned Arabella, faintly.

' And,' added he, ' you will of courfe like to hear of all that paffes material in our neighbourhood?'

' Certainly

' Certainly I fhall,' replied fhe. ' Adieu, dear fir. I cannot fay much, but you know what I feel for you all.'

The Rev. Mr. Devaynes had taken her hand to lead her down ftairs; but fhe difengaged it from him, and faid to Mr. Peter Perkins, as fhe gave it to *him*, ' Let us go to your fifter.' He led her to the door of the room; where at that moment Amelia entered pale and breathlefs; her eyes were heavy, and fixed on Arabella, but fhe did not weep. Arabella's tears, however, were more ready, and as fhe embraced her friend, they choaked the trembling adieu fhe would have ut-

F 3   tered,

tered, and fell in fhowers on her bofom. The emotion was too painful; and Mr. Peter Perkins defirous to end it for both their fakes, difengaged Amelia from the arms of the trembling Arabella, while Mr. Devaynes feizing Amelia by the hand, hurried her down ftairs, and as he put her into the coach, told her he fhould wait upon her the next day. She would have befought him not to do it, as a liberty he ought not to take in the houfe whither fhe was going; but before fhe could fufficiently recover herfelf to find words, the coach was driven away, and in a fhort time, fhe found herfelf at the door of the Marchionefs of Oakley, at Fairy Lodge, and it became necef-

fary

fary for her to collect her fpirits, to acquit herfelf as fo much kind attention deferved.

F 4   Chapter

105

Chapter 14.

A SCENE OF HORROR, A GHOST,
AND A SUPPER.

IT is now neceſſary to return to
Henry Lambert, who purſued his
journey with unabating perſeverance,
and at midnight found himſelf in an
immenſe foreſt through which there
was no traƈt, and the thickneſs of
which prevented the ſmalleſt glimmering of light from penetrating the
' palpable obſcure'. On every ſide
were heard ſtrange murmurs as of
perſons in anguiſh, and now and
then the mournful gale brought to his
aſtoniſhed ear ſome faint female la-
F 5   mentations.

106

mentations. The river had overflowed
its banks with a ſpreading inundation, and the ſtupendous rocks that
ſeemed to prop the ſkies, colleƈted
dreadful thunders over his head.
There appeared to his wondering faculties, to be a chaſm in all nature,
and the howling wolf, as if conſcious
of the general deſolation of the ſcene,
added terror to the perturbation he
endured.

Philip Duvergois his faithful valet
was advanced only a few paces, when
a bloody ſpeƈtre with a countenance
of the moſt inconceivable diſmay and
agony, glided by, bearing in its hand
a ſcroll on which was written—
DEATH.—A ſudden flaſh of lightning
threw

107

threw a luſtre upon the parchment at
the moment. Henry's heart felt involuntary depreſſion, but colleƈting
all his fortitude, he called to Duvergois, ſaying,—' Saw you that figure,
what was it ?'—' You aſk me vat it
vas, by Saint Jeronimo it vas a live
ghoſt.' A long ſilence now enſued,
when the two travellers arrived at an
old abbey that was mouldering in
decay, and which ſeemed the abode
of ſome banditti who frequented the
foreſt, as none but the outcaſts of
ſociety could inhabit ſo melancholy
and dreary an abode.

On approaching the ſouth aiſle
which was over-run with ivy, and
covered with moſs, the ornaments of
F 6   time;

time; Henry's horfe began to neigh, and immediately a light appeared at the chapel window and the bell tolled. Henry rufhed forward with an animated courage, and in a few feconds, found himfelf in an ancient hall in which was a table with fome covered difhes placed thereon, but no perfon appeared. A pendant lamp from the fretted roof, difcovered to the terrified Henry the awful folemnity of the place. He called Duvergois, but received no anfwer, when on a fudden an unnatural burft of laughter was heard in the adjoining apartment. Henry, not difmayed, fmote with the handle of his fword againft the door of the room from whence the noife had iffued. Another burft of laughter

ter more fhocking than the former ftruck upon his heart. Anon the portal opened and an appearance fo exquifitely horrible prefented itfelf to his fight, that all refolution failed him, and he fled. Henry traverfed the great hall with the fwiftnefs of an Antelope, he arrived at a marble ftair-cafe which he afcended, till he came into a long gallery. By a glimpfe of the moon which now darted a tranfient luftre through an antiquated cafement he thought he difcovered a female at fome diftance on her knees before a crucifix. He paufed, uncertain whether to advance or not, when a man before unfeen caught him in his arms. It was Duvergois; ' O mine Got' faid he ' let us efcape from dis abominable

minable abbey, I have feen de Tifel himfelf, O my dear mafter, in dat cell is de body of a murdered man, I faw him lie dere gafhed vit vounds, O vat will become of us?' During this parley, a child of about feven years of age came out of a fmall clofet on the right fide of the gallery with a lighted torch in his hand. The infant looked earneftly in Henry's face and faid ' will you come to the banquet, fupper is ferved up, there are only feven; the widow, my dear mother, is at prayers, but the Baron will be there, and I wifh the foup may pleafe your palates.' They now followed the child in fpeechlefs amazement till they arrived at a fpacious faloon, round which were arrayed a number

number of figures in armour; the infant pointed to them and exclaimed ' Henry Lambert, thefe may all be called your predeceffors, for they came hither and departed no more.' At thefe words he gave a loud fhriek and difappeared, leaving Henry and Duvergois to ruminate on what had paffed. It was totally dark, yet the near and frequent trampling of feet convinced them that there were perfons moving about.' Who paffes there?' faid Henry. ' Only your lordfhip's fervants,' replied a female voice, ' who are going to bid the ftrangers welcome, and to give them the reception you wifh, be not uneafy, my lord! they will foon be fafe.' Immediately after, a large pair of folding doors

doors at the end of the faloon flew open, and difcovered feven perfons at fupper, five ladies and two gentlemen, all magnificently dreffed, but mafked: there were two vacant feats, which furprized Henry, as it appeared that he and Duvergois were expected to complete the party. One of the ladies on obferving the two travellers, left the table and lightly tripping towards them, took Henry gracefully by the hand, and prefented him to the company, faying ' This courteous gentleman deferves your notice, his attendant alfo fhall partake of our repaft. ' Worthy ftrangers be feated, you may depend upon having excellent fare with us, thofe who vifit us never know how to leave us.' The mafked

mafked figure who fat at the head of the table now helped Henry and Duvergois to fome foup, and earneftly entreated them to fall to, which they did fomewhat reluctantly notwithftanding the keennefs of their appetites. One of the ladies after a little while took a rofe from her bofom and prefented it to Henry at the fame time finging with great fweetnefs the following lines:

With blufhing modefty fhe glows,
And from her bofom takes a rofe,
Accept my Corydon! fhe cries,
With fweeteft look, and downcaft eyes,
Accept from me this fading flower—
He fcarce can live another hour,

Yet

Yet while 'tis frefh, O let it be
A dear remembrancer of me!
Rafh fleep,
Slafh deep,
Loory loory loo.

A loud and general applaufe teftified the company's delight at this fong, and in a little time afterwards, the principal male figure chaunted with a bafs voice the enfuing ftanza.

The Mufes nine, and Graces three,
Do all unanimous agree:
The Mufes firft, that all they can impart
Of excellence is in your heart;
That all their wit and fenfe is in your mind
Pure as the golden ore, and as refined:
The Graces next, with reverence declare,
By merit you have ta'en their fhape and air,
Thus

Thus the Nine Mufes in your mind we fee,
And in your lovely form the Graces Three.
Ever dare,
Never fpare,
Hooly, cooly, kill.

This laft fong occafioned a vaft expanfion of merriment, when one of the ladies dropped her mafk.— Henry in aftonifhment cried out ' What! Mifs Louifa Singleton?' To which fhe replied, ' Yes, fir, the very fame whom you ufed to vifit at her papa's, near Rochefter.' All the company now unmafked, and the Duke de Belcour explained the whole joke, Madame Lebon rallying Henry prodigi_oufly on his late alarm. They all enquired eagerly after Arabella, and the nature of his hopes.

He

He gave them in consequence a full account of the last campaign, and then taking Madmoiselle Roubilliere by the hand, began the ball without further ceremony. The peasants of the neighbouring districts hastened at the sound of the merry tabor, and Duvergois watched an opportunity to give his master's letter to the gardiner, with the strictest injunction to be careful. The pictures now were all brought out and examined with a critical eye both by the corporal and the innkeeper, on which account the sale was deferred till the morrow, and the Commandant politely invited them all to dinner on the succeeding Tuesday.

Thus

So ended this tragical adventure, and Henry's spirits having been recruited by nine hours sleep, he attended the parade with more than his usual alacrity, thus dedicating his soul to honor and Arabella, and proving at least the truth of the sublime lines in Cato.

'Tis not for mortals to command success,
But we'll do more, Sempronius, we'll deserve it.'

Chapter

Chapter 15.

THE STRUGGLES OF VIRTUE PREVAIL.

FOR several days Arabella devoted her whole thoughts to her dearly beloved Henry, and regretted more and more the fatal cause of their separation. Sometimes grief would rise to its achmé in her mind, and she was frantic with despair; again she would sink into the soft calm of melancholy. But time with its rapid wing kept flying by, yet brought her no intelligence of the object that most interested her feeling heart. At the end of the week, however,

120

however, she received a letter from the valuable suffering Amelia; but O! what was the agitation of her mind when she perused the contents.

THE LETTER.

'My dear, amiable, lovely and excellent Arabella,

For the future I will always mistrust most when appearances look fairest. O your poor friend! what has she not suffered since she left you, and Oh! you shall hear what a vile and unwomanly part that wicked Marchioness has acted. Take, then, the dreadful story, as well as I can relate it.

The

121

The maid. Martha is a little apt to drink if she can get at liquor, and having chanced to find a bottle of cherry brandy, the wench drank more of it than she should, for which she was soundly rated by the Marchioness, who ordered her to go and sleep off her liquor before we came to bed.

About two hours after, which was near eleven o'clock, the Marchioness and I went up to go to bed; I pleasing myself with what a charming night I should have. Poor Martha was sitting fast asleep, in an elbow chair, in a dark corner of the room, with her apron thrown over her head and neck. The Marchioness said,

G   'there

122

'there is that beast of a wench fast asleep, instead of being abed! I knew, she had taken a fine dose.' 'I'll wake her,' said I. 'No don't,' said she, ' let her sleep on, we shall lie better without her,' and indeed I thought so, for it appeared to me rather strange to sleep three in a bed.

The Marchioness by this time was got to-bed, on the farther side, to make room for the maid when she should awake. I got into bed and lay close to her. ' Put your arm under mine, said the wicked Marchioness; so I did, and the abominable Lady held my hand with her right-

123

right-hand, as my right arm was under her left.

In less than a quarter of an hour, I said, ' There's poor Martha awake, I hear her stir.' ' Let us go to sleep,' said her Ladyship, ' and not mind her.'

At that, Martha sat down by the bed-side and began to undress. I heard her, as I thought, breathe all quick and short: 'Indeed,' said I, ' the poor maid is not well; what ails you, Mrs. Martha?' but no answer was given.

But I shudder to relate it. She came into bed, trembling like an

G 2   Aspen-

Aspen-leaf, and I, poor fool that I was, pitied her much. What words shall I find, my dear Arabella, to describe the rest, and my confusion, when the guilty wretch, (who was no other than Lord Mahogany himself) took my left arm, and laid it under his neck, and the vile Marchioness held my right, and then he clasped me round the waist.

Said I ' Is the wench mad?' Why how now Confidence!' thinking still it had been Martha. But he kissed me with frightful vehemence; and then his voice broke upon me like a clap of thunder. ' Now Amelia,' said his Lordship, ' is the dreadful time of reckoning come'. I screamed out

out in such a manner, as never any body heard the like. But there was nobody to help me, and both my hands were secured, as I said. Sure never poor soul was in such agonies as I.

Says he, ' One word with you, Amelia! hear me but one word, and hitherto you see I offer nothing to you? ' Is this *nothing?*' said I, ' to be in bed here? to hold my hands between you! I *will hear*, if you will both instantly leave the bed.'

Said the Marchioness (O disgrace of womankind!) ' What you do, my Lord, do; do'nt stand dilly-dallying; she cannot exclaim worse than she

G 3   has

has done: and she'll be quieter when she knows the worst.'

He now put his hand in my bosom: with struggling and forrow I fainted away quite, and did not come to myself soon; so that they both, from the cold sweats that I was in, thought me dying.

Your poor Amelia cannot answer for the liberties taken with her, in her deplorable state of death, but when I recovered my senses, his Lordship solemnly, and with a bitter imprecation vowed that he had not offered the least indecency, that he was frightened at the terrible manner I was taken with the fit: that he should

should desist from his attempt, and begged but to see me easy and quiet; and he would leave me directly and go to his own bed. ' O then,' said I, ' take with you this vile Marchioness, as an earnest that I may believe you.'

' And will you, my Lord,' said the wicked Lady, ' for a fit or two, give up such an opportunity as this? I thought you had known the sex better. She is now, you see, quite well again!'

This I heard; more she might say; but I fainted away once more, at these words, and at his clasping his arms about me again. When I

G 4   came

came a little to myself, I found that his Lordship was gone, and Mrs. Dorothy Webster holding a smelling bottle to my nose, and no Marchioness.

This O my beloved Arabella, was a most dreadful trial! I tremble still to think of it, and dare not recal all the horrid circumstances, though I hope, as his lordship assures me, that he was not guilty of indecency.

I shall leave this naughty house to-morrow, and go to my cousin Filby's at Margate. I fear you will not think the lace fine enough, but it was the best the picklesalmon man had to dispose of, or you may be sure I should have

have waited till Miss St. George had returned from the north; but that not having been the case, I will no longer trespass on your patience than to subscribe myself, dearest Arabella,

Your truly affectionate

AMELIA DE GONZALES.'

Fairy-Lodge, Friday 17th.

Having perused this lamentable epistle, the blooming Arabella wrapped in the insensibility of private sorrow, suffered herself to be arrayed for dinner. Serene dejection sat upon her countenance, and her mild eyes were expressive of the resignation she had imposed upon a heart alive to every sentiment of friendship and benevolence.

G 5   As

As soon as dinner was at an end, Arabella, in company with the eldest Miss Appleby, took a walk upon the common, and near farmer Rigby's stile, she observed a small piece of folded paper on the ground, which she took up, and to her great surprize, found it to contain the following lively verses addressed to herself.

TO THE HEAVENLY MISS ARABELLA BLOOMVILLE.

What proof shall I give of my passion,
  Or how shall I struggle with fate?
Arabella! since cards came in fashion,
  You've mark'd me an object of hate.

I'd have willingly fought with the devil,
  And grateful have been, to be slain,

For

For I suffer indefinite evil,
  And warble alone to complain.

Like a madman I scour o'er the vallies,
  Unobserv'd like a mite in a cheese,
For 'tis the criterion of malice
  To laugh at my efforts to please.

Now I snuff the fresh air of the morning,
  In a transport of sorrow—because
You treat me with flouting and scorning,
  But hold, it is time I should pause.
           ENDYMION.

Arabella now returned home more tranquil and serene than she had been for many months.

G 6   Chapter

Chapter 16.

A MISTAKE, AND A MOST INTERESTING ARRIVAL.

IT was one of thofe foft mild evenings when fcarcely a wandering zephyr prefumes to difturb the tranquility of nature. The fetting fun had thrown a yellow glow on the huge maffes of grey marble, whofe crevices here and there afforded a fcanty fubfiftence to lickens and mofs campion, while the defolate barrennefs of other parts added to that threatening afpect with which they feemed to hang over the wandering traveller, when Henry leaping from his horfe, caft himfelf at
the

the foot of an aged oak, in a ftate between indifference and defpair. ' How long' cried he ' am I to be the fport of fortune, how long feparated from the arms of the angelic Arabella the fole miftrefs of my heart? Had my uncle Parkinfon forefeen my fufferings, he would never have permitted the bafe triumph of Lord Mahogany to have embittered all my hopes, nor have relied upon the promifes of Sir Matthew Sullivan to extricate me from my difficulties. Peace will now probably be foon eftablifhed, and thofe who fell in battle will be mourned in vain, more efpecially fince the ridiculous and difaftrous war has been fo completely unfuccefsful. Yet what of that? If I return home
can

can I be fure of the fettled confolation which all my endeavours have tended to procure me? Is not General Barton my bitter enemy, and can I ftand alone againft fo powerful a confederacy ?'

Here an involuntary figh efcaped him, for he looked back with foft regret to thofe times, when Mrs. Marmaduke cherifhed his youthful propenfities in her fweet retirement. He called to mind the interefting period when the tear of friendfhip bedewed her bridal eye—fuddenly he recollected that fhe was now no more, that fhe was alas! the filent tenant of the grave. The conflict was too much to bear, for his love for Arabella

bella was more ardent than ever, and the pangs of abfence more infupportable.

He therefore determined to unbofom himfelf to his friend Ferguffon, and confult with him what was beft to be done in the prefent crifis of his fituation. Ferguffon he knew to be a tall well-looking young man with a good heart and an excellent underftanding, but he dreaded left the influence of fome artful female might draw his fecret forth, if he fhould confide in him too far, and thus ruin all his projeĉts. At times indeed he felt fome little indignation both againft Jennings and him for the trick they had put upon him relative to the venifon

nifon feaft, but that matter had now blown over, and he generoufly made allowances for their inconfiderate inattention.

While he was yet wavering, the landlord waited upon him, and offered to purchafe his greyhounds, affuring him at the fame time, that Lord Thomas Groves had flept there the night before, and had praifed the wine very much.

Henry however was deaf to all his entreaties, and totally forgot to make the neceffary enquiries after Lucinda Howard, which mortified the old Baronet's pride a good deal, for though he was of an open jovial charaĉter,

charaĉter, yet he knew the value of land as well as any man, and had abfolutely refufed a peerage from principle.

In a paroxyfm of grief therefore Henry retired early to his chamber, and calling for a boiled fowl and a bottle of Burton ale, in a few hours compofed the following beautiful acroftic, as a tribute of admiration and efteem to the unrivalled excellence of Arabella.

LINES ADDRESSED TO THE LOVELY
ARABELLA.

May all the gods approve my tender love,
Yes, all the gods, the Pagan gods above!
Wife fhe is truly, gentle, good, and kind,
In body aĉtive, and fublime in mind;
Fond

Fond as a turtle dove—O may fhe be
Eternally, what this acroftic means, to me !

The waiter now ran into the room with a note, which he faid a little boy had that moment left at the bar— Henry broke open the feal with eager anxiety and read as follows :

' My dear friend,

It is with great grief, I confefs, that I heard, the quantity of goofe you ate yefterday has occafioned you a pain in your fide; you fhould keep yourfelf warm by a good fire, and fit quiet in an elbow chair. I have feen a receipt for this diforder in a book that is now out of print. But I will

I will not tire your patience any further; left you grow melancholy, and lofe the memory of former amufements, which we are apt to regret when they have taken flight from us. I fhall therefore lay down my pen for the prefent, though I would refume it in a fecond, had I any good news to fend you.

> I am, dear Doctor,
> Yours affectionately,
> BRIDGET CAWTHORNE.'

Henry Lambert was very much irritated by this foolifh miftake, and curfing heartily both the Doctor and Bridget Cawthorne, ftepped into a poft chaife, and defiring the lad to make all poffible hafte, fell afleep in the

the corner, while his ftill active imagination was delighted with the hovering phantom of Arabella. The blufh of innocence, the glow of artlefs beauty, bloomed on her cherub cheek, the milk of fweetnefs hung upon her tongue.

In the mean time, Arabella had not been out long before the chill and gloomy appearance encreafed, and darknefs coming on, fhe flowly and reluctantly returned to the houfe. She heard a little before fhe quitted the road, the rattling of a chaife, but not attending to it, fhe did not even diftinguifh whether it might belong to any perfon of the place, or to fome traveller. She entered the parlour,

parlour, and fat down by the card table, where the Earl having performed his evening's tafk, had juft refigned his place to Mr. M'Intofh. Suddenly a voice was heard in the paffage, enquiring for Lady Langley. ' My Lady is within fir,' replied the man. ' And who are with her?' ' The Earl of Pocklington, Mr. Paul Dodfworth, Mrs. Kemp, the three Mifs Bernards, Doctor Browne, Mifs Bloomville, General Barton, Sir Obediah Loftus'—the fervant was going on, when the enquirer faid vehemently, ' It is enough—let me however fee them.' Arabella at the found of this voice, had ftarted from her chair—the fecond fentence it uttered, affected her ftill more; but fhe

fhe had no time to anfwer the eager enquiry of Mr. Thomas Jackfon, ' What is the matter?' before the parlour door opened; and pale, breathlefs, with an expreffion to which only the pencil can do juftice, fhe faw before her the figure of Henry Lambert.

There was agony and defperation in his looks. He gafped, like a fifh in fits—he would have fpoken but could not. The company all rofe in filence. Lady Langley who hardly knew him even by fight, looked at Arabella for an explanation, which fhe was unable to give.—At length, Henry, as if by an effort of paffionate phrenzy, approached Arabella,

49

bella, and ſaid in a hurried and inar-
ticulate way, ' I would ſpeak to you,
Madam,—though—to—this gentleman, I ſuppoſe,' and he turned to
General Barton, ' I muſt apply for
permiſſion.'

Arabella could not conjecture why
he looked ſo little in his ſenſes—She
ſat down—for her limbs refuſed to
ſupport her—and faintly ſaid or tried
to ſay, ' I hope I ſee Captain Lambert well.'

Lady Langley then addreſſed herſelf to him—deſired him to take a
chair, and to do her the honor of
ſtaying ſupper with her.   He heard
or heeded her not—but, with fixed
eyes,

eyes, gazing on Arabella, he ſtruck
his hands together, and cried—while
the violence of his emotion choaked
him—' It is all over then—I have
loſt her—and have nothing to do
here—No, by heaven I cannot bear
it.' He then turned away, and left
the room as haſtily as he had entered
it.

' My dear Arabella!' cried Lady
Langley, ' what does all this mean?
Do, General Barton--for Miſs Bloomville is, I perceive, much alarmed—
do, ſpeak to Mr. Lambert— I am
really concerned to ſee him in ſuch
a ſituation.'

' No,' ſaid Arabella, who would

H   not

not for the world have had General
Barton follow him—' No; I will go
myſelf after him.'—Her fears gave
her reſolution, and without heeding
General Barton, who would have
prevented her, ſhe hurrried after
Henry, and overtook him juſt as he
was quitting the houſe.

' Dear ſir,' ſaid ſhe, ' Dear
Henry!' At thoſe well known ſounds
once ſo precious to him, he turned
round—She took his hand—' I am
very ſorry to ſee you' continued
ſhe, ' in ſuch agitation of ſpirits—I
am afraid ſomething is wrong.'

' Wrong,' cried he, ' wrong! and
do you Arabella, inhuman Arabella,
inſult

inſult me with ſuch an enquiry?
Wrong!—am I not the moſt curſed
of human beings?'

' I hope not' interrupted ſhe, ' for
your happineſs'—ſhe knew no longer
what ſhe meant to ſay; nor did he
give her time to recollect; for eagerly rivetting his eyes on her face,
and graſping her hands between his—
he cried ' My happineſs!—and what
of my happineſs? Is it not gone, loſt
for ever?—Have you not deſtroyed
it? Damnation and diſtraction—Why
do I linger here?' He then plunged
away, and ruſhed out of the door,
where Duvergois waited for him with
the chaiſe.

H 2   Chapter

149

Chapter 17.

REGRET AND LAMENTATION.

GENERAL Barton's grandmother had been long in a declining ſtate, and for the laſt thirty years had afforded little hopes of a permanent recovery—but ſhe was now rapidly approaching

' That undiſcovered country, from whoſe bourne,
No traveller returns.* '

Lucinda Howard deſcended haſtily to fetch the General—prepared him

* Shakeſpeare.

H 3   for

150

for the pity-moving ſpectacle, and introduced him to his dying grandmother. She had requeſted to be raiſed, and ſupported by her pillows: ſtrong agitation convulſed her frame, and, for a few moments, ſhe was deprived of the power of utterance. An interval of calm ſucceeded—ſhe extended her emaciated arms.—The General who underſtood the ſign, ſuffered her to embrace him; the drops of ſoft humanity, wrung from his feeling heart, fell upon her cheek. A ghoſtly ſmile illumined her haggard eyes—ſhe looſed her feeble hold— then faintly articulated ' I am forgiven, I am happy !' and ſinking on her pillow, inſtantly expired.

A ſcene

151

A ſcene ſo mournful, and a death ſo ſudden, awfully affected the gay Sir Charles Atkinſon, and the lovely Lucinda Howard. The General ſupported the latter from the breathleſs corpſe of his grandmother. Lady Langley was no leſs ſhocked at an event, little expected to take place ſo ſoon. She ſent a complimentary meſſage, but was herſelf too much indiſpoſed to admit an interview. At length, being tolerably recovered, ſhe was attended to the carriage by her two companions, and ſet out on her return to London. The ſpirits of this amiable woman had been ſo much affected by the penitence and death of Lady Barton, for whom ſhe once felt the tendereſt friendſhip,

H 4   that

that she was some time confined to her chamber. There she shed fresh tears to the renewed remembrance of her beloved husband, whose injurious conduct never could erase him from her affections.

During this interval, Mr. Simon Walford, the steward of the late Lady Barton, attended his new master, who was soon fixed in the secure possession of the inheritance of his ancestors: but the General was dead to every pleasure fortune could bestow. This amiable man whose attentions during her illness, and anxiety for her recovery, could not have been exceeded even towards the wife of his choice, was sensibly touched

touched by her sudden fate!—With undissembled tears he mourned her death, and tenderly regretted her removal from a world, to which she had been too fondly attached! In contemplating the ghastly form, that once glowed with animated beauty, how does the thinking mind moralize upon the vanity of short-lived pleasures!

The grief, the anguish of the General, is not to be described: that heart alone can sympathize with such sensations, which has experienced such a loss. The revival of his grandmother's virtues obliterated the impression of her failings:—he remembered only the dignity of her form, and the graces of her mind!—

H 5   nor

nor could all his philosophic resolution support with fortitude, this unexpected stroke of fortune! He felt, bereaved of every social joy, the comfort of his life—deserted and forlorn! Thus the fair blooming branches cropped from the venerable tree, are left unsheltered, to the rude elements and boisterous tempest!

Scarce could the gentle force of friendship drag this heart-stricken General from the deformed remains of what was once his grandmother. Fixed like a statue, he gazed upon her face! then smote his gallant breast, and with a smile of anguish thus exclaimed.

' Yes,

' Yes, it is past! the only tie of nature that remained to attach me to existence, is now dissolved!—Life has no more a charm, nor death a pang for me! O thou who lately wert so kind, so talkative, so venerable!— thou art fled for ever—the ravages of sickness have defaced thine awe-inspiring wrinkles, and left thee a spectacle of horror! O my grandmother! my grandmother!'

Thus did the afflicted General vent his soul's anguish; neither when borne from this scene of desolation, did his piercing lamentation cease:— still he addressed the invisible object of his sorrows, till overwhelmed with grief, he sunk into a silent stupor.

H 6   Several

Several gentlemen of a neighbouring county who were only acquainted with her Ladyſhip's merit, but had no perſonal knowledge of her, cauſed an elegant marble monument to be erected to her memory in Langley church, and one of the firſt poets of the age furniſhed the following beautiful epitaph, which for dirge-like ſimplicity, and ſtriking pathos, has ſeldom been equalled, and never excelled. Every line goes directly to the heart. Lady Barton had a fine poetical vein herſelf, and had unfortunately been ſubject to fits of inſanity, beſides which it is reported of her, that in her latter days ſhe would never read any book but the bible. All theſe circumſtances are feelingly

feelingly touched upon by the above-mentioned bard.

The Epitaph.

Ye who the merits of the dead revere,
Who hold misfortune ſacred, genius dear,
Regard this tomb, where Lady Barton's name
Solicits kindneſs with a double claim!
Tho' nature gave her, ard tho' ſcience taught
The fire of fancy, and the reach of thought;
Severely, doom'd to ſuffer grief's extreme,
She paſs'd, in madd'ning pain, life's fev'riſh
    dream;
While rays of genius only ſerv'd to ſhew
The thick'ning horror, and exalt her woe.
Ye walls that eccho'd to her frantic moan,
Guard the due records of this grateful ſtone!
Strangers to her, enamour'd of her lays,
This fond memorial to her talents raiſe.
For this the aſhes of a Fair require
Who touch'd the tend'reſt notes of pity's lyre;
                                    Who

Who join'd pure faith to ſtrong poetic powers,
Who in reviving reaſon's lucid hours
Sought on one book her troubled mind to reſt,
And rightly deem'd the book of God the beſt.

Chapter 18.

NEW CHARACTERS, AND A LEARNED DISSERTATION.

MRS. DE MALTHE was a Lady of very ſhining qualities, and the fineſt ariſtocratic ſenſations; her noble ambition was to form ſplendid connections, and to be admitted into the ſociety of the great. To gratify this wiſe wiſh, ſhe ſacrificed all other conſiderations. She wrote books, ſhe gave balls and concerts, and ſhe dreſſed, for no other purpoſe, but the attainment of this her favourite object. She was fully and properly perſuaded that kings can do no wrong,

wrong, and that they were autho-
rized by heaven to maſſacre and
plunder their own ſubjeĉts, and to
deſolate the world at their pleaſure.
She profeſſed herſelf the moſt loyal
of all human Beings; was a praiſe-
worthy, orthodox believer, yet with
religious enthuſiaſm ſhe would have
doomed all men to the flames, who
even ſuffered themſelves to doubt
on any article of faith which ſhe
had adopted. For the majority of
mankind, who languiſh in hovels, and
wither away by hard labour, ſhe had
little compaſſion. She thought that
they were only ſent into the world to
pay tithes and taxes, and by their
inceſſant exertions to procure lux-
uries and amuſements for the rich
and

and powerful. To be diſtinguiſhed
as a woman of learning, ſhe had
ranſacked all the indexes of books
of ſcience, and of the claſſics; her
writings and diſcourſe were larded
with ſcraps of Latin and Greek, with
far-fetched alluſions, and obſolete
quotations. Her manners were af-
feĉtedly eaſy, and vulgarly refined;
ſhe was alſo more remarkable for her
profeſſions of ſincerity, than for the
ſincerity of her profeſſions. In her
converſation ſhe was frequently lively and ſometimes entertaining, and
at all times knew better how to pleaſe
than to attach. She had confirmed
all her old prejudices by travelling,
and had acquired new ones, and
hated a philoſopher as much as ſhe
feared the devil.

To this Lady, who was now retired
into Wales, having been diſguſted
by the negleĉt of the faſhionable
world, the intereſting and lovely Miſs
Lucinda Howard went to pay a viſit,
hoping, amidſt the wild ſcenery of
mountains and natural caſcades, to
be able to indulge her romantic paſſion more tranquilly, than ſhe could
do among large aſſemblies, and the
public amuſements of high life.

Mrs. De Malthe received her with
ſmiles and apparent gratitude, and
endeavoured to ſoothe her tender
grief, by every ſpecies of rural entertainment. She introduced her to
all her Welch friends, and ſtrove to
gratify her by Cambrian feſtivity,
but

but in vain—the penetrating flame of
jealouſy had congealed her heart,
and the lightning flaſhes of ſtruggling
virtue dragged her heavily on through
a chaos of diſappointment. The lake
might bubble on the valley's breaſt,
or the pine-grove ſhake its hoary ho-
nours through the glade, but without
effeĉt. The diſtant water-fall loſt its
mild murmurs in the air, and feebly
died upon her ſenſes.

Lucinda felt with additional anxiety
for the fate of her Arabella, and
mingling her friend's ſenſations with
her own, arrived ſpeedily at that
ſtate of rending apathy, when the
nerves relax before the tempeſt of
diſappointment.

Muſick

164

Musick and poetry were now her only resources, but from these she found occasional relief, from these she learnt that solemn patience which submits to what it cannot resist, and flies from an ungrateful and turbulent world, to the calm and silent abyss of solitude and oblivion.

Henry's duel, she well knew, must rend the feelings of the too susceptible Arabella, with ineffable distress, and though the consequences had been less fatal than might at first have been suspected, yet she dared not mention the circumstance to Mrs. De Malthe, lest her extatic sensibility should be shaken in the extreme.

She

165

She sometimes thought of hastily returning to the metropolis, but then again her heart failed her, and she determined to carry the secret with her to the grave.

On one of these awful occasions, she composed the subsequent poem, which Mrs. De Malthe declared, was equal in imagery to any of the most admired works of Jeremiah Drexelius himself, had all the rich colouring which distinguished the animated pencil of Giotto, and was indeed a bright exanthema of the muse.

The Poem.

Where will at last my wretched wand'rings end?
Where shall I find contentment and a friend?

Not

166

Not such as grandeur, in its polish'd trim,
Lends honest faith in charities of whim:
Not such as Clodio, with a boasting mood,
Affords his nearest relatives in blood;
Whom famish'd nature to his gates has borne,
The bitter pittance of his hand to mourn:
Not such as sycophants from fools obtain,
The transient earnest of a venal strain!
Or new created insolence affords,*
Mongrels in rank, and visionary lords!
But such as freedom, with unclouded mind
Can dare receive, and publish to mankind:
Where friendship, careful of its friend in need,
Prevents the burning blush, and hides the deed.

On every side by disappointment foil'd,
With hopes deceiv'd, and promises turmoil'd,
Misfortune gathers on my sick'ning eye,
And melancholy prompts the gnawing sigh.

* Mrs. De Malthe rather objected to this and the five following lines as being *low*, and denoting an improper democratic spirit.

And

167

And can my friend, whom heav'n has kindly blest
With ev'ry comfort of the human breast,
Whose dearest pleasure is to soothe distress,
Its sorrow soften, and its sigh repress,
To ease, by stealth the miseries of life,
And scatter roses o'er the thorns of strife—
And can my friend the memory renew
Of scenes to which I breath'd a long adieu!
When anguish visiting secluded care,
Within the deep recesses of despair
Her dwelling takes; ah! what avails it then
To talk of friendship or the ties of men?
Ah! what avails it from ourselves to fly,
Or mingle comfort with affliction's sigh?
Lull'd for a time the bitt'rest grief may rest,
To wake with tenfold anguish in the breast.

And if the solace of De Malthe is vain,
What other balm can mitigate my pain?
Oh that oblivion could enwrap the whole,
And close each information of my soul!

Contented

168

Contented then, this refiles heart at eafe,
No friends to promife, and no views to teafe;
Unknown to all the flatt'ry which beguiles
Full many a youth, and ruins with its fmiles;
Unknown to luxury's deceitful ways,
The wanton libertine, the villain's praife,
In rural peace my fpotlefs hours might run,
My wifhes equal, and my profpects one!
E'en thou, mad love! thou tyrant of mankind,
Faithlefs to all, to *me* the moft unkind;
Save education, firft and direft foe!
From which, with knowledge, all my forrows flow—
E'en thou, mad love! my troubled heart wouldft
        fpare,
And fcatter comfort LIKE A RUSSIAN BEAR.

When the tender-hearted Lucinda
had finifhed the reading of her delightful compofition, Mrs. De Malthe
thus affectionately addreffed her.

' I have

169

' I have liftened my dear love!
with the utmoft attention to your
fweet and fuperexcellent poem, and
am fo convinced of your tafte and abilities that I would advife you to extend
your reading through the whole circle of fcience and literature. Amongft
other things I would recommend the
ftudy of medals, for experience has
taught us that there are fome medals of
Herod I. furnamed the great, on one
fide whereof is found Ἡρωδον, and on the
other Εθναρχου, that is, Herod *the ethnarch.* After the battle of Philippi,
we read that Anthony paffing over
into Syria, conftituted Herod and
Phafael his brother *tetrarchs,* and in
that quality committed to them the
adminiftration of the affairs of Judea.

I   Jofephus

170

Jofephus indeed gives Herod the appellation of *tetrarch* inftead of that of
ethnarch; but the two terms come
fo near each other, that it is eafy to
confound them together. With regard to the word *gehenna,* which is
a fcripture term, and if I miftake not
occurs in St Matthew, it has given
the critics fome pain. The authors of
the Louvain and Geneva verfions
retain the word *gehenna* as it ftands in
the Greek; the like does Monfieur
Simon: the Englifh tranflators render
it by hell and hell-fire, and fo do the
tranflators of Mons and father Bo-
hours. The word in my opinion is
formed from the Hebrew *gehinnon,*
that is, valley of Hinnom. In that
valley which was near Jerufalem,
                                there

171

there was a place named *Tophet* where
fome Jews facrificed their children
to Moloch, by making them pafs
through the fire—King Jofias, to
render this place for ever abominable,
made a cloaca or common fewer there-
of, where all the filth and carcaffes
in the city were thrown. Now you
muft know, my dear! the Jews obferve farther, that there was a continual fire kept up there to burn and
confume thofe carcaffes fomehow;
for which reafon, as they had no proper term in their language to fignify
hell, I cannot but believe that they
made ufe of the expreffion *gehenna* or
gehinnon, to denote a fire unextin-
guifhable. You have heard my
charming dear! of the two forts of

I 2   *fafti,*

faſti, the greater and the leſs, the former being diſtinguiſhed by the appellation *faſti magiſtrales*, and the latter by that of *faſti kalendares*. *Faſti*, or *dies faſti*, alſo denoted court days. The words *faſti faſtorum* is formed of the verb *fari*, to ſpeak, becauſe during thoſe days, the courts were opened, cauſes might be heard, and the Prætor was allowed *fari*, to pronounce the three words, *do*, *dico*, *addico*: the other days wherein this was prohibited were called *nefaſti*: thus Ovid

Ille nefaſtus erit, per quem tria verba ſilentur:
Faſtus erit, per quem lege licebit agi.

But I fear my charming Precious! that I fatigue you by theſe fooliſh learned

learned alluſions; you had much rather I doubt not, ſweet dear! diſcuſs the *ſit* of a cap, and the fall of a flounce, becauſe, you have ſo correct a taſte in muſick, and ſing ſo ſeraphically, that you run away with all the mens' hearts, pretty love!'

' Hah!' ſaid Miſs Maleverer, ſmiling on Mrs. De Malthe, ' you have hit the right nail upon the head, believe me, madam!' Lucinda could not ſtand it, ſhe turned away to conceal her bluſhes, and the Parſon, pitying her embarraſſment, broke up the party.

I 3 Chapter

175

Chapter 19.

THE BEAUTIES OF LETTER
WRITING.

THE ſorrows of the penſive Arabella encreaſed every hour—ſhe knew not where to look for conſolation—all was dreary—no ſunny ray to gild the diſtant proſpect. Her Henry gone—Ah whither? Mrs. Marmaduke totally forgotten—and no news whatever from her beloved Amelia de Gonzales. The clouds of woe that inundated her afflicted heart, would never more, ſhe feared, bloſſom into hope—but her chain of reaſoning was now interrupted by the

I 4 entrance

entrance of Margaret Grimes who prefented her with a letter, and who having feated herfelf in an arm-chair, with her fcalded leg upon a ftool, liftened with great attention to its contents.

To Miss Arabella Bloomville.

' My dear Arabella!

A thoufand thanks are due to my deareft friend for her kind kind letter. If ever I deviate from the path of duty I fhould be inexcufable: I write without referve, and indeed I never harboured a thought I wifh to conceal from you: no my dear Bloomville! you fhall ever be the repofitory of

of my thoughts, and the guide of my actions.

I was fo delighted on the receipt of your letter that I retired to my chamber to give it an attentive perufal. The gay Mifs Macnamara, hearing where I was, burft into the room, ' Hey-day!' fhe cried, ' what but ten days in town, and have already received a love epiftle as long as a law indenture? Well who is it?

' Oh! anfwer me,
' Let me not burft in ignorance.'

Indeed, faid I, my dear Mifs Macnamara, you are miftaken: this is from my Arabella. To convince, her, I

I 5   read

read fome parts of it, and will fend you a few of her comments. The firft general one was ' Your Arabella, child, is certainly the offspring of Jupiter's brain, I wifh you would lend her letter to Mr. Danby, to take into the pulpit with him next Sunday. I'll fwear he never preached fo exquifite a fermon. Lord, how my head would have ached after writing fo much.' My dear Arabella, faid I, is fond of writing and reading, and we have, by a country life, a great deal of time for thefe amufements; and for my own part I muft confefs, though I like town for a few weeks, yet the country is my choice for conftant refidence. What charming walks! how pleafant to hear the whiftling

whiftling of birds, the bleating of fheep, and to fee the people employed in ruftic bufinefs.

' No more, no more,' exclaimed Mifs Macnamara: ' O! defend me from being buried in the country.'

' Sans balls, fans plays, fans tafte, fans every
' thing.'

Take my word for it, as honeft Ranger fays, thou art a mighty filly girl. You find I do read—I have read plays, child, innumerable. Romances are too long and tirefome. Novels that are full of the marvellous and furprifing, I can't attend to.'

I 6   In

In this manner she ran on till it was time to go to the play, ' What is the play, Emily?' said she with her usual vivacity; I could not inform her— ' Why, it is the Fool, written by Captain Vatafs, do you know the Captain?—he is an amazing *quis*— great whifkers—no fkirts. Ha ha ha!'

And when we were at the play, every gentleman who came into the box was an *ugly devil*, or a *handsome toad*; but with Sir Peter Mapletoft, the affiduous Sir Peter, she was inceffantly chatting, sometimes laughing at him, at other times enquiring after every unknown face. Then ridiculing every difagreeable or unfafhionable appearance with fo much humour,

humour, that though I was vexed at the interruption, and could not approve her fatirical talents, it was impoffible to forbear laughing.

I called on her next morning, and found her playing with her monkey, and lap-dog. I afked her how she could chufe to lofe time fo. ' Child,' said she, with an affeᵈ gravity, ' do you underftand the nature of time ? Time, as Mr. Lock obferves, is a fucceffion of ideas. Now, my dear, it is evident no perfon can have a quicker fucceffion of ideas than I ; *confequently* I can't lofe time, fince I enjoy its very effence, what conftitutes *its exiftence*. Heigh ho! I have almoft done tormenting the men,

men, poor devils—I am almoft married;—why furely, faid I, you are fatisfied with your choice? ' Satisfied ! you little foolatum,' interrupted she, ' why to be fure, I fhould not have given the man fuch hopes of happinefs, if I had preferred any other—but I had, notwithftanding, rather live fingle. Though, on fecond thoughts, I don't know what to fay—he is a good-natured genteel creature enough —a fimpleton, *I believe*. You are perhaps convinced of it ; but no matter; many a hufband is made a fool of; now my *intended* is naturally fuch, more reputable for me, let me tell you.'

Our

Our converfation was here interrupted by the monkey, who having obferved her playing with a beautiful drefs cap, fnatched it out of her hands, and pulling it with his teeth and fingers, foon rendered it unfit for ufe. O you mifchievous little devil,' she cried, ' what are you about? See, Amelia! nay don't interrupt him, how prettily the toad holds the lace. My fweet pug, if it had been worth a thoufand pounds, I muft have laughed as I do now at thy roguery!'

She then catched him up, and in the prefence of George Stapleton kiffed him feveral times. The little animal feemed to enjoy the frolic, and

184

and looked as if he wished for another prey. I was fearful my muslin petticoat might be his next attempt, and I found Miss Macnamara did not chuse to disappoint him. I took leave sooner than I should have done, if she had been quite alone, or had had better company.

I shall expect another letter from my dear Arabella, with as much impatience as the first; and while I wish to merit her approbation, I entreat her never to spare any deserved reproof. It can be only by pursuing the advice of the best of friends, and attempting to copy the model of her example, I can become worthy of her esteem; which, with a continuance

185

nuance of her affection, is essentially necessary to complete the happiness of

her ever affectionate friend
AMELIA DE GONZALES.'

P. S. I yesterday was in company with the young Charles Grandison; he is a wild spirited youth, and totally unlike his grandfather the celebrated Sir Charles, who is still alive. He said, which made us all laugh, ‘ The old square toes continues to wear a full suit of gold laced cloaths, with bag and sword; he bows upon Lady Grandison's shrivelled hand twenty times in an hour, gives every body advice, and takes the air in his chariot and six.' Adieu.

Margaret

186

Margaret Grimes being fast asleep, and Arabella herself feeling much inclined to yawn, she drew from her pocket the miniature portrait of her adorable Henry, and gazing on it with a steadfast look, fetched a deep sigh, and retired.

Chapter

187

Chapter 20.

ARABELLA'S EMBARRASSMENT, AND THE BEGINNING OF A VOYAGE.

SOLITUDE is the nurse of sorrow, and therefore Arabella loved to be alone; her affection for her dear Henry every hour increased, in spite of the sly remarks of Miss Dawkins, and the artful insinuations of Miles Matthews—she was convinced that his heart was good; and though the custards were all spoiled, yet she was persuaded that Lady Fairville was innocence itself. It is not possible to separate ideas where there is prevarication,

rication, and diforders accumulate in proportion to defultory opinion. For this reafon, when the ftar of evening began its gradual courfe to the antipodes, fhe fauntered from her cottage in that frame of mind, which difappointment naturally inculcates.

As fhe was elegantly leaning with her forehead againft a beech tree, in the vicinity of Mr. Pafley's park, fhe obferved a youth approach her of an interefting countenance, and engaging mien. He was dreffed in a light robe of green taffety, and a bonnet of yellow farfenet, and had in his hand a hop-pole, hung with bunches of grapes. He gazed at her with admiration and delight; then throwing

ing himfelf at her feet, implored that beneficence which fo fingularly marked her character. As fhe looked at his large black eyes, a new and tender emotion took poffeffion of her foul, and for a moment fhe forgot the fuperiority of Henry. 'Ah! Madam,' faid the youth, 'if your condefcenfion knew the agitation of my intellect, a feebler tone might fuffice, but as it is, nature may pafs away, before this pulfe fhall ceafe to throb with love and adoration.'

She replied with a half fmile, that was inexpreffibly fweet, 'Indeed, young gentleman, your behaviour entitles you to confideration and refpect; your whole conduct is unexceptionably

ceptionably correct; but my little cottage is the abode of peace. Removed from the idle occupations of fplendid greatnefs, and the commercial buftle of felf-intereft, I there devote myfelf to contemplation and retirement. 'Ah me! I am the moft difconfolate of women.' Here a flood of tears came feafonably to her relief, and the youth catching her in his arms, vowed eternal conftancy, and affection without end.

He inftantly mounted his horfe, which was a forrel nag of confiderable value, and giving the view-hollow, difappeared in an inftant.

Margaret Grimes had been fent to Amelia,

Amelia, who was juft returned into the country, when the Bifhop received the cheefes by the London Carrier, and confequently fhe had no time to enter into any difcuffion upon the matter. Henry, it is certain, had been twice hunting in that neighbourhood, and fupped at Parfon Grigfby's, with Major Ellerby and fome other officers, totally unconcerned as to the refult of the Weft-India expedition. At leaft it appeared fo by his conduct, for George Simms declared he had been thrafhing all day, and had not dined when the accident happened.

When Arabella heard thefe ftrange circumftances, fhe was at a lofs what plan

192

plan to pursue; yet she thought it would be the wisest way, to pay a visit to Lady Fairville, as if nothing had happened. Taking up her pen, therefore, as usual, and bending her left knee to the ground, to give herself a greater spring, she produced the following verses.

On a dead Goldfinch.

Poor little bird that died one day,
As kings and other people may!
Ah! what would gentle Henry say
To find your life thus past away?

But Henry, O my pretty dear!
Is gone far off, and is not here,
Therefore does Arabella fear,
He is not overmuch sincere.

When

193

When next the moon begins to rise,
Again thou wilt not ope thine eyes,
And thus my faithless Henry flies,
And leaves me looking at the skies.

Begone then balmy zephyrs, go,
And let my cruel Henry know
That on this fruitful earth below,
No other man could use me so!

My Goldfinch died—how did he dare,
To leave me lost in deep despair?
Then let each maiden, sunk in care,
Of Lovers such as mine, beware.

Having relieved her anxious mind by the above soft effusion, Arabella wrote a long letter to the Countess, and offered to submit the whole matter to arbitration; she also re-

K   quested

194

quested the loan of her Ladyship's telescope, for the purpose, if possible, of shaming Henry out of his present pursuit; for she well knew the impossibility he laboured under of collecting fossils in that part of Lincolnshire, and rather wished to have it in his own hand writing, than through any other medium whatever.

Such was the situation of these two unfortunate lovers, and so sure was she of his fidelity, that no power on earth could have tempted her beyond the boundary of her garden, for the remainder of that week.

This precaution was however premature, for General Barton made a point

195

point of the whole party coming to the ball, and as Amelia had promised to introduce Don Pedro, who had but just arrived from Spain, so it was expected that Arabella would have sent an express to Henry, and earnestly have requested him to try the effect of the Bath waters, if the pain in his side continued.

Henry obeyed the summons with the utmost alacrity, and the wind being fair, towards evening, the vessel got out of the harbour. As the shore lessened from his view, he offered up one sigh to Love and Arabella, and then retired to his cabin in all the silent bitterness of anguish and dismay.

K 2   Chapter

197

Chapter 21.

A WISE LECTURE.

LUCINDA Howard now removed to the houſe of Mrs. Maltrever in Portman Square, was introduced into all the firſt company in London. Her engagements were endleſs, and what with dinners, aſſemblies, and public places, ſhe was almoſt harraſſed out of her life, and the conſtant attention and invariable purſuit of Sir Sidney Walker diſguſted her extremely. Mrs. Maltrever endeavoured to comfort her, and being a woman of ſuperior underſtanding and uncommon penetration, one morn-

K 3   ing,

ing, after they had been to Wandſworth, in Captain Harland's phaeton, took her into a private ſtudy, and thus with emotion addreſſed her. ' My dear and amiable Lucinda, it is impoſſible for a young woman entering life, whatever may be her connections, to avoid that ſort of petulance and incongruity, which is but too often the reſult of ill-placed ambition, and a deſire to diſtinguiſh herſelf in literary compoſition. Dreſs, for inſtance, is a natural propenſity, but if diſpenſed with too liberal a hand, degenerates by degrees into a ſpecious kind of contumely. I was once myſelf a giddy girl, and at the time Mr. Maltrever fell a victim to my charms, was perhaps

as

as fond of fields ſports, as any alderman amongſt them. I had been at Spa with Lady Green and her family, when I firſt entered upon the plan of life, which unfortunately was my chief inconvenience, for had I known the world well, I certainly ſhould not have built this houſe during my huſband's abſence, nor ſhould I have written thoſe works which have impreſſed the public with a ſenſe of impropriety which certainly does not belong to me. Here then lies the error of your conduct, and ſorry am I to ſay, Miſs Howard, in many inſtances of late, I have diſcovered a careleſſneſs in your outline that totally deſtroys the effect of crayon painting. For the principal

K 4   beauty

beauty of it confifts in a certain harmony, and an attention to general agreement, as I fear I have frequently before been obliged to obferve to you.

' Now Sir Sydney Walker it muft be owned, has a fine eftate, and in point of family, is unexceptionable; but you know, Lucinda, that he is not in parliament, and that he goes into the North every other year to pafs feveral weeks with Lady Fairville. On this, therefore, I fhall make no comment, but you, my dear, are the beft judge, how far you could be happy with a man, who has, perhaps, the fineft collection of pictures in Europe, and who went to Copenhagen,

hagen, to fettle the herring fifhery on a more permanent eftablifhment. It is irkfome, it is painful to me, to fpeak to you in this manner, becaufe I know the goodnefs of your heart, and I am fure for my own part, I am only actuated by the intereft I take in what concerns you, for I made no objection to their cutting down Hadleigh Grove, nor did I wifh you to go to America, even at the time when your poor father was fuch a martyr to the gout. You will, therefore, no doubt, do juftice to my pretenfions, and in fome degree, relieve me from that corroding anxiety, which has too long and too feverely preyed upon my health. A love of pleafure is the bane of the youthful mind, and a too

K 5   great

great earneftnefs in worldly matters, gives a tone of reftleffnefs to moft people, which, in their latter days, they cannot readily difcufs with any fort of coolnefs, or difefteem.

" Beyond the fix'd and fettled rules
Of vice and virtue in our fchools."

' As the poet fays, lies all the difference between immorality and that fatal chafm in human affairs, which tends to overcharge the brain, and diffeminate erroneous opinions.— Then do not, my dear girl, miftake my motives; my only wifh in life is to fee you well eftablifhed on a permanent foundation, that may defy the biteing blafts of calumny, and avoid

avoid by its efficacy the abfurdities of fociety in general. In the country, it is true, we efcape thofe fcenes of folly, which diflocate the capital, but there alfo we are fubject to the ill effects of climate, and the frequent variations which the beft of us cannot refift or fubdue. In the intercourfe with the gay and diffipated, the moral obligations fubfide, and reafon triumphantly prevails over the wild extravagancies, which pervert the general well-being of the human race. I have now done with reproach, I am confident, my beloved Lucinda fees her own conduct in its true point of view, and will not enter into any engagements, that, originating in impropriety, can only tend

K 6   to

to tarnifh the pure luftre of virtue, and to occafion that fpecies of regret, which is irrefiftible in the extreme.'

Here the old lady paufed, and with much feeming contrition, wiped away the falling tears, that copioufly bedewed her aged cheeks, while Lucinda exprefled her gratitude in the warmeft terms of acknowledgement, and, actuated by the moft graceful impulfe, fpontaneoufly drank her health in a bumper of Tokay, which had been fent as a prefent to Mrs. Maltrever, by a celebrated merchant of Hamburgh, who, during the whole war, had fupplied the Britifh navy, with indigo, cocoa nuts, and cochineal.

The door of the room now burft open with a fudden jerk, and Arabella Bloomville, with a haggard countenance and difhevelled hair, rufhed in, and a moment after, fell lifelefs upon the carpet. By the care and attention of Mrs. Maltrever and Lucinda, fhe was foon reftored to fome appearance of fenfation, and was carried to bed by the butler, who feemed tenderly to intereft himfelf in her recovery. In confequence of this awful event, the party was put off, the mantua-maker was difmifled, five phyficians were called in to her relief, and the lap-dog was locked up in the pantry.

Chapter

Chapter 22.

A DUEL.

AT fix o'clock in the morning, Don Pedro with the Chevalier de Berlingier, repaired to Kenfington Gravel Pits, according to appointment, where they were foon joined by Lord Mahogany and Sir Paul Danbury. The ground being meafured, which was fixteen paces, Lord Mahogany afked Sir Paul if the Oxford coach was gone by; this difconcerted Don Pedro, who fired his piftol in the air, and the Chevalier leaping over the ditch, feized the bull by the horns. Lord Mahogany had climbed

climbed up a tree in the utmoſt
conſternation, but ſeeing the milk-
woman drop upon her knees to Sir
Paul, he took a pinch of ſnuff, and
returned to the attack. He, therefore, with cool reſolution and determined rage, pointed his piſtol at his
antagoniſt; but the pheaſant flew
away at the report of the piece, and
the link boy throwing a ſquib into
his Lordſhip's right eye, put him off
his bias, of which Don Pedro inſtantly took advantage; for pulling
out his memorandum book, he wrote
down every particular with unde-
niable preciſion. As Lord Mahogany declared he was by no means
ſatisfied, the ſeconds interpoſed, and
begged Don Pedro to conſider that
ſuch

ſuch a diſplay of horſemanſhip at this
time, was totally unneceſſary. In
conſequence of freſh difficulties ari-
ſing, Don Pedro fired, and the pigeon fell; which convinced Lord
Mahogany of his miſtake, and induced him ſo far to apologize, as to
ſay, ‘ That he thought Amelia's hair
of the moſt beautiful color, and that
he would have ſaid the ſame in Spain,
or any other part of Europe. That
as for any evil intention, he diſ-
claimed it; he acknowledged, indeed,
that he had ſpoken highly of Amelia's
perſonal accompliſhments, but that
he actually had not propoſed the
party of pleaſure on the water, and
that if Don Pedro thought he had,
he was extremely ſorry for it. The
Chevalier

Chevalier objected to this part of the
propoſal; in conſequence of which,
they again renewed the combat. Don
Pedro's piſtols were Spaniſh, and
Lord Mahogany had a pair of Wog-
den's, which having the air of an advantage on his part, he offered to bet
a thouſand pounds, that Sir Paul
Danbury had not been preſent at
the dinner. Don Pedro now caſt a
look of ineffable contempt on his
Lordſhip, and artfully inſinuated that
the Liſbon Mail had been loſt the
preceding week; but this Lord Mahogany totally denied; ſo that as the
matter was not likely to be otherwiſe
accommodated, they fired a third
round. Lord Mahogany having on
a large cocked hat, his adverſary's
ball

ball paſſed innocently by; but Don
Pedro was not ſo fortunate, for his
Lordſhip's ſhot ſtruck an oak tree
within twenty yards of him, thence
glanced into a horſe pond, and killed
an old woman's pig, that was aſleep
in its ſtye.

The combatants became more furious than ever, at this juncture, their
eyes flaſhed hatred and deſtruction,
and Lord Mahogany with a firm
tone demanded, whether Don Pedro
really ſuppoſed him capable of libelling an Archbiſhop, who had never
been guilty of one good action in
the whole courſe of his life. This
queſtion was ill timed, for Don Pedro, foaming with fury, entreated
the

the Chevalier to attend particularly to this laſt denunciation. Again therefore, with wonderful accuracy, Don Pedro diſcharged his piſtol, and Lord Mahogany bounding three feet from the ground, pitched perpendicularly upon his toe, and ſpun round for ſome time like the flyer of a jack, then putting the little finger of his left hand into his ear, and with the other hand gracefully taking off his hat, he vociferouſly called out ' God ſave the king.' This immediately ſoftened the ſanguinary temper of Don Pedro, who was the moſt loyal grandee in Spain, he ſlung himſelf into the arms of Lord Mahogany, and declaring that the diſpute was now

now perfectly accommodated, begged that they might exchange neckcloths.

Sir Paul Danbury and the Chevalier Berlingier, waited with extreme earneſtneſs for his lordſhip's reply, who drawing his ſword, inſtantly preſented it with the moſt engaging politeneſs to a barber's wife, who was opening oyſters for a Scotch pedlar at the corner of the meadow.

The whole affair being thus amicably adjuſted, they all entered the boat together, which glided rapidly down the ſtream towards the place of their deſtination, where the lovely and agonizing Amelia expected them, with

with doubt and trepidation. In their progreſs Don Pedro ſaw a bird ſwimming upon the ſurface of the water, and aſked Lord Mahogany to inform him of its Engliſh appellation. His Lordſhip anſwered him with wonderful readineſs, by the following extemporary enigma:

    The fourth letter of the alphabet,
    What every body is often called,
    A ſimple ſound expreſſive of the ocean,
    And the beginning of all Kings.

Thus this tremendous day, the dawn of which was ſo overcaſt, the morning of which loured ſo much, and came on heavily with clouds, was now

now changed to ſoft ſerenity, mild tranquility, ſober peace, meek harmony, and concluded with general ſatisfaction.

Chapter

Chapter 23.

THE DANGERS OF A MASQUERADE.

THE ladies were all in high prepa-
ration for the enfuing mafquerade,
Mrs. Maltrever who had vifited in
her early days the coaft of Malabar,
fixed upon the drefs of a peafant of
the Alps, as moft fuitable to her fituation in life. Lucinda chofe to af-
fume the character of Queen Elizabeth, Margaret Grimes was difguifed
as Cardinal Wolfey, and the celeftial
Arabella, like a fimple dairy-maid,
in white fattin, with a little black
feather, perking over her left ear,

L   ' Appear'd

218

' Appear'd like an angel, new drop'd from the
fkies.'

General Barton went as an old
cloaths man, Sir Sydney Walker as
a pair of nutcrackers, and Captain
Harland as a blackfmith. When
they arrived at the Theatre in the
Haymarket, the gayety of the lights,
the proportions of that elegant building, and the fplendor of the furrounding company delighted them beyond
meafure. Arabella felt an unufual
flow of fpirits, and Lucinda whifpered
a blue domino with particular emotion. The devil now feized Arabella
by the hand, and ftanding upon his
head drank up a whole bottle of
champagne without flinching. This
occafioned

219

occafioned great merriment on both
fides, and Sir Sydney being quite
intoxicated, added a frefh ftimulus
to her vivacity. Sterne's melancholy
Maria, dreffed in ftraw, now advanced
with a crowd of admirers in her
train; then toffing her head at fight
of Arabella fhe faid, ' well to be fure,
I dare to fay this *here creter* thinks
herfelf the *biggeft* beauty in the
place.' Arabella no fooner heard
this rude attack of the lovely maniac,
than fhe fwooned away, which threw
three gentlemen into fits, and fhat-
tered the great luftre that was fufpended from the dome. This was
indeed a chance, but the pathetic
Maria paid little attention to the alarming confufion fhe had occafioned.

L 2   On

220

On the contrary, she took her guitar and sung the following mournful elegy with such invincible pathos, that Lord Mahogany himself, who was there in the character of a mile-stone, burst into tears:

Elegy.

Where flow meand'ring thro' the verdant plain,
  Yon rill with murm'ring melancholy flows,
Contiguous to the spot where, hapless swain!
  Young William's straw-clad cottage once arose.

Lost in incomprehensibility
  Of those dire pangs which rent his tortured
    breast,
When on his death-bed laid with many a sigh,
  His soul departed, leaving me unblest,

I gaily

221

I gaily hasten'd to the well-known spot,
  Where I had oft partaken curds and tart,
Untir'd by repetition, 'twas my lot,
  To share the dainties of his dairy's art.

The slipp'ry butter which in daily course,
  Was by his pretty sister Mary made,
Ah happy days, but now distress, remorse,
  In sad perfection my torn thoughts invade.

For gone alas! are this once blissful pair,
  And anguish only now remains for me;
He left a monkey, that my griefs shall share,
  And mourn the season I no more shall see.

This beautiful effusion was received with unbounded plaudits, when Mrs. Maltrever screamed out ' O heavens! she's gone, she's gone,' at which a sailor exclaim'd ' yes, damme

L 3   she's

222

she's off.' This occasioned a violent burst of laughter, while Mrs. Maltrever and Lucinda fell into the orchestra, and unfortunately broke Signor Corvino's capital violoncello.

When the ladies got home, the horror of the scene is not to be described, the servants were dispatched to Pimlico and Bear-key, Mrs. Maltrever's own woman went to Billingsgate, but all in vain, no tidings of the celestial fugitive could in any manner be procured. Towards noon a lad of about eighteen, who was a brickmaker in the environs of London came to Mrs. Maltrever's house, and informed her, that being at work about five o'clock in the morning, he

223

he saw a chaise and four drive by, in which were two old ladies and a child. ' That being the case, my lady!' said he, ' I looked after them a good bit, and saw a gelman ride past on a grey mare, and in a brown coat, so said I to Bet, I'll be a bob-stock of ale, if you have a mind, so she said, says she, with all my gizzard, now we had not been at the sow and harrow above ten minutes, before a livery servant came in for a pint of twopenny, whereby says I where are you going sir? Now he was a black looking man to be sure, and says he, we have lost our Miss from Mol Traver's in Portman Square, and whoever can give count of her shall have ten quids. Now my lady, I

L 4   does

does believe, she was in the *chay*
with a great squire that I seed an
hour afterwards, for she was des-
perate pretty and screamed out main-
ly, so I hopes you'll give me the
bounty for my *dickscovery*.' The
whole company were so entertained
by the lad's naiveté, that they presented him with a shilling, and all
agreeing that he possessed infinite
humour, advised him, if possible to
get into the church; Lucinda smiled
inwardly at the comicality of the
idea, and vowing eternal enmity to
all masquerades, took her diamond
ring from her finger, and wishing
Arabella all possible success, danced
a Scotch reel with Lord Mongomery
to the admiration of all the spectators.

' Now

' Now pursuing, now retreating,
' Now in airy circles meet,
' To brisk notes in cadence beating,
' Glance their many twinkling feet.'

L 5   Chapter

227

Chapter 24.

A TERRIBLE LOSS, AND A PRO
JECTED JOURNEY.

WILHELMINA Countess of
Fairville was the descendant of an
ancient and honourable house in
North Wales. Her father, the Marquis of Mushroom, inherited all those
brave qualities and stern virtues,
which had so eminently distinguished
his ancestor's breed of sheep, from
the cows of Spain, or the heavy
beasts of the low countries. Early
in life he lost a wife whom he tenderly loved, and he seemed to derive his sole consolation from playing

L 6   at

228

at leap-frog with the children she
had left behind. His son whom he
had brought up to the arms himself
so honourably bore, fell out of a
back garret before he reached his
nineteenth year; an elder daughter
died of the whooping cough in her
infancy. Wilhelmina, who had recovered from the measles, was his
sole surviving child. His castle was
situated in one of those delightful
vallies in Wales, in which the beautiful and the sublime are so happily
united; where the magnificent features of the scenery are contrasted,
and their effect heightened by the
blooming luxuriance of woods and
pasturage, by the gentle windings
of the stream, and the ruinous aspect of
the falling cottages.

229

The Marquis was now retired from
the service, grey age having overtaken him one day in an expedition
to the West Indies. His residence
was the resort of all foreigners of
distinction, who had fled from their
own country to escape the horrors of
liberty, and who, attracted by the
united talents of the soldier, the phi-
losopher, and the cook, under his
hospitable roof, enjoyed good beef
and pudding, eels, mutton cutlets,
Irish stew, and pigeon pie, besides
strong beer, vegetables and pastry.

Among the visitors of this description, was the late Earl of Fairville,
who was then on his travels through
Wales, very much pitted with the
small-pox.

230

small-pox. The beauty of Wilhelmina, whose hair was rather sandy,
embellished by a mind, highly and
elegantly cultivated, touched his
heart, as it were with the tip of an
eagle's feather, and he instantly so-
licited her hand and glove in marriage.

The manly sense of the Earl, who
was allowed to be the best shot in
the county, and the excellencies of
his disposition, had not passed unobserved, or unapproved by the Marquis or his steward, while the graces
of his person, and of his mind, had
anticipated for him in the heart of
Wilhelmina, a pre-eminence over
every church dignitary that she knew.
The

231

The Marquis of Mushroom had
but one objection to the marriage,
which was his hatred of leeks in general, and this was likewise the
objection of Louisa, who had an
equal aversion from potatoes, neither the one nor the other could
endure the idea of a mode of nou-
rishment which would be so disagreeable to them.

Wilhelmina was to the Marquis the
last prop of his declining age. The
Marquis was to Wilhelmina the father, the doctor, and the friend, to
whom her heart had hitherto been
solely devoted, and from whom it
could not now be torn, but in a
multiplied ratio of the unknown
quantity.

232

This remained an infurmountable obftacle till it was removed with the garden wall by the tendernefs of the Earl, who entreated the Marquis to quit North Wales, and refide with his daughter in Berkfhire. The attachment of the Marquis to his natal land, and the pride of hereditary confequence, were too powerful to fuffer him to acquiefce in the propofal, without a violent diforder in his bowels, and fome appearance of the ague.

The defire of fecuring the drawings of his child, by a union with fuch a charaûer as the Earl's, and of feeing her eftablifhed in all her conjugal rights, before death fhould deprive

233

prive her of the inveftigation of a father, at length fubdued him to the loweft pitch of defpondency, and he refigned the hand and feal of his daughter to the rapturous avidity of the amorous Earl.

The Marquis adjufted his affairs, and affigning his eftates to the care of fome old rufty agents, bade a laft adieu to the landed intereft, which, during fixty years, had been the principal objeû of his happinefs, and of his regrets. The courfe of years had not obliterated from his heart the early affeûions of his youth: he took a hop—ftep—and—jump over that grave, which enclofed the reliques of hie wife, from which it was not his leaft effort

234

effort to depart, and whither he ordered all letters and parcels to be conveyed.

Wilhelmina quitted Wales, with a pain in her head, fcarcely lefs acute than that of her father; the poignancy of which, however, was greatly foftened down, by the tender affiduities of her lord and mafter, whofe affectionate attentions hourly heightened her expeûations, and encreafed her love for the handfomeft, moft induftrious, and beft of men.

They arrived in Berkfhire without any accident, where the Earl welcomed Wilhelmina, as the miftrefs of his

235

his domains, and immediately prefented her with this delightful

Sonnet.

O Wilhelmina ! 'tis with double joy,
   I fee thee here, both as my friend and wife,
My future hours, my dear ! I will employ,
   To make thee bleft, I will upon my life.

Ah ! fhould'ft thou nine months hence, produce
      a boy ;
   To fing the cherub, I'd refume my fife,
For then my happinefs could never cloy,
   And then I'd bid adieu to war and ftrife.

The Marquis, too, fhould liften to my fong,
   Thy worthy father, and the beft of men !
While beef and beer fhould cheer the peafant
      throng.
   But I will now a moment drop my pen,
And wait the time, for which I fo much long,
   When, without fail, I'll take it up agen.

The

The Marquis of Mushroom had apartments in the castle, and a magic lantern to amuse him when out of spirits, and there the evening of his days declined in a very decent sort of happiness.

Before his death, he had the exquisite pleasure of seeing his race renovated in a child of the Countess, a daughter, who was a little ricketty or so, but of a clear complexion, and rather plump.

On the decease of the Marquis, it was necessary for the Earl to visit North Wales, in order to take possession of his estates, which, from neglect, had a good deal run to seed, and

and which, owing to his long absence, in many places, wanted new paleing.

He, with all his pointers, two churchwardens, and a bookseller, attended the remains of the Marquis to their last abode.

The Countess, desirous of once more beholding her young ducks and the old pigeon house, as well as anxious to pay her compliments to the memory of her Papa, entrusted her child to the care of the gamekeeper, who had made her caps in her early childhood, and had accompanied the Marquis to Whitechapel on a Sunday.

Having

Having deposited the remains of the Marquis in the coal-hole, according to his wish, and had their hair cut, they returned to Berkshire, where the first intelligence they received on their arrival at the vestry, was of the death of their daughter, and of the old game-keeper, her attendant. The poor fellow had died of the mumps, soon after their departure, the child only a fortnight before their return.

This disastrous event gave the Countess a violent creak in her neck, and afflicted the disconsolate Earl with a white swelling on his knee, and they never ceased to ridicule each other, for having entrusted their infant to a game-keeper. Time, however,

ever, subdued the poignancy of the cholic, but came fraught with another evil, more acute; this was the death of the Earl, who, in the pride of youth, with seventeen pipes of old port in his cellar, and constituting the felicity of his family, died, as he was dancing a hornpipe. He left the Countess to bewail his loss, and to wear spectacles, if ever she should attempt to read by candle light.

As soon as the Countess was arrayed in her becoming weeds; the first thought that darted across her imagination, was her much valued Lucinda Howard, to whom she immediately sent a most impressive letter, earnestly requesting her company, on

240

on a journey to Naples, which she meant instantaneously to undertake. Meanwhile, as she wished for nothing more ardently, than a fair wind to waft them across the Channel, she occupied herself in penning the following sublime and incomparable ode to Eolus, which for novelty of expression, harmony of versification, plenitude of idea, and dignity of sentiment, is not to be equalled in the English language:

Ode to Eolus.*

O Thou! to whom great Jove † assign'd
The empire of each stubborn wind

* The God of the Winds, according to the accounts given by Heathen poets.
† A Pagan Deity, and the first of all the Gods,

And

241

And bade them own thy sway;
'Tis thou who giv'st them leave to rage,
Thy voice their fury can assuage,
And check their headlong way.

When Juno, ‡ Heaven's imperial Dame,
A suppliant at thy feet became,
Thou didst admit her pray'r;
For her the surges lash'd the shore,
For her thou bad'st the tempest roar
Wide thro' the troubled air.

But now a nymph whose matchless mien
Surpasses that of Jove's proud queen
Is venturing on the deep;
O then each adverse wind restrain,
Let favouring zephyrs skim the main,
And hush the storms to sleep!

Love at the helm shall take his stand,
And guide the bark with skillful hand

‡ A Pagan Deity, wife and sister to Jupiter.

M

242

Along the watry way,
The cestus which adorn'd her waist,
By Venus § on the topmast plac'd,
Shall like a pendant play.

Their green locks dripping briny dew,
The Nereids ‖ rising to the view,
Shall each gay art employ,
And Ocean, † conscious of his freight,
Proud to subside beneath her weight, ¶
Soft murmuring tell his joy!

The beautiful Countess Dowager had strained her left leg so much in the composition of the above harmo-

§ The Goddess of Beauty, and wife of Vulcan, who used to wear a cestus.
‖ Pagan mermaids, who lived in the salt sea.
† Alias Neptune, who is always proud on such occasions, being King of the sea.
¶ She was very bulky woman

nious

243

nious and affecting ode, that she ate a plate of prawns, drank a pot of porter, and retired to bed, agitated in the extreme.

END OF THE FIRST VOLUME.

Modern Novel Writing,

OR THE

ELEGANT ENTHUSIAST;

AND

Interesting Emotions

OF

Arabella Bloomville.

A RHAPSODICAL ROMANCE:

INTERSPERSED WITH

Poetry.

IN TWO VOLUMES.

Vol. 2.

BY THE RIGHT HON.

LADY HARRIET MARLOW.

I nod in company, I wake at night,
Fools rush into my head, and so I write.

Pope.

London:

PRINTED FOR G. G. AND J. ROBINSON.

MDCCXCVI.

CONTENTS.

Vol. 2.

Meeting

TEXAS WOMAN'S UNIVERSITY LIBRARY

76

CONTENTS.

ERRATUM.

Col. 2.

PAGE 64 LINE 17 for *moifter*, read *moifture*

The

The

ELEGANT ENTHUSIAST.

Chapter 1.

AN IMPORTANT DISCOVERY.

AFTER a journey of much fatigue and unpleafant rumination, Lucinda Howard, accompanied by the melodious Arabella, arrived at the Countefs's elegant abode. They were fhewn into the drawing room, the walls of which her Ladyfhip had fpent two years and a half in ornamenting with her own dear hands.

2

It was entirely painted over with birds, beafts, fifhes, urns, flowerpots, and arabefque figures in a moft aftonifhing manner, fo that the praifes for her ingenuity, and for the laudable occupation of her time, was a conftant fource of vanity to her Ladyfhip, and a ready fubject of converfation to all her vifitors. But alas; the Countefs, fince the expediting her letter, had endured a ftate of dreadful fufpence, although Mrs. de Malthe in friendfhip had endeavoured to foothe her Ladyfhip's diftrefs, by her conftant prefence, and the moft unbounded admiration of the pictures and pier glaffes, and particularly the curtains. She was entering into an elaborate treatife on tafte, when the noife

3

noife of horfes at the gate reached her ears. ' It is my Lucinda,' faid Mrs. de Malthe, rifing from her chair, ' it is my dear Lucinda, fhe brings us life or death.' She faid no more, but winking at Captain Harland, and with a comical fnap of her fingers, rufhed forwards, and with an oval movement, clafped the almoft expiring Lucinda to her bofom. The tranfport of the fcene repelled utterance; fobs, tears, and chocolate drops, were all that could be given. Let thofe who have experienced fuch fuperabundant blifs, declare, how inconceivably gratifying are the encomiums of virtue, when foftened by the breezes of content.

4

The general joy, however, was fuddenly diffipated by the Countefs, who fell fenfelefs to the floor; delight yielded to furprife, and to the bufinefs of affiftance. On recovering, the Countefs looked wildly round her, and Doctor Philbert took a cup of coffee. This giving the whole company breathing time, Lord Damplin objected to the manœuvre, and her Ladyfhip exclaimed, ‘ Was it a vifion that I faw, or a reality?’ Every body put on their fpectacles, but could not difcover any thing extraordinary. ‘ It was Mr. Bloomville himfelf, my firft hufband, his very hair, his features, under a female form; that benign countenance which I have fo often contemplated in

5

in imagination.’ Her fine eyes ftill feemed in fearch of fome ideal object, and they began to doubt whether a fudden frenzy had not feized her brain. ‘ Ah! again!’ faid fhe, and inftantly relapfed, with an engaging motion of her head. Their eyes were now turned towards Arabella, who was bringing a glafs of water for the Countefs’s parrot, and on *her* the attention of all prefent was now centered. She approached, ignorant of what had happened, and her furprife was great, when the Countefs, reviving, fixed her eyes mournfully upon her, and afked her to take off her glove. ‘ It is,—it is my Arabella!’ faid fhe, with a ftrong emotion; ‘ I have, indeed, found

B 3   my

6

my long loft child; that ftrawberry on her arm confirms the decifion.’ The whole company crowded round them, and Jack Deepley crammed his hankerchief in his mouth. Arabella fell at the feet of her new Mamma, and bathed her hand with tears. ‘ Gracious me! for what have I been referved!’ She could fay no more. The Countefs raifed, and preffed her to her heart. It was upwards of feven minutes and a half, before either of them could fpeak, and all prefent were too much affected to interrupt the filence. At length the Countefs gazing tenderly upon Arabella faid ‘ My beloved girl, within thefe laft fifteen months, I have taught myfelf German.

7

man. ‘ Aye,’ cried Doctor Philbert, ‘ the man who can be infenfible to the charms of virtue, muft be a bad moral character, and vicioufly inclined.’ Arabella wept filently upon the neck of her mamma, while Jack Deepley exclaimed, ‘ Well, Poll, what have you got to fay to all this?’ The bird looked up archly and replied ‘ What’s o’clock.’ This gave a turn to the converfation, and fortunate indeed it was for poor Mrs. de Malthe, whofe emotions almoft overcame her, and were too powerful for utterance.

The company now adjourned to the cedar parlour, and Arabella withdrew to take that repofe fhe fo much

B 4   required.

8

required. She was sufficiently recovered in a few hours to join her friends in the green-house.

After they had eat up the ice cream, and washed their faces in vinegar, the transports of the scene became a little more calm. 'I have much to hope, and much to fear', said Lord Damplin, taking off his coat, and jerking his hat out of the window, 'You, Madam', addressing the Countess, 'you will willingly undertake to be my advocate with her whom I have so long and so ardently adored.' What, are we going to have a funeral,' cried Jack Deepley, 'that your Lordship wants the Countess to be an undertaker?' This

9

This remark occasioned a roar of laughter, but his Lordship looking very serious thus continued, 'May I hope,' taking tenderly the hand of Arabella, who stood trembling by, 'May I hope, that you have not been insensible to my long attachment, and that you will confirm the happiness which is now offered me?' A smile of ineffable sweetness broke through the melancholy which had long clouded her angelic features, and which even the present discovery had not been able entirely to dissipate; then lightly scratching her back with the end of her fan, and heaving a profound sigh, she thus replied, 'No, my Lord, I never can be yours, my affections are engaged to

B 5   another

10

another gentleman, and I will never bestow my hand, where I cannot give my heart.' This answer, so sentimental and so new, charmed the attentive audience; his Lordship was not equal to the shock, but bursting into a flood of tears, declared, that had he suspected matters would have turned out so, he would certainly have gone to the boxing match, which was to be on that day at Rumford, between Johnson and the Jew.

The discourse for the remainder of the day, was occupied by the subject of the discovery, and by a recital of Arabella's adventures, during which Jack Deepley would frequently entertain the company with some facetious

11

tious remarks on the crest-fallen lover. He called him a suspirating senator, a perplexed peer, a lordly lollypop, a neglected nobleman, and a love-sick legislator in hereditary hopelessness. These lively sallies restored the good humour of the company, and induced the amiable Lucinda to favor them with the following

Song.

What is this sentimental love—
  This spell of the romantic mind,
Whose flimsy texture fancy wove
Too weak th' impassion'd heart to bind!

Does it from nature spring? Ah! no;
  Nature the airy form denies—
Is it by reason bred? If so,
  Why always hid from reason's eyes?

B 6   Is

12

Is it a quick inspiring flame
  That animates with love the *heart* ?
No—its cold dictates strangely aim
  A mental fervour to impart.

Dull apathy, or frozen age,
  The phantom conjur'd first to view ;
The policy or envious rage
  Of those who ne'er true rapture knew.

Away ! no more my thoughts detain,
  Illusive, visionary sprite !
May love's warm stream thro' ev'ry vein
  Roll gay desire and fond delight.

And may the youth whose sparkling eyes
  For love and mutual bliss were sent,
Ne'er damp my ardours as they rise,
  With the chill clouds of sentiment.

Every

13

Every body testified the highest approbation of Lucinda's voice, and exquisite mode of singing—but Mrs. de Malthe objected to the words, as having too much meaning in them to please persons of fashion, and the Countess herself glancing her eyes upwards exclaimed—' Well! Miss Howard! indeed I wonder at you.' This observation set the diffident Lucinda a crying ready to break her heart, which Major Pemberton observing, he slyly looked at Jack Deepley and said ' you see, my dear boy! we are up to you.' The gloom of the moment was consequently dispersed, as the heavy vapours of morning fly before the beams of the sun.

On

14

On account of this happy discovery the Countess ordered her house to be thrown open; mirth and festivity resounded through the walls; and the evening closed by a plentiful supper given to all her Ladyship's tradespeople, who, to promote gaiety, were arranged at a long table in the servant's hall, in alphabetical order as follows: an attorney, a baker, a cheesemonger, a dustman, an engraver, a fishwoman, a grocer, a haberdasher, an informer, a joiner, a kitchen-maid, a lapidary, a mercer, a nightman, an optician, a poulterer, a quack, a reviewer, a silversmith, a taylor, a vintner, an undertaker, a writing-master, an xciseman, a yeoman, and a Zealander, who had

emigrated

15

emigrated with the Stadtholder from Holland, and was a maker of Dutch tiles. Thus ended the most brilliant and blissful day the Countess had experienced for many months; a day which will long be remembered by all the guests, for Arabella's restoration to happiness, and for the hospitality, and dignified affability of her ladyship's own woman.

Chapter

Chapter 2.

A LORD IN TRIBULATION.

THE next morning the whole party set off to pay a visit to Arabella's humble cottage, where the watchful Margaret Grimes regaled them with apple dumplings and a syllabub, to the unspeakable satisfaction of little Master Burton, and Sophy Warley.

While they were here engaged in an instructive conversation, two rustics of the neighbourhood, knocked at the door for admittance; they supported between them, on a hurdle, a gentleman

gentleman in great apparent agony. They stated they had found him in a wood, writhing under a tree; that he had implored their charitable aid, and they thought the greatest kindness they could render him, would be to bring him to that place. Arabella's humanity would not permit her to refuse any assistance she could render to a person under such circumstances. She was making the necessary arrangements for that purpose, when Amelia entered, and, with a loud shriek, announced her recognition of Lord Mahogany.

He had returned into the country the very day Lucinda had arrived at the Countess's, and had received the letter

letter Amelia left for him; but the servant informing him from whom it came, he had thrust it carelessly into his pocket unopened, saying, he was engaged in matters of greater import, and could not attend to her messages.

La Contessa Negri had enquired for her foot-boy in the morning, and hearing he had absconded, readily conjectured the reason, though being totally unacquainted with Amelia, she could not suppose her to have any hand in the business, as Arabella very properly remarked, when the circumstance was mentioned. Well, this Italian Signora, who was deeply enamoured of Lord Mahogany, fancying that

20

that her former project might be discovered, determined, if his Lordship put himself again in her power, to trust to no other hand, but perpetrate her intention herself, and cursed her timidity, which had so far disabled her resolution and better judgment, as to make her trust such a matter to a silly boy. If Lord Mahogany, on his first visit, discovered any fear or suspicion of her, she resolved to anticipate the event of a second, by going immediately abroad; for which purpose, she packed up her jewels and money, and made all necessary arrangements; and if he fell into the snare, she thought a very short time, and a few seasonable donations, would prevent all enquiry.

Little

21

Little did the Signora imagine, while she walked in the garden, that the very fate she prepared for him, was, by a counterplot, of which she could have no possible notion, impending over her own head.

In a mind, hardened by successful practice, in a course of iniquity, no scruple intruded itself to prevent the adoption of the most nefarious ones; Lord Mahogany, therefore, resolved to poison La Contessa; and to prevent all suspicion of a musical tendency, gave the answer he did to the servant, and introduced himself into her house by a private way, known and open to himself alone.

The

22

The maids and the shoe-boy were playing at blindman's buff, as he passed the Brewhouse, yet he entered carelessly into the apartment of La Contessa, eating some conserves, of which he held a box in his left hand. After the ordinary salutations, and kissing the back of her neck, he asked her to partake of his sweetmeats, which she did chearfully, foreseeing it would be a reason for her offering him some wine, in which she had infused the fatal venom.

La Contessa, overjoyed at the prospect of success, ate the conserves with avidity, and those which he took care to give her were poisoned, then immediately complaining of thirst,
filled

23

filled two large glasses with wine, and presented one to his Lordship which he drank off without hesitation. Thus perfectly satisfied with the event, he went away, but first he borrowed an umbrella of the coachman, because he had promised to meet General Barton at the bowling green that they might crack a bottle together, and talk over old stories.

Both La Contessa and Lord Mahogany, from an excessive solicitude to avoid suspicion, had given a poison which would not operate for some days. His lordship therefore resolved to employ the interval in travelling, and set out immediately, without its being known that he had visited La Contessa.

24

On the fourth day, as he was riding alone, having fent his fervants forward by the waggon, and his books in the ftage coach; he happened to put his hand into his pocket, and drew out the letter, which Amelia had fent him, and for want of fomething elfe to do, opened and read it.

Language is inadequate, nor would the beft wrought fimilies afford fufficient affiftance, to defcribe the furprize, horror, and regret, which feized him on the perufal of this paper, in which his projected murder was fo far defcribed, that his Lordfhip could not help feeling he had fallen a victim to the treachery of another, at the very moment he was rejoicing in

25

in the fuccefs of his own. He fpurred his horfe forward that he might get to fome place to procure relief, but the violence of this exercife accelerated the effects of the venom. He felt parched with fever; a cruel pain feized his bowels; his eyes feemed burning in their fockets; and his ftrength began to fail him, fo that he was obliged to difmount, and lean againft a ftile, he then took out his pencil and fome affes fkin, and in a fhort time compofed the following illegitimate fonnet without rhime:

26

To the Lark.

Hail lofty Pindar* of the feather'd choir!
Whether at heaven's bleft gate, on mattin wing,
Soaring thou warbleft, when young Maï† firft
Pours forth the gay luxuriance of her dies,
And hill and valley fmile with fudden bloom.

Whether blithe foaring o'er the warring field,
Where bounteous Ceres‡ pours forth all her ftore,
Veiling glad nature's form in living gold§,
Thy pipe, unfailing, roves thro' ev'ry change,
Lofty or *fofty*, melody divine!

* Pindar was called the Theban Eagle, and therefore very like a Lark.
† Some affected portafters of the prefent day have called her Maia, but furely Maï is much more agreeable to the ear.
‡ Ceres, the goddefs of corn.
§ The moft malignant critic will hardly deny this line to have fublimity.

Or

27

Or whether, 'fcaping from the fatal tube,
What time the plunder'd ftubble dufky mourns‖,
Still attic fongfter ¶! to the lift'ning foul
Thy ftrains fhall warble gratitude and love.

This fonnet, which his Lordfhip wrote without rhime or reafon, may, perhaps, be beft excufed by the lamentable fituation in which he found himfelf. He had fcarcely finifhed it, when he fell at the foot of a tree, where the clowns difcovered him, and brought him to the retreat of Arabella.

‖ Though this verfe may be totally unintelligible to the vulgar, it may, perhaps, not be deemed the lefs beautiful by perfons of tafte.
¶ The Nightingale and the Owl have been hitherto called the attic birds, but furely the term is more appropriate to the Lark, which fings up aloft, i. e. in the attic ftory of the fkies.

Chapter 3.

A DIGRESSION ON PATRIOTISM,
AND A STAG HUNT.

' I WISH,' said Lord Charles Oakley, as he came out of Covent Garden Theatre, I wish I knew for certain whether or no Lucinda Howard is with my mother at Fairy Lodge. ' Why so" replied Colonel Birch, ' are you one of her admirers?' ' Faith Frank' returned Lord Charles, ' I can but little bear joking upon that head: though I am a profligate dog, to all appearance, yet the remnants of virtue still actuate a heart, too deeply interested in the peace and

C 3   welfare

welfare of mankind to conform to all the current prejudices of the world.' ' Why, how now! my lord! surely you are not a democrat? what say you, shall we go to orator Gabble's political lectures, he *preaches* to night, *pro bono publico,* come along Citizen Oakley.' You *may* laugh, yet the title of Citizen is as respectable to my ears, as Lord, or any other that folly may have invented, but talk not to me of the orator and his lectures, I am only attached to principles; I hate an egotist in every situation, whatever may be his professions; nay, believe me, when I see a man putting himself forward as the *greatest* sufferer in the cause of liberty, as its *best* friend, as its *firmest* support, when he harrangues

rangues a gaping multitude with an air of the *utmost importance,* tells them all the wrongs they endure, and exaggerates if possible all the oppressions they labour under, and at the same time entreats them to be orderly, patient, and submissive— when I hear and see this, Frank, I say the man cannot be sincere. ' Why in truth,' returned the Colonel, ' if a friend was to come and tell me that Mr. Smith had called me a coward and a scoundrel, and afterwards request me to behave kindly and civilly to the said Mr. Smith, I should think my friend to be either a fool or a madman, or an impostor.' ' Besides Frank,' continued Lord Charles, ' a true patriot can have neither

C 4   vanity,

vanity, nor oftentation, nor ambition,
his only motive to exert himfelf is
philanthropy, his only objeſt, to me-
liorate the wretched condition of the
majority of the human race. If he
difcover weaknefs or abfurdity in any
fellow-labourers in the vineyard he
will endeavour to glofs over their
errors, and not hold them up to contempt, he will feel indignation only
againft unblufhing tyranny, and felfifh
affumption: but is this the cafe with
Gabble? No—if his deareft friend
were to gain more applaufe than he
did for public fpeaking, that inftant
he would look upon him as a rival and
treat him as an enemy.—Does a writer in fupport of freedom and truth
either in profe or verfe obtain any
degree

degree of popular confideration? the
rancour, the jealoufy of Gabble immediately burft out againft him;
he will attack him with a malignant,
though feeble ridicule, with a virulent
though inefficacious criticifm, and
hate him more fincerely than he does
either Pitt, Dundas, Windham, Mansfield, or even all of them together.
Like Pantagruel he thinks to cover a
whole nation with his tongue—In
fhort, this vain orator reminds me in
a flight degree, *parvis componere
magna*, of Robefpierre, who ftrenuoufly employed the energies of
France, oppofed its external ene-
mics, and wifhed to overthrow all the
tyrants of Europe, that he might remain the fole hero of the piece, and

C 5   be

be ftiled MAXIMILIAN THE FIRST,
GREAT PATRIOT OF THE WORLD.
' Why you grow warm Charles,' faid
the Colonel, laughing, ' what fay you
to a couple of fine girls and a dozen
of Champagne?' Here an Irifh chair-
man interrupted their difcourfe, by
informing them, that they had better
be upon their guard and not talk
fedition, for that there was a *blind* man
walking under the Piazza, whom he
fufpeſted to be a *fpy*.

In confequence of this intelligence,
the orange-woman dropped the Cou-
rier, and firft afking the Hackney
coachman's leave, finifhed the tankard
of porter at one draught—which fo
provoked a paftry-cook, who wanted
to

to fell Lord Charles a couple of ra-
zors, that he took no notice of the
Colonel, which was the more extraordinary, as the market was beginning
to fill, and one of the watchmen had
fallen down in an apoplexy.

They both mounted their horfes
with great eagernefs, and though the
ftag took to the North, and led them
a chace of five hours, and though
his moft facred majefty was not prefent, which took much from the
pleafure and intereft of the day, yet
they got fet down to dinner, at Parfon Hornby's before dark. The
dove-houfe having been deftroyed in
their abfence, there could be no
fifhing that evening; fo Lord Charles
C 6   drank

36

drank a large bumper of brandy to the health of his favourite Lucinda Howard, and was pledged by the Colonel, in a pint of old port.

As their hopes and wifhes were now deferred till the morrow, they juft treated the Parfon with a few jovial fongs, and were carried up to bed by the houfe-maid, at half paft two in the morning.

Chapter

37

Chapter 4.

PHRENZY, DESPAIR, AND DEATH.

LORD Mahogany, when he was brought to the abode of Arabella, was in a ftate of infenfibility. The violence of his agitations had exhaufted him; but as foon as General Barton was informed of his fituation, he prepared a decoftion of fimples, which he faid, would, if the poifon was not very ftrong, or had not been long taken, operate as an antidote, but would, at all events, reftore his reafon and quiet. This was adminiftered, and foon produced a return of fenfe in his Lordfhip: he opened his

38

his eyes, and ftaring wildly at the General, exclaimed with a fhriek of agony—

' I am not dead. Why art thou come to torment me before my time? I know thee well; thou art an elephant.—Hah! how he handles the cards—help, help—my poor pig is in convulfions—how the tree laughs—the duck whifpering that bifhop is La Conteffa Negri—fee, fee! they make bulrufhes of her hair—Torment me not—I did not kill her!'

General Barton was fo aftonifhed, that for fome moments he could not fpeak; but, at length, he told Lord Mahogany,

39

Mahogany, he was miftaken, and that *he* was endeavouring to do him all the fervices that lay in his power.

' Forgive me, holy man! forgive me,' faid his Lordfhip. ' I am a wretch! I have thrown away a jewel! I'll give a hundred guineas for a filver muffin! what a ftorm it blows! and the mule fpeaks Greek! can you dig up the world? had I met her in the grave, for fhe has fweet lips, perhaps—I might have given my vote for peace! but O! 'twas war, war, war! how they bleed! thoufands, ten thoufands dead! fuch a wafte of murder! bring the wheel barrow! for I will fly to Naples.' Here a tear or two rolled down

down his glowing cheek, and seemed to relieve him. He recollected himself, and in a composed tone of voice, said, ' I know not where I am; my ideas wander! is this my head? look! the warming pan is on fire! Is there any body will go for me to Wapping, and bring me a bason full of stockings?

General Barton answered, ' there is.'

' Will he be faithful?' asked Lord Mahogany.

' I will be responsible for him with my life, he is a brother fox-hunter,' said the General. ' Give him these keys,'

keys,' said his Lordship. And then describing, very minutely, every place, directed him to a particular part of the garden, where he would find a well, which he requested might be brought him without delay, as his life depended on it.

Amelia now entered the room. Her presence calmed and relieved him more than any other thing could have done. He called her to his bedside, and entreated her to sit, and stay with him while the General left the chamber.

' My dear woman,' said he, ' had you but lighted the fire in time, we might have gone to Banbury in a nut-shell

nut-shell—but O! this cursed war— I voted for it—how it burns my brain. Bring me a feather, for I would fain speak a word to the pigeon house.'

His delirium now returned, and Amelia was obliged to call in the General, who restored him to a state of quiet, by a further dose of the decoction; but this was not easily effected, and he entertained no hopes of his recovery.

Lord Mahogany, when he came to himself again, desired every one to leave the room except Amelia, he declared he could not bear to look at the features of any other person,

as they all inspired him with gloomy recollections. He implored her to watch with him that night, and urged this point so earnestly, that she was obliged to submit, though not by any means fond of the employment.

The bed the miserable Peer occupied, was that where Margaret Grimes had lain the night before. General Barton and Major Pemberton sat up till a late hour, playing at backgammon; while Arabella resolved to render her patient every assistance in her power.

Lord Mahogany slept for some hours, but the little strength he gained by this refreshment heightened

ened his fever, and when he awoke he raved with more violence than before. Amelia was obliged to call for affiftance, as he threatened the moft dreadful vengeance on himfelf. Thefe fits of delirium fupplied him with fuch amazing force, that the united efforts of the General and Major Pemberton could hardly keep him in bed.

' Ah!' he would exclaim, ' look how fiercely the faggots blaze—O! confcience, confcience! —the troops march—alas !—the war is mine—and the fight of that collyflower breaks my heart-ftrings. Do you imagine I am blind? He ftands by the curtains of my bed, and afks me to buy a ferret.

a ferret. Ah! that's a ferious queftion. Look at the blooming bride; fhe is watchìng the flames, with her nofe in a gallipot—now fhe is going off—fee, in what agony fhe dies; but fhe did not go to war—fhe was a grafhopper.'

Lord Mahogany now appeared more eafy, and took fome refrefhment from the hands of the gentle Arabella. But this tranfient calm was only the forerunner of a more violent ftorm. His phrenzy returned, and before proper help could be procured, he had jumped out of bed, and bruifed himfelf dreadfully againft the walls of the room—' To drive away,' as he faid, a fala-

' a falamander that was playing on the harpfichord ; look,' cried he, ' look at that pelican, how it fmiles upon the imps of darknefs—they chain the fun to a coal-tub—what a world it is, who can tell but it may be given to me, for my library is full of jackals, and virtue is a mere carpet —murder, war, murder cannot go unpunifhed.'

In this manner he continued to rave at different periods, till he grew more weak, and life feemed to ebb apace. His recollection was better, but his horrors of mind were more fhocking than were before witneffed. He would not be a moment alone, and at night could not reft without three

three or four perfons about him. The flighteft noife terrified him, and he would fometimes cry out ' What is that? furely I faw a lady-bird undraw my curtains.—No, it could not be, for fhe was without her mackarel.' Then he would figh deeply. He flept but a little in the night; if he did for a few minutes, he would ftart, and wake in the greateft agonies, and relate the moft hideous and unconnected dreams.

The return of morning prefented a certainty, that he could not long furvive. His tongue and lips were parched and dry, fpite of his frequent recourfe to decoctions of General Barton's preparing. The furface

88

48

face of his fkin exhibited a leprous appearance, and his eyes wild, glowing and deep funk in his head, glared difmally on all around. ' Let me meafure the moon,' faid he, 'tis full of marrow, faugh! but O this torrent of lobfters—ftop them, they curl the Heavens. Bottle up the war in a corn-field, and put my vote in hell. Hold me—the room is in flames, and the caftle totters, what a ferpent is the minifter, he has ftung mankind—I am a crocodile.' He now caught hold of the bed cloaths, as if to fave himfelf, and giving a dreadful fhriek, EXPIRED.

Major Pemberton was much difconcerted at the fuddennefs of the event,

49

event, as it prevented his going out a fhooting. The reft of the company walked forth upon the terrace to vent their reflections on the extraordinary events they had witneffed, and in the evening there was a concert.

VOL. II.　　D　　Chapter

51

Chapter 5.

VARIETY OF SINGULAR EVENTS.

IT is a tafk by no means eafy, to develope the workings of the human heart in all its progreffive motions, yet furely the moft interefting endeavour is, to divulge the perverfion of the paffions, and to hold out a beacon to mifguided men, which fhall controul the irregularities of fancy, and hourly generate the voice of wifdom, the dignity of virtue, and the incomprehenfibility of fhame.

Henry Lambert, feduced by the gay diffipation of the metropolis, foon

D 2　　launched

launched out into every fashionable folly and extravagance; he associated with the Toms the Charleses and the Georges who exhibited their elegant persons in Bond Street every day, he became a member of the first clubs, drove a *vastly neat* curricle, and nodded familiarity to every woman of the town whether he knew her or not. He had also the credit of an intrigue with a Duchess. He was, (what is called) in a good stile. One day as he was riding carelessly in Hyde Park, he observed a beautiful young woman selling nuts to an old cloaths man; he was so much struck by her appearance, that he immediately set spurs to his horse and taking off his hat with a respectful air, saluted Mrs. Wallingford,

Wallingford, (who was just then passing in a low phaeton) as follows. ' It is a charming day ma'em, I think the air is wonderfully mild for the season.' ' Quite so indeed,' replied the Lady, ' but dear Harry! where have you been? Lady Sambrook's party was extremely dull last night, can you guess why I thought so?' ' Have n't an idea, upon my word, what can you allude to.' ' O you sly man, to pretend ignorance—I have a great mind not to tell you; shall I tell you, Harry?' ' You will oblige me infinitely, you don't know how much you'll oblige me, you can't conceive the obligation I should think it—can the finest woman in England be so hard-hearted?' ' O

D 3   you

you monster, O you flatterer, do you know that you now make me really angry—and so you can't guess? well, however I won't tell you.' ' Yes do now, have compassion upon me, tell me why you thought it dull, pray do.' ' And so you absolutely have not the smallest notion what could be the cause of my thinking it dull.'—Upon my credit, have not any conception of what it can be.' ' I'd lay fifty guineas', continued the Lady, ' that in your heart, you are perfectly convinced of what I mean.' ' No, indeed, I am upon my *parole*, I cannot discover the reason why you thought it dull last night—I am entirely at a loss.' ' Well you may protest, but I don't believe you—however, not to tantalize

lize you, the only reason why I thought it dull last night at Lady Sambrook's was—I think I had better keep it to myself—was—now I will not say a word more about it.' ' How can you be so severe upon me?— Have mercy, my sweet woman, I shall die if you don't tell me.' ' Well then the truth shall out, I thought it dull at Lady Sambrook's for no other reason but,—O you wretch!—because *you* were not there. Now are you satisfied?'

Henry professed himself in raptures at this discovery, and instantly standing with one foot upon the saddle, set off full speed, till he reached the Serpentine river, when plunging in,

D 4   he

he fwam his horfe to the oppofite
fhore, then took a flying leap over the
wall on the Uxbridge road, croffed
the fields till he came near Harrow,
turned to the left, and in half an hour
found himfelf by Windfor—thence
he bent his courfe to Henley, and
reached Banbury at the very moment
Major Pemberton had his tooth
drawn. The foup was not yet taken
away, fo that Henry had juft time to
wafh his hands, and to enquire with a
faultering tone, ‘ how is the divine
Arabella?’

The Curtain at Drury Lane Theatre had been up fome time, and the
great Kemble, was in the very act of
being fuperior to Garrick, when
                                   Henry

Henry Lambert entered the ftage
box covered with duft, and looking
dreadfully fatigued. As the houfe
was uncommonly crowded, and as a
butcher from Leaden-hall Market
was in hyfterics in the center of the
pit, fo Henry did not difcover Lady
Fairville till towards the conclufion
of the fourth act. She faw Henry
with a fmile of complacency, being
fully convinced of the fincerity of his
paffion. She therefore advanced to
the front of the box, tall, admirably
proportioned, and with a dignity of
carriage peculiar to herfelf. A loofe
circaffian drefs of gold muflin ferved
juft to give an idea of the outline of
her perfect form, her fnowy arms
were bare to within an inch of her
D 5   fhoulders,

fhoulders, a girdle of diamonds marked the fituation of her fwelling bofom,
and her fine brown hair fell in profufion far below her middle. A plume
of oftrich, lefs white than her fkin,
rofe from her forehead in lofty pride,
and in the midft ftood a heron's feather
triumphant. A *couche* of Paris *rouge*,
appeared upon thofe cheeks, whofe
natural bloom required no fuch aid,
yet it muft be owned, her eyes from
this circumftance received additional
brilliancy, though their luftre was
fomewhat tempered by the dark fringe
that furrounded them. Her eye-
brows too were as charming as her
eyes, they were much darker than
her hair, and nature had penciled
them with fuch peculiar exactnefs,
                                   they

they needed not the aid of art. Her
nofe—it was not perfect—it had however as good pretenfions to pleafe as
that *petit né retrouffé* which overthrew
the laws of a potent empire. Two
ruby lips occafionally opened to fhew
the fineft teeth in the world; and her
chin, and the turn of her face were
more pleafing than can be imagined:
her royal highnefs the Duchefs of
York's fhoemaker had the honour of
making her Ladyfhip's fhoes, and her
foot was ftill lefs, if poffible, and more
to be admired than even that of the
incomparable Princefs. Add to all
thefe charms, the vivacity of forty, the
felf complacency that dwells on the
countenance of a beauty, on the
fcene of her triumph; the little airs
D 6   and

and graces of a coquette, embellished
with her lover's presence; picture to
yourself all this, and you will see Lady
Fairville gaining the admiration of
the whole audience, and gradually
effacing from the mind of Henry those
unfavourable impressions which Arabella's dissertation had occasioned.

Her Ladyship got through the
crowd with the greatest difficulty, and
did not reach her own house till two
o'clock in the morning, when throwing herself upon a marble hearth before the fire, she poured fourth a
deluge of tears, and declared to Mrs.
Marmalade, her own woman, that
she was the most miserable creature
upon earth.

Henry,

Henry, on the contrary, passed the
night in deep play, and having won
fourteen hundred and sixty guineas,
set off at five o'clock, for Mahogany
Castle, the residence of the late Lord
Mahogany, and which was now become the inheritance of the right
honorable Lord Charles Oakley.

Chapter

63

Chapter 6.

CAPTIVATING SCENERY.

MAHOGANY Castle was an ancient gothic building of the most im-
posing and venerable appearance, it
had towers and battlements, and a
moat: but never was there a spot
more calculated for tender meditations
than the extensive gardens which surrounded it.

From the eminence on which the
house was placed, as far as the eye
could reach, it traced a silver mean-
dering stream. In the distribution of
the grounds, the hand of KNIGHT
had

had affifted, but not forced nature; each mafterly ftroke of his art had only ferved to bring to light beauties that lay concealed before, and to improve and cherifh each gift the bounteous Goddefs had lavifhed on this charming place.

A velvet lawn, gently floped from the houfe down to the river, and ferved for pafture to fome hundreds of fheep, which enriched the land, while they animated the fcene. A rifing wood ftretched itfelf to a confiderable diftance on the eaft, its ftems were wafhed by the river, and its feathered branches feemed to bend to receive the refrefhing moifter. On the weft, the eye wandered over an
immenfe

immenfe park; the ground was beautifully irregular; wild, and diverfified with fcattered herds of deer and cattle, groups of trees, with here and there a fpire or a fteeple peeping over their heads, and the view was terminated by rifing hills.

The cold blafts of the North were kept off by fome fheltering mountains; the fides were covered with the ilex, the laurel and the arbutus; and the fummits were crowned with firs.

The fhrubbery fkirting the wood on the Eaft, extended far to the South. It was adorned with a prodigious variety of flowering fhrubs and curious plants, collected from
various

various parts of the world. A few temples, defigned after the beft ancient models, were judicioufly placed, and a bridge, particularly light and elegant, thrown over the river.

But amongft the beauties of the fcene, Lord Mahogany's cave was the moft delightful fpot.—In the fpring, the approach to it feemed a terreftrial paradife. A gradual defcent carried you from the houfe, through a winding path irregularly planted with firs and foreft trees, fkirted with laurels and flowering fhrubs. Here and there the eye caught thorns in all the pride of bloffom; their reign of beauty is but fhort, yet they ftood alone on diftinguifhed

guifhed fpots, and wreathed their trunks into many fantaftic fhapes.

The purple lilac in lovely clufters, and the unfullied white, vied with the Portugal laurel, and gelder rofe, in beauty. Here feftoons of libernum, and there the elegant acacia pleafed the eye, while the air was perfumed with the united fragrance of fweet-briar and violets;

' The mufk-rofe, and the well-attired wood-bine, With cowflips wan that hang the penfive head.'

In wandering thus through a labyrinth of fweets, fometimes you caught a view of the adjacent country, and
faw

faw the water glitter through the trees; but often the clofing branches confined the eye to the delightful fpot around. As you advanced, the fhrubs gave way entirely to foreft trees—majeftic oaks, elms, chefnuts, and beeches formed into a fpacious grove. At firft their tall ftraight ftems appeared like columns fet at convenient diftances from each other; by degrees they preffed clofer together; their bright tints difappeared; the deep receffes of the grove were darkened with the folemn gloom of cedars, and mournful cypreffes, now quite impervious to the rays of the fun. The paths became more numerous and intricate, till they brought you

you to fome irregular fteps cut in a rock; the light infenfibly ftole upon you as you defcended; and at the foot of the fteps you found the entrance of a fpacious cave. All here was hufhed and filent, fave that the trickling drops of a purling rill ftruck your ear, while it foftly bent its way toward the parent ftream. A broken arch opened to your view the broad clear expanfe of the lake, covered with numerous aquatic fowl, and weeping willows adorning its banks.

Round this cave no gaudy flowers were ever permitted to bloom; this fpot was facred to pale lilies and violets. An outlet, at firft fcarcely perceived

perceived in the cave, carried you through a winding paffage to an immenfe amphitheatre, formed by a multitude of irregular rocks; fome bold and abrupt, others covered with ivy, perriwinkles, and wall-flowers. One of thefe grottos was deftined for a bath, and ornamented with branches of coral, brilliant fpars, and curious fhells. A lucid fpring filled a marble bafon in the centre, and then lofing itfelf for a moment under ground, came dafhing and fparkling forth at the extremity of the cave, and took its courfe over fome fhining pebbles to the lake below. Here ftretched fupinely on a bed of mofs, the late Lord Mahogany would frequently

quently pafs the fultry hours of the day, and here its prefent worthy poffeffor Lord Charles Oakley would fometimes alfo indulge himfelf. The grove, though lefs charming than when enlivened by the fweet fong of the nightingale, and adorned with the tender foliage of the fpring, was ftill delightful. His Lordfhip, to compenfate for the lofs of the lily and the violet, had fubftituted the tuberofe, jeffamine, and orange trees. The pots were concealed in the earth, and they appeared natives of the cave. Here all his thoughts were engroffed by the objeft of his flame. Here he formed fchemes of delufive joys, ftifled the rifing figh, ftopped the

72

the flowing tear, and in focial con-
verfe with his dear friend Henry
Lambert would oftentimes fmoke a
comfortable pipe, when the foft radiance of the moon played upon the
pearly bofom of the adjacent waters.

Chapter

73

Chapter 7.

SEVERE TREATMENT.

DON PEDRO having returned
to Spain on very important bufinefs,
the wretchedly forlorn Amelia knew
not how to fill up the miferable interval that muft neceffarily pafs before his return, when one day, having
taken it into her head to go a
trout fifhing, at the corner of a
copfe of hazle and brufh wood, fhe
was fuddenly furrounded by fix men
with black crape over their faces,
who, gagged her, having bore her
to a diftant manfion, which fhe
did not at firft recognife, but which
Vol. II.   E   fhe

74

fhe foon difcovered to be the abode
of the Marchionefs of Oakley.
Having entered, they croffed a prodigious large hall, which in days of
yore, had often feafted hundreds
of vaffals and dependents of the
Oakley family, but its neglefted walls
fhewed it had long been deferted.—
A folemn ftillnefs reigned through
the building, no noife was heard but
the echoing found of their footfteps
on the pavement, and the diftant
crowing of that domeftic male bird,
which with piercing note cried, Cock-
a-doodle-do.

Having paffed through many windings and paffages, and afcended a
vaft ftaircafe covered with old family
pictures,

75

pictures, and after traverfing a *fuite*
of rooms, fome without windows,
others unfurnifhed, at length they
arrived at an apartment wainfcoted
with oak, with old-fafhioned chairs,
covered with dark blue velvet, and
which received its light from grated
cafements, nearly as far from the
floor as from the ceiling.

Within, was a bedchamber in the
fame ftyle, with an enormous fized
bed, the tefter of which was faftened
to the ceiling, and the walls hung
with old-fafhioned tapeftry.

One of the men, fhewed her a
fmall fervant's chamber, and taking
the gag out of her delicate mouth
E 2   informed

informed her that thefe were her apartments. They then all joined in a loud chorus of " Rule Britannia," and departed.

Amelia who had trembled from head to foot ever fince fhe had entered this odious houfe, and had a *prefentment* of her fate, caft a mournful look around, and burft into a violent agony of tears.

Dinner was foon after ferved by an old woman, whom Arabella could not get to fpeak a word, for in fact, fhe was both deaf and dumb, befides the having a nafty whitlow on her middle finger which had tormented her above a fortnight. The repaft confifted

confifted of a difh of fprats, a bafon of boiled tripe, a dozen roafted larks, fome broiled kidnies, a fuet pudding, and a roaft duck.

In the evening the Marchionefs made her appearance, with a ftern countenance, and faid fhe had fome bufinefs to fettle, but that fhe fhould fee her again before her departure. ' Your departure,' cried the terrified Amelia, ' can you think of leaving me here? you had better kill me at once.' The Marchionefs made no anfwer, but immediately left the room.

She returned, however, to fupper;

no

no converfation paffed, and as foon as it was over, retired, and fent Mrs. Dorothy Webfter to Amelia, whofe fpirits were fo totally fubdued, that fhe fuffered herfelf, without fpeaking, to be put to bed.

The next morning the Marchionefs came to take her leave, when Amelia, with a torrent of tears, flung herfelf upon her knees, and in the humbleft accents fued for mercy. Lady Oakley raifed her up, and placing her on a chair, ' Compofe yourfelf, Madam,' faid fhe, ' and fubmit patiently to your fate; *here* I am determined you fhall remain; and your behavior will decide, whether your imprifonment

prifonment fhall be temporary, or only terminate with your life. Your reafonable commands Mrs. Dorothy Webfter will obey, your wants fhall be fupplied, but nothing more.

She then haftily rufhed out of the room, and after fending Mrs. Dorothy Webfter to Arabella, immediately quitted the houfe.

Nothing could be more deplorable than Amelia's condition, fhe raved, fcreamed, tore her hair, and refufed all confolation. Alone in this difmal prifon, never feeing any creature but Mrs. Dorothy Webfter; from frantic fits of defpair, fhe fell

into

into a ftupid melancholy, would frequently whiftle ' Britons ftrike home'
for the hour together, talked about
the Rights of Man like a maniac,
and drank lemonade like a fifh.

Chapter

Chapter 8.

A WATER PARTY.

AFTER fome days paffed in a difagreeable confinement, Amelia turned her thoughts on fpeculative philofophy, and foon difcovered the
power of the human Will, by a proper exertion of which, fhe could
conquer the approach of fleep and
hunger with a marvellous facility.

The Marchionefs in confequence
of thefe favourable fymptoms in her
fair prifoner's mind, invited a large
party to go upon the lake, in a very
magnificent barge, which had for-

E 5   merly

merly belonged to the ftationer's
company, and which had been
knocked down to her Ladyfhip at a
private auction, for fourteen pounds
twelve fhillings and ninepence half-
penny.

The company was very brilliant,
and the weather prodigioufly fine;
they were all dreffed in their richeft
cloathes, and looked as elegant as
carrots when newly fcraped by the
induftrious care of a handfome cook-
maid. The wind was South-Weft,
and the little fifhes fported in the
veffel's filver *wake* with a fafcinating
gaiety; when unfortunately Lucinda
Howard, ftretching forward to catch a
cormorant, flipped overboard, and in

a moment

a moment difappeared. General
Barton immediately burft into tears,
the Marchionefs fainted, and Amelia fell into ftrong hyftericks. At
this interefting moment the Rev.
Mr. Squares, fo renowned for his valuable criticifms, for his love of
royalty, and deteftation of liberty,
jumped upon the deck, and jerking
away his fpectacles with uncommon
grace, exclaimed ' Good lack a day,'
then curling up his nofe with a cy-
nical twift peculiar to himfelf, plunged
beneath the waves, and feized the
drowning Lucinda by the locks,

' Like a rich triumph in one hand he bore her,
' And with the other dafh'd the faucy waves,
' That throng'd and prefs'd to rob him of his
prize.'

E 6 Mr. Bilbo,

Mr. Bilbo, a learned coadjutor of the Divine, was for some time so shocked and overcome, that he could not speak. At length, pointing his left foot towards the dangerous element, he cried out in original Greek Βεαυω; then seizing a heavy translation of Herodotus, in a fit of distraction he hurled it furiously at the celebrated Mr. Gifford's head, which being of a very solid texture, received no kind of injury. The blow, however, awakened the spleen of the satirist, who immediately expressed his sensations by the two following excellent and extemporaneous verses.

' By Jove I will lampoon you all,
' Except Sam Slybore—great and small.'

Now

Now Sam Slybore was laughing in his sleeve during the whole transaction, and declared he would in the course of twenty-four hours produce a painting of the whole scene with his accustomed *sincerity*. This alarmed the Marchioness and the rest of the Ladies, when Amelia archly demanded of the Limner ' were not you educated at Buckingham House?' Every body took the joke, and in a few moments they all landed with the utmost harmony and good humour.

During this period of time, the Reverend Mr. Squares who had dragged Lucinda to the shore, was endeavouring to recover her by putting in practice all the means which have been

been directed by the Humane Society, and at length he happily succeeded—It was then that the meek Lucinda gazing on the Parson with ineffable rapture, exclaimed, ' now the secret is discovered, the cat is let out of the bag, you my charming Squares, you are the man I love and have long loved—' I have languished many months, but now I look to you for comfort, you have saved my life, you know my mind, O Squares!'

The divine, though very much flattered to find that Lucinda Howard was so deeply smitten, yet being terribly drenched by the water, stood mournfully drooping, and had a similar appearance to a rat half-drowned.

His

His natural asperity however soon returned, and he declared that he would be —— if he did not cut them all up in his next Review, which determination the great Gifford highly approved of, and Sam Slybore

' Grinn'd horribly a ghastly smile, to find
His friends would be abused.'

Bilbo said nothing, but he paid it off with thinking—and Amelia wittily observed to him—' The still sow sucks the most draught.' Lucinda, having thanked Mr. Squares, the Marchioness, Sam Slybore, and the rest of the company, for their kind solicitude, retired—being determined to prepare a copy of verses fit for the eye of the immortal

88

immortal Squares. She therefore took a dofe of falts, and after feven or eight *movements*, produced the following panegyrical ode, which fhe prefented to her beloved Squares the next morning at breakfaft, and which was highly applauded by all the company, but efpecially by Mr. Gifford and the Painter.

Ode to my Dear Squares.

O thou, my Squares! beft formed to fhow,
The right and wrong of things below,
  To thee I dedicate the fong—
Prime Parfon of this happy land,
The foremoft of the critic band,
  The terror of the fcribbling throng!

Whether in pride of mental might,
Thou wageft literary fight,
          With

89

With fpectacles upon thy nofe,
Or quaffing gay Sam Slybore's glafs.
Thou toafteft many a buxom lafs,
  Alike for thee my bofom glows.

Whether thou teacheft readers vile,
When they fhould frown, and when fhould
  fmile,
By thy fcholaftic rigid rules;
Or in a haughty cleric paffion
Mendeft the judgment of the nation,
  Proving it but a neft of fools;

Still will I love thee, Squares fo dear!
Still will I heave the figh fincere,
  Thou haft preferved Lucinda's life!
And as thou plunged'ft in the water,
To fave an honeft Perfon's daughter,
  Make her an honeft Parfon's wife!

And I, my love! will join with thee,
Againft the caufe of liberty,
          And

90

And all its daring friends to fcold,
Tyrants and fycophants we'll praife,
To penfioners our voices raife,
  And touch like them the BRITISH GOLD.

Then Gifford, with his lumbring line,
Shall fwear our efforts are divine,
  Bilbo fhall gaze with look demure;
Sam Slybore kindeft, beft of men!
Shall add his pencil to the pen,
  And paint us all in car'cature.

89

Whether in pride of mental might,
Thou wageft literary fight,
  With fpectacles upon thy nofe,
Or quaffing gay *my* Hopner's glafs,
Thou toafteft many a buxom lafs,
  Alike for thee my bofom glows.

Whether thou teacheft readers vile,
When they fhould frown, and when fhould
  fmile,
By thy fcholaftic rigid rules;
Or in a haughty cleric paffion
Mendeft the judgment of the nation,
  Proving it but a neft of fools;

Still will I love thee, Noftrils dear!
Still will I heave the figh fincere,
  Thou haft preferved Lucinda's life!
And as thou plunged'ft in the water,
To fave an honeft Perfon's daughter,
  Make her an honeft Parfon's wife!

Chapter   And

And I, my love! will join with thee,
Againſt the cauſe of liberty,
  And all its daring friends to ſcold,
Tyrants and ſycophants we'll praiſe,
To penſioners our voices raiſe,
  And touch like them the BRITISH GOLD.

Then Gifford with his lumbring line,
Shall ſwear our efforts are divine,
  Beloe ſhall gaze with look demure;
My Hopner kindeſt, beſt of men!
Shall add his pencil to the pen,
  And paint us all in car'cature.

Chapter

' She pined in thought.'

She did indeed, and in a few weeks
grew ſo extremely ' green and yellow,' that it was diſagreeable to look
upon her. Had Mr. Squares felt for
her thoſe gentle ſenſations which cor-
reſpond with her internal emotions,
no doubt they might have been happy in the extreme: but alas! in this
tranſitory world, the faireſt hopes are
too frequently blighted, and the beſt
pretenſions not ſeldom obumbrated
by deſpair. Lucinda Howard was
beautifully pathetic, and poſſeſſed a
mind of the fineſt texture, therefore
the coldneſs of her beloved Clergyman affected her too deeply, and in
                      her

her exquiſite agitations ſhe wandered
through the wilds of fancy with marvellous pertinacity. Not but ſhe had
hopes of ſoftening his obdurate nature by time and opportunity, yet
the difficulty was great, and in the
interim ſhe was liable to all thoſe
little incidental inconveniencies which
ariſe from ill requited affection, and
the workings of a generous, but a too
tender, heart. She therefore ſeized
the firſt occaſion that offered to ſend
him the following compoſition.

Ode to the Moon.

Meek Queen of Night! who gliding o'er tho
    glade,
Art ſo averſe from ſhade,
All hail!
Whether upon the flow'ry vale,
                  Or

Or on the Woodland height,
Thou ſhed'ſt thy ſtream of ſilver light;—
I ſtill admire thee, very much,
Or when thou deign'ſt to touch
The rocks magnificent that o'er the ſea
Riſe in ſublime deformity;—
For thou art wondrous fair; and thy full Orb
Can all mankind entrance, and this rich globe
    abſorb.

Thy ſoft Eye gliſtering on the vernal grove,
Awakes its feather'd Choireſters to love,
Or when the nightingale begins to pauſe,
And the lone Shepherd's mild attention draws,
Thou addeſt to th' enchanting ſcene,
By telling thy pale beams to intervene—
Thus when my Critic Clergyman appears,
I melt in anguiſh, and in tears,
Becauſe he is indifferent and cold,
Nor am I very young, nor is he very old.

                        Strike

Strike the loud drum, and wake the merry flute,
With dub-a-dub-a-dub, and toot, toot, toot,
Let the shrill trumpet Tarra-tarra cry,
And the sweet viol breath its melody.
While to the glancing moon my song I pour,
And tell of him I ever must adore;
Whose winning smiles, whose voice, whose gait
    to me
Are one eternal source of joy and extasy.

When the wondering Mr. Squares had read this delightful effusion, he called for a glass of gin and water, and with more than his usual good nature, exclaimed, ' Thus endeth the second lesson !'

Chapter

Chapter 10.

A DIGRESSION AND A DREAM.

DURING the progress of this little work, the greatest care has been taken to avoid confusion, and to establish throughout, a general consistency of character, and a regular succession of events. To this praise the publication must have some claim, whatever defects may be found in the style, the sentiments, or the poetry. But to return.

Henry Lambert having obtained the rank of Colonel became an object of much interest to the first socie-

Vol. II.   F   ties

ties in London, where a number of elegant young Ladies, who have perhaps more beauty than fortune, are always to be disposed of to Gentlemen of honor and consideration. He however, was totally absorbed in the contemplation of the happiness he might have shared with the incomparable and lovely Arabella, if such a succession of untoward circumstances had not prevented him. As his affection for the glorious constitution of his country was unbounded, and as he had at all times a proper contempt for the hunger and sufferings of the poor, so in an equal degree he respected the ornamental part of society, consisting of Lords, Aldermen, Parliament Men, Crimps, Justices

Justices of the Peace, Bishops, Deans, Arch-deacons, and Attorneys.

One evening Henry finding himself indisposed, retired early to his bed, and presently fell asleep. The dream he had this night made such an impression upon him, that the very moment day-light appeared, he wrote it down as follows, for the entertainment and instruction of his friends.

THE DREAM.

' Methought I was thrown upon an island in the Atlantic ocean which was crowded with inhabitants, and the ports of which were full of vessels from all parts of the world. Its sur-

F 2   face

face was covered with abundance, and every countenance I faw denoted chearfulnefs, profperity, and content : But after a little time I beheld a band of ruffians poffefs themfelves of all the power of government, and divide amongft themfelves the riches of the land. The liberties of the people were fpeedily annihilated, they were plunged into deftructive wars to gratify the felfifhnefs and ambition of their rulers, they were reduced to famine by every fpecies of the bafeft monopoly, and the honeft and induftrious poor were configned to ignomity and treated with contempt. Then the people affembled in great multitudes to complain, and petitioned their oppreffors to grant them fome relief,

relief, but they found none, their juft remonftrances were deemed feditious and treafonable, and the men who had thus feized the reigns of authority, publifhed an order forbidding all perfons to affemble, or even to murmur ; and afterwards a decree was paffed that all the tongues of all the complainants fhould be cut out as a proper punifhment for their audacity. When this *ftrong meafure* was carried into execution, there was a dead filence throughout the nation, and order and tranquility were pretty generally reftored. Now methought the name of this ftrange country was, THE ISLAND OF MUM'.

F 3   Chapter

103

Chapter II.

FEMALE FRAILTY, AND A MISFORTUNE.

AS the elegant Lucinda was one morning walking upon the terrace of Lady Fairville's garden, ruminating upon her fad and hopelefs deftiny, fhe obferved a youth fleeping on a bank of daifeys, fafhionably attired. She ftarted at the fight and faintly fcreamed, while he, at the found of her angelic voice fprang towards her, and folding his fond arms around her, profeffed himfelf the eternal flave of her beauty and attraction. ' O!' exclaimed he with the moft wild and energetic paffion, ' O

F 4   thou

thou mirror of fuperhuman excellence, thou foft fuftainer of all earthly good, to every zone I will declare the ardor of that flame which now confumes my heart, thou art a divinity of the firft order, a lambent fire of exquifite delight that plays upon the wings of fancy, and fettles both the judgment and the wifh ! How beautifully fall thofe luxuriant treffes in foft profufion on a neck of fnow, which feems as it were juft tinged by the laft weak blufh of evening. Ha ! thofe lips, how inconceivably tempting, thofe eyes how penetrating, how brilliant, how expreffive—chin, nofe, mouth, teeth, arms, elbows, breaft and fhape, how beyond all conception captivating and enchanting ! She now reclined her head upon

upon his burning bofom, while many a dewy drop moiftened her glowing cheek. Her fenfibility yielded to the impreffion of fo much tendernefs and truth, fhe clafped him tenderly in a foft embrace and almoft fainted.

There happened to be a hermitage at no great diftance from the fcene of aftion—it was made of mofs, and in it was a couch for Lady Fairville to repofe herfelf, after the fatigues of company and cards. Thither the gallant handfome youth bore the yielding Lucinda ' nothing loth', and there, if we may ufe the words of Shakefpeare, he

' Robbed her of that which naught enriched him,
And made her poor indeed'.

F 5   The

The two lovers paffed feveral hours in this heavenly retreat, vowing eternal fidelity to each other,

' And mingling foft difcourfe with kiffes fweet.'

As at length, however, it became neceffary for them to put a period to fo interefting a tete-a-tete. Lucinda, with her accuftomed prudence, reminded him that it was time to depart, and he inftantly obeyed her command, but not till fhe had given him one balmy parting falute, and had promifed to marry him the firft opportunity. To which, the enamoured youth being overcome by the finenefs of his fenfations, could make no reply.

As

As Lucinda was tripping acrofs the lawn towards the houfe, fhe unfortunately met Mr. Squares and Mr. Gifford, who were taking an *abufive* walk,

' As is their cuftom in an afternoon.'

She was fhocked at the fight of thefe two cynics, and though fhe was fomewhat relieved to find that Sam Slybore was not with them, yet the feverity of their afpeft had fuch an effeft upon her delicate nerves, that fhe immediately fell fick with a bilious fever, and notwithftanding all the care of the Satirift, and the pious prayers of the Parfon, before twelve o'clock on the next day, fhe was as

F 6   dead

dead as Julius Cæsar. The following beautiful epitaph upon her was written by a learned and ingenious fchoolmaſter of Dedham in Eſſex; it was compofed in lefs than eight months, and is engraved upon her tombſtone in Banbury church-yard.

The Epitaph.

Here lies the body of Lucinda Howard,
Who neither ugly was, nor falſe, nor froward;
But good and pretty, as this verſe declares,
And fav'd from drowning by his Reverence
    Squares.
But fmall the 'vantage, for fhe fcarce was *dried*,
Before fhe made a fad faux pas—and DIED.

Chapter

the wife Lord Grenville and the humane Mr. Windham, fo he paffed his time in the moſt fplendid luxury amongſt the principal placemen, penfioners, and other worthies of the court. There is however no accounting for accidents as we all know by fatal experience, for on the third day after the arrival of the party, owing to a copper ſtew-pan in which fome celery had been cooked; every perfon prefent was feized with convulfions about eleven o'clock at night, and the following Ladies and Gentlemen departed this life in the courfe of twenty four hours; Amelia de Gonzales, General Barton, Lady Langley, Major Pemberton, the Marchionefs of Oakley, Lord Charles Oakley,

Chapter 12.

A WIDE SPREADING CALAMITY.

THE fudden death of the unfortunate Lucinda Howard, having thrown a great damp over the company, it was thought advifeable to adjourn to the manfion of Don Pedro de Gonzales, who having been appointed Ambaffador from Spain, led his charming Amelia through every round of animating pleafures which his fituation enabled him to purfue.

As his attachment to the heavenborn Mr. Pitt was great, and as he honoured the tranfparent virtues of the

Oakley, Doctor Philberd, Mifs Warley, the two Mifs Pebleys, Mifs Maleverer, and Sir Sidney Walker. This terrible cataſtrophe occafioned much buſtle throughout the county, and various opinions were formed upon the fubject; however, as the coroner's inqueſt brought them all in lunatics, fo the affair went off with more fpirit and decorum than could at firſt have been imagined. Fortunately none of the great political perfonages were prefent at this fatal dinner, otherwife the country at large would have fuffered an irreparable lofs.

Chapter

Chapter 13.

A PHILOSOPHER.

WHEN Arabella heard of the dreadful misfortune that had befallen her friends, she resigned herself to the most excruciating sorrow, and frequently reflected with all the poignancy of despair, on the conduct of her beloved Henry. To Colonel and Lady Maria Lambert she therefore determined to apply for that consolation which her immediate agonies demanded.

Having dressed herself a blue robe with a yellow sash, she departed with the faithful Margaret Grimes, in quest

quest of him who could alone administer relief to her perturbed soul.

It was now autumn, and the harvest was every where got in, when tempted by the beauty of a rich country, the two fair travellers descended one evening from their chaise, to repose themselves upon the bank of a rivulet that ran murmuring with a shallow stream among groves, and lawns, and flowers. While they were here enjoying the rural solitude of the scene, and imbibing the wholesome freshness of the air, they were surprized by the appearance of a man very much worn with years, leaning upon a staff, who advanced slowly towards

towards them. His beard was long, full, and white as the mountain snow, his eyes were sunk deep in his head, his countenance was melancholy, and with a faultering voice he thus addressed them.

‘ Ladies, it is now above sixty years since I retired from the world into yonder neighbouring wood, where I have built a hut which defends me from the inclemencies of the season. My food consists of the simplest herbs, and I slake my thirst at the lucid spring. I was turned of thirty years when I quitted the unmeaning bustle of the world, to dedicate my life to solitude and reflection. I had found alas! that my friends

friends were falfe, and the woman of my heart was faithlefs; I therefore fhunned the fociety of mankind ; for to live in a croud without confidence or attachment, is a mifery infupportable. Here I have employed myfelf in ufeful ftudy, and occupied my mind with deep refearches, which, though they fhall never benefit the human race, have ferved to enlarge my foul, and to render it more capable of future happinefs. I have calculated the fucceffion of feconds paffed fince the creation of the world, I have difcovered the average number of hairs that grow upon the heads of all mankind, I have found out with great trouble how many half pints of water are contained in this

this terraqueous globe; the leaves in yonder foreft have all been counted by me, and I hope in a little time to be exactly informed, how many millions of words womankind utter every twenty-four hours throughout all the world. This, with afterwards reducing the words into letters, will be the occupation of the enfuing year, and you muft allow that it will be time nobly and meritorioufly employed. I find that at four o'clock this morning, I had lived precifely 2,932,848,000 feconds, yet how foon are they fled! a portion of life concontaining 33945 days is granted unto few, but how fhort is even fuch a period! nor do my tears ever ceafe to flow, when I reflect upon the deftruction

ftruction of animal life, made by the human inhabitants of this earth. More rapacious than the mountain wolf, more favage than the tyger of the defert, each individual gorges himfelf with blood. I can prove that the moft delicate female by the time fhe attains the age of twenty five, never fails to have eaten to her own fhare a flock of fheep confifting of 267, beeves 39, calves 48, hogs, 51, chickens 3256, befides 1840 ducks, with turkeys, pigeons, partridges, pheafants, hares, and wildfowl, in proportion—add to thefe as many fifhes as would fatisfy the largeft whale for a twelve month, together with an abundance of corn, wine, oil, herbs, fruit, and other neceffaries'.

neceffaries'. At thefe words Arabella and Margaret Grimes burft into an immoderate fit of laughing, which fo much affected the old man that he walked off in difdain. The two travellers now began to make fome fhrewd remarks upon the different occupations of men, and the various caufes of their purfuits and ftudies, when Arabella inftantly called to mind the excellence of her Henry, and feizing Margaret Grimes by the hair with great energy, vowed eternal fidelity to him.

On the following day they purfued their journey in the waggon, and arrived at length in perfect fafety at their lodgings in Conduit Street, which

120

which had been previously taken for a Bishop's daughter, by an Alderman. The promised pleasures of the grand metropolis delighted the tender heart of Arabella, and the hopes of again seeing her dear Henry, conveyed the strongest sensation of rapture to her breast, while Margaret, the faithful Margaret, formed schemes of conquest, to which, through life she had hitherto been a stranger.

Chapter

121

Chapter 14.

A VISIT TO A MINISTER OF STATE.

SINCE the fatal rencontre with Arabella that had so disturbed the peace of Henry, he had left off many of those idle amusements which add but little to the general stock of harmless pleasure, and too frequently mislead the mind into a labyrinth of woe.

He therefore called upon Dr. Sanderson at his elegant villa, to ask his advice relative to his own future conduct with Arabella; besides he

Vol. II.　　C　　wished

122

wished to be informed whether the worthy Doctor had really adopted those democratic principles which he had been reported to have done, for Henry was very unwilling to withdraw his friendship and regard from any man without very sufficient reason. Lawyer Blackingson had indeed circulated many cruel reports to the injury of the poor Doctor's reputation, but the general opinion of Blackingson was so unfavourable, that Henry thought it beneath him to pay much attention to his malignant stories, knowing that the fellow, though himself a bit of a Farmer, had no greater delight upon earth than to oppress the poor to the utmost of his power, and to beat his maids when occasion offered.

In

123

In this emergency therefore Henry cropped his hair according to the prevailing mode, and pulling on his boots and spurs waited on Mr. Pitt to thank him for the care he had so kindly taken of the British nation. As Henry, by the death of the Marchioness of Oakley, was become a man of immense property, with two Boroughs at his command, so the heaven-born minister received him with more than his common candour, and presented him with a goblet of sherry and two macaroons. Henry, overcome by such a testimony of regard, and captivated by the condescension of so great a man, politely offered him in return a pinch of snuff, and with pleasing diffidence demanded

G 2　　　　if

124

if THE ACT FOR GENERAL SILENCE was paſſed. The great Roſe aſſured him it was, and that Lord Grenville, Lord Mansfield, Mr. Windham and himſelf were the happieſt of men, in ſpite of the high price of bread, and the encreaſing weight of taxes, which he jocularly obſerved did not affect them. Henry getting more intimate, and more eaſy in the preſence of ſuch ſublime perſonages, earneſtly entreated to have a baſon of pea ſoup, but this Pitt abſolutely refuſed, becauſe he was under the neceſſity of going to the houſe.

Here then the conference ended for the preſent, and Henry returned home in the higheſt ſpirits, and being in

126

ſcattered her pale yellow tints on the ſycamore grove, ſhe wandered forth to all appearance a

    ' Penſive Nun devout and pure,
    Sober, ſteadfaſt and demure.'

Seated upon a favourite green bench on the margin of a bubbling ſtream, ſhe would remain for hours reading her beloved Arioſto and eating golden pippins, while the tears would inceſſantly ' chaſe one another down her ' innocent noſe,' as ſhe reflected on the capricious inſtability of her heart's dear lord, her handſome gallant Henry Lambert. To divert her melancholy ſhe at times would yield her ſoul to the deluſions of poetry. And one evening

125

in a finely animated mood, immediately wrote a comedy which he carried the next morning to the manager of Covent Garden theatre, who received it favourably, and as it had no plot, and was full of tumbling, kicking, breaking, and buffonery, ſo it met with univerſal applauſe, and gained the approbation of Mr. Aſtley the elder, who has long preſided over the amuſements of the Public with wonderful eclat; and who enjoys the holy patronage of his Royal Highneſs the Biſhop of Oſnabourg, Duke of York.

Arabella in the mean time indulged her delicate fancy in all the ſoftneſs of romantic love, and when the moon

G 3   ſcattered

127

evening being rather in better ſpirits than uſual, produced the following enigma, which thoſe perſons who can diſcover its meaning will find to be a *chef d'œuvre* of the art.

Enigma.

I'm as firm as a rock, and as weak as a reed,
As ſlow as a ſnail, and as ſwift as a ſteed,
As fat as a porpoiſe, yet thin as a rake,
As pliant as ozier, though ſtiff as a flake.
I'm a giant, a dwarf, a lion, a hare,
And by fetters conſtrain'd, am as free as the air.
Extremely deform'd, yet a beauty complete,
Very fat, very thin, and tho' dirty am neat.
I can fly like an eagle, but can't leave the ground,
Am exactly a ſquare, and am perfectly round,
I'm as heavy as lead, and as light as a fly,
And am at a diſtance whenever I'm nigh.
Tho' I talk all day long, I'm as mute as a fiſh,

G 4   And

128

And tho' wanting all things have nothing to wish.
I'm as red as a rose, yet as black as a crow,
Am the friend of mankind, yet am every man's foe.
I'm a king and a beggar, a drab and a queen,
And while charming *all eyes*, am not fit to be seen.

Chapter

129

Chapter 15.

A PLEASANT EVENING.

THERE is but little resource in the human heart in times of emergency, unless nature adds a redundancy of imagination to regulate the impetuosity that springs from discordant sentiments. Of this the dear fascinating Arabella was more convinced than ever, and therefore determined to open her little cottage for the reception of a small party, whose conversation and remarks might tend to withdraw her agitated mind from the contemplation of her adorable Henry.

G 5   The

130

The card table was accordingly *set*, and Mr. Beloe, having cut in as partner with the beautiful Miss Hook, for a rubber at whist, was asked by that Lady if he had written his Arabian story books himself. The pride of the Author revolted at the question, and he begged leave to observe, that however he might like to cut up the works of other persons, he was nevertheless as *sore* as any body when his own were attacked. As the growling Gifford saw that matters began to wear a serious aspect, he wished to enliven the company by reading a few extracts from his ode to the Reverend Mr. Ireland, written in imitation of Horace. Taking therefore a pinch of black-guard from Mr. Nares's

---

131

Nares's box, and nodding gracefully to *my* Hopner, he began as follows.

When howling winds and louring skies,
The light *untimber'd* bark *surprize*,
　Near Orkney's boisterous seas;
The trembling crew *forget to swear*,
And bend their knees, unused to prayer,
＊ To ask a little ease.

For ease the Turk ferocious, *prays*,
For ease The barbarous Russe,—for *ease*,
　Which P— could ne'er obtain,

＊ The *surprize* in which a light-timbered, or as *the Poet* has it a *light-untimbered* bark must be in when overtaken by a *storm* is most happily expressed. The sailors forgetting their oaths is a fine conception. In the concluding lines, the returning sounds of *seas, knees*, and *ease*, so near together, have a pretty effect upon the ear.

G 6   Which

132

Which Bedford lack'd amidſt his ſtore,
And liberal Clive with mines of ore,
  † Oſt bade for—but in vain.

For not the liveried troops that wait
Around the manſions of THE GREAT,
  Can keep, my friend! aloof
Fear; that attacks the mind by fits,
And Care, that like a raven *flits*,
  ‡ Around the lordly roof.

O well

+ The two laſt lines of the firſt ſtanza end with the
words, *prayer* and *eaſe*, and the two firſt of the ſecond
ſtanza end with *prays* and *eaſe*, (or rather Hibernice
aiſe) which is beautiful in the extreme. The idea of
putting *eaſe* up to auction, and making Lᴏᴅ. Clive an
unſucceſsful *bidder*, is certainly original—it is grand—
it is ſublime.

‡ The *liveried troops* here mentioned, mean *livery ſervants*, and not *ſencible regiments*,—THE GREAT, means
all

133

O well is he; to whom kind Heaven
A *decent competence* has given,
  Rich in the bleſſing ſent;
He graſps not anxiouſly at more,
Dreads not to uſe his little ſtore,
  And *fattens* on content.

N. B. A contented mind is a continual feaſt,
and continual feaſting makes a man fat..

all titled and rich men in general, which brings to our
mind a couplet, written by a Lady.
  I have no deſire to reflect on *the ſtate*,
  But little Lord Montford is one of THE GREAT.
The happy mode of expreſſion—Can keep, my friend!
aloof fear! is moſt charmingly melodious, and the re-
preſenting the raven *flitting* about the lordly roof like a
bat, is new, and beyond all praiſe. Surely Gray ſhould
have written,
  Far far aloof the *bat* affrighted ſails.
Such appropriation of *non appertaining* properties gives
an exquiſite beauty to poetry.

O well

134

O well is he! for *life is loſt*,
Amidſt a whirl of paſſions *toſt:*
  Then why, *dear Jack*, ſhould man
Magnanimous ephemera! *ſtretch*
His views beyond the narrow *reach*,
  * Of his contracted ſpan?

Why ſhould he from his country run,
In hopes beneath a foreign ſun
  Serener hours to find?
Was never man in this *wild chace?*
Who changed his nature with his place,
  † And left himſelf behind.

* The idea of the Magnanimous Ephemera ſtretching
his *views* beyond the narrow reach of his *ſpan*, is worthy
of Homer.

+ A chace to find ſerene hours, is very well hit off
indeed, common ſportſmen find their game firſt and
chace it afterwards, but here the chace is to find—this
is ſuperior to any thing extant.

135

For winged with all the lightning's ſpeed,
Care climbs the bark, Care *mounts 'the ſteed*,
  An inmate of the breaſt:
Nor Barca's heat, nor Zembla's cold,
Can drive from *that pernicious hold*,
  The too tenacious gueſt.

They, *whom no anxious thoughts annoy*,
Grateful the preſent hour enjoy,
  Nor ſeek the next to know:
† *To lighten ev'ry ill they ſtrive*,
Nor, ere misfortune's *hand* arrive,
  Anticipate the *blow* ‡.

* An inmate of the breaſt mounting a ſteed, is good.
† i. e. Thoſe who are not annoyed by any ills ſtrive
to lighten them. Good again!
‡ That a *blow* ſhould neceſſarily follow the *arrival of
a hand* few perſons would anticipate.—A *word* and a
blow we have heard of,—This paſſage therefore denotes
genius.

For

Something

136

Something muſt ever be amiſs,
Man has his joys; but *perfect bliſs*
   Lives only in the *brain ;*
We cannot all have all we want
And chance unaſk'd to THIS may grant,
   What THAT has begg'd in vain.

WOLF ruſh'd on death in manhood's *bloom,*
PAULET crept ſlowly to the tomb ;
   * *Here* BREATH, *there* FAME was given;
And that wiſe power who weighs our lives
+ By *contras* and by *pers* contrives
   To make the balance even.

To THEE ſhe gave *two piercing eyes* §,
A body—juſt of Tydeus' ſize,
   A judgment ſound and clear,

---

* Breath here means length of days, which has the recommendation of novelty. *Fame* inſtead of *breath* is a grand conception.
+ This is ſurely one of the fineſt lines in the Engliſh language.
§ How prettily complementary to his friend !

A mind,

137

A mind, with various ſcience *fraught* *,
A liberal ſoul and threadbare *coat,*
   And forty pounds a year.

To ME, one eye, not over good,
Two ſides, that to their coſt have *ſtood* +.
   A ten years hectic cough.
§ *Aches, ſtitches, all the numerous ills,*
That ſwell the dev'liſh Doctor's bills,
   And ſweep poor mortals off:

A coat more bare than thine, a ſoul
That ſpurns the croud's malign controul,
   A fix'd contempt of wrong;

---

* *Fraught* and *coat* are allowable rhimes.
+ *Stood,* here means *withſtood*—for two ſides ſtanding a cough, might otherwiſe be deemed harſh.
§ It has generally been ſuppoſed that *the medicines* taken ſwelled the deviliſh Doctor's bills, but it is here evident they are ſwelled by *diſeaſes.*

Spirits

138

Spirits *above* affliction's *pow'r,*
And ſtill to charm the lonely hour,
   ‡ WITH NO INGLORIOUS SONG!

Mr. Gifford having finiſhed the reading of this excellent production, received the congratulations of the company, with a modeſty peculiar to himſelf. Their applauſes were long and reiterated, which encouraged him to bring forth another performance,

---

‡ The author's deſcription of himſelf elucidates his own character, in the happieſt and moſt fortunate manner. Every body muſt ſurely reſpect and honor a man who gives it under his own hand, that his ſoul ſpurns the *malign controul* of the croud, that he has a fixed contempt for every thing wrong, that his chearfulneſs can ſubdue affliction, and that he can ſing like a nightingale to charm the lonely hour. This it muſt be acknowledged is indeed a *glorious ſong* !!!

written

139

written as he ſaid in his younger days, ‘ Upon the pleaſures of malignity.' But the attentive Arabella perceiving his drift, incontinently ſnuffed the candles, and the ſervant at the ſame moment informing them that ſupper was on the table, all parties were ſatisfied, and every body becoming jocoſe, the evening was concluded with the utmoſt feſtivity.

It happened that a maſtiff dog which Arabella had brought up from a puppy, had gone mad the preceding day. She therefore was afraid to indulge any further ſpeculations on Henry's fate for the preſent. After a long night paſſed in the utmoſt diſquiet, ſhe aroſe with the lark, and determined

140

determined to fet out on a pilgrimage of love to find the dear objeﬅ of her affeﬅions, if he ﬅill exiﬅed an inhabitant of this globe. Dreﬄing herﬄelf therefore in a green Joﬄeph which had been made for her grandmother, and tying a little ﬅraw hat upon her head, ﬄhe ﬄat off with a ﬄhepherd's crook in her hand, and her pockets full of turnips.

Chapter

142

might have continued in this tranquil ﬅate, it would be difficult to aﬄcertain, and how frequently his ﬄighs aroﬄe in contemplation of his loﬄs, it might be equally impolitic to deﬄcribe. But the reﬄult was ever advantageous to his feelings, and his honour in every confliﬅ remained not only unimpeached, but even more conﬄpicuous than before.

Henry's maternal uncle who was very feeble and infirm, was alﬄo a Peer of the Realm, with the rank of an Earl; and ﬄhould his Lordﬄhip die without iﬄﬄue, it was evident that an ancient barony would deﬄcend to him in right of his mother. This therefore cheered his drooping ﬄpirits, as he

141

Chapter 16.

A MEETING OF EXTASY.

HENRY LAMBERT had conﬅantly purﬄued the grand objeﬅ of his enquiries, and had never relinquiﬄhed a moment the fond hope of being united to the lovely Arabella. Ardent in all extremes, he found the dear idea vivify his heart. Early in the morning he was leading his high ﬄcented hounds to cover, and when evening caﬅ her faded gloom over the face of nature, his library was his unfailing reﬄource, while his cultivated mind trod the various paths of ﬄcience with indefatigable perﬄeverance. How long he might

143

he truﬅed the time might not be far diﬅant, when he ﬄhould be able to come forward with that rank and dignity, which would eﬅabliﬄh his former pretentions to the divine Arabella.

While Henry remained in this ﬄituation of ﬄuﬄpence, he received intelligence of his mother's death, who departed this tranﬄitory life in the middle of a rubber of whiﬅ, with Lady Di Danvers, Lord Ginger, and Colonel Saﬄh.

No ﬄooner had he heard the fatal news, than he mounted his beﬅ hunter, and rode forward to the cottage of Arabella, that he might diﬄcover

cover how far his expectations were likely to be realized in the poſſeſſion of that excellent young Lady.

In the mean time Arabella had got a violent ſwelled face, by ſitting out all night to liſten to the mournful ſong of the nightingale, whoſe gentle warblings were echoed from grove to grove, and ſweetly floated on the balmy zephyr to ſooth her raviſhed ear.

All was ſtill as death, the watch dog was ſilent in the yard, and the owl was mute in the aged oak, when ſhe ſuddenly ſtarted from the bank of violets on which ſhe was repoſing, and exclaimed, ‘ O Heavens! was ‘ that

that a ſpirit paſſed me ?’ Henry now ruſhed forward, and ſeizing the enchanting Arabella by the hair, thus tenderly expreſſed himſelf; ‘ O matchleſs efferveſcence of human happineſs, divine empreſs of my ſoul, I have languiſhed for ages to behold thee, I have been burnt up and conſumed by the unquenchable fire of exhauſtleſs paſſion. Every moment that paſſed, ſeemed to me to have the duration of a century. The ſports of the field were vain in thy abſence. I ſeemed like a forſaken doe on the banks of the Tigris. The golden glory of the ſun when darting his meridian ſplendor on the ſycamore ſhade, had no ſolace for my diſtracted heart. In ſleep, the dainty viſions

VOL. II.   H   of

of thy lovelineſs, played on my ſecluded ſenſes, and irritated my hopes to the madneſs of deſpair. There was no muſic in the murmuring of the ſilver rivulet that babbled through the flowery brake ; the pale moon glared on me with the dimneſs of death. O Queen of all my wiſhes, O incomparable Arabella, O thou moſt beautiful of the human race, what will become of me, if your frowns ſhould fall upon me! one kiſs from thy ſweet lips would raiſe me to a height of joy, that the proudeſt earthly potentate never yet experienced in his gilded palace, or his outrageous miniſters in the wide plunderings of official power. Wilt thou be mine, wilt thou bleſs thy Henry

Henry by accepting his proffered hand ? Wilt thou become myſelf, the chief portion of my being, the light of my eyes, the rapture of my ſoul ? I will hug thee to my heart, 'till it burſt with extaſy, I will play with the tangles of thy hair till faintneſs overſhadows me.’ To this eloquent rhapſody, the mild and invincible Arabella prepared a ſuitable reply. She had nearly eat up all her turnips, and therefore looked at him with commanding ſweetneſs, while ſhe ſaid, ‘ To be the object of the adoration of ſuch a mind as thine is, my Henry, of itſelf ſufficient to raiſe the moſt humble to the pinnacle of human greatneſs! The tone of thy melodious voice falls on my

H 2   nerves,

nerves, like the calm operation of opium on the wretch in pain. Sweet Henry, pretty youth, fine gentleman! I will, I will be thy wife, immediately—let no time intervene till we are ONE. I have waited a long while, and began almoft to be out of patience—therefore let us lofe no more time—had we been married on our firft acquaintance, at this period we might have been the parents of two girls and a boy, I am fure we might—here is my hand, take it and welcome. She then fang gaily,

Away to the church, to the church lead away,
And to morrow at furtheft, be our wedding day.

The enraptured lovers now returned hand

hand in hand to the elegant cottage of Arabella, where orders were immediately given to prepare every thing neceffary for the happy nuptials. Margaret Grimes was ready to jump out of her fkin for joy—the old dog looked piteoufly upon them, and the villagers met in the neighbourhood to talk the matter over, and to get drunk with decent delight in honour of their good patron's felicity. Doctor Dedrick procured a licence, and the clerk bought a new wig upon the occafion, while Sir Timothy Rattle-fnake offered generoufly to give her away. This kind propofal was inftantly acceded to, and the next morning was fixed for the celebration of the holy rites of Wedlock. Henry

H 3 and

and Arabella paffed the evening alone in mutual endearments—they had a roaft fowl, eggs and fpinnage for fupper, he drank three pints of port, to prove the fervency of his paffion, and fhe toafted his health in liberal potations of gin and water. Two happier beings never lived upon earth —they danced, they fung, they romped, till midnight, when with engaging gravity they feparated to go to bed, and to dream of the delights of the coming day. The only unfortunate event was that Henry had forgot his night-cap.

Chapter

Chapter 17.

A WEDDING.

IN the morning Arabella appeared more blooming than the vernal rofe, when bathed in the glittering dew of May. She was dreffed in a pale fea green fpencer, elegantly trimmed with blue flowers and gold fpangles, her petticoat was of lilac filk covered with a yellow gauze, that produced the moft beautiful effect. Her lovely locks were bound with a fillet of fcarlet fattin, mixed with ftraw and artificial nettles, and her enchanting arms, bare above the elbow, fafcinated the eyes of every obferver—

H 4 her

her shoes were pink ornamented with white roses and silver spangles—she appeared a perfect divinity, her smiles, her dimples, her soft looks of pathetic languor, were very much applauded, as Henry led her to the altar. We have in a former part of this work described his person, we therefore shall only now say that he was fashionably attired in boots and leather breeches, and a rough great coat with nineteen capes. The clergyman went through the ceremony with great decency, though Arabella was so much agitated that she hardly knew how to keep her countenance. The clerk having a cousin in the pay office rather gave himself more airs than the circumstances could justify, but

but every body admired Arabella's unaffected attire and virgin modesty. Henry looked grave at times, and a silent tear stole down his cheek not entirely unobserved, for a farmer's man stept up to him withgreat caution, and in a whisper informed him, that he had found a hare sitting, this a good deal disconcerted the Doctor, who shook his wig with disdain, and eagerly enquired, if there was any extraordinary news from the Continent. They therefore hastily returned home when a sumptuous entertainment was prepared which all the Militia regiments were invited to partake of.

After dinner Arabella, at the earnest request of Captain Malmsbury,

bury, favoured the company with the following song, which penetrated the hearts of all the spectators.

Ah well-a-day!
It is not now the month of May,
Yet let us all be gay,
Ah well-a-day!

Yes, we will sing
The praise of every living thing,
And for each other we will bring
The flow'rs of spring.

Ah well-a-day!
I must not sport with virgin play,
I'm married as they say,
Ah well-a-day!

This charming song received the most animated applause from all the company,

company, particularly from Serjeant Tomlinson, who declared he would rather be Henry than an Ensign. At eleven o'clock precisely, Arabella was led weeping to her chamber, and a quarter before twelve, Henry flew to her longing arms and found all his fondest expectations realized in the possession, of youth, beauty, innocence, and love. The remainder of the party kept it up till a late hour and then marched off at open files, singing in a grand chorus, ' Britons strike home.'

Nothing ever equalled the bliss of Henry and Arabella, they passed their time in the sweetest reciprocity of affection, till at the end of six

months,

months, his fair wife prefented him with a lovely boy, that confolidated their affe&ions, and gave new interest to their exiftence. The babe was conftantly in the arms of Henry, who feemed to transfer a part of his adoration for Arabella to the dear little innocent, who early difcovered fymptoms of the moft furprizing genius, and grew fatter and more thriving every day, notwithftanding that in one year it had the jaundice, the meafles, the whooping-cough, the fmall pox, the chicken pox, the nervous fever, the rickets, the mumps, the pleurify, the ftone, the gout, the bilious cholic, the dropfy, and St. Anthony's fire.

Chapter

Chapter 18.

A MELANCHOLY INCIDENT.

HENRY had gone to London on particular bufinefs, and had not written to his dear Arabella, for more than three weeks, when one evening, full of the idea of her beloved hufband, fhe wandered to an adjacent grove, and feating herfelf under a fweet-briar, on a bank of camomile, at the very entrance of an old hermitage, fhe thought fhe heard the diftant trampling of horfes' feet. She liftened,—in an awful folitude, feemingly facred to filence every found excites attention; again

fhe

fhe liftened, and took off her gloves. The grove with which fhe was furrounded, obftru&ed her view, but the horfeman whoever he was, fhe was now convinced drew nearer.

' Could it be her Henry? fhe foftly exclaimed: O no! that is impoffible, he cannot yet have even left London.'

But gentle reader! think of her aftonifhment when fhe faw not indeed her Henry, but Mr. Peter Perkins (for it was he) leap from his horfe, and with a lover's fpeed, for he had defcried her from the avenue, fly to the romantic little fpot, on which fhe was feated! He fell at her knees;—fhe fainted in his arms.

' O my

' O my Arabella! 'tis thy Perkins, my angel look up. What has my rafhnefs done?—I was to blame to take thy foftnefs unprepared!'

She now began to revive, when withdrawing herfelf gently from his arms, fhe foftly exclaimed, ' O Mr. Perkins how could you furprize me thus?'

A tender converfation now enfued, in which Mr. Peter Perkins faid all that the moft honourable paffion could di&ate (for he was ignorant of her marriage with Henry) or the moft refined generofity could fuggeft; and Arabella, who was above the little affe&ations

of

of her fex) readily acknowledged that her efteem for him was permanent and fincere. Mr. Perkins ftaid two hours in this fweet retreat, and in all that time the circumftance of her being already married never once entered her head. So true it is, that *love* abforbs all other confiderations. He informed *his* Arabella he was going to the houfe of a friend, only a few miles diftant, and that he fhould, with her permiffion, vifit her frequently.

The moon now beginning to rife in all the beauty of ' clouded majefty' warned Mr. Peter Perkins to depart, which he immediately did; whilft the lovely Arabella flowly walked towards her

her cottage, and before fhe had reached it, the idea of her prefent fituation intruded on her thoughts, and banifhed every pleafant reflection.

' Why,' faid fhe, ' did I not think of this before? why did I indulge a foftnefs that muft be fuppreffed? Ah tyrant love! thofe who fincerely feel thy power too often facrifice every other confideration to thy all ruling fway.'

Arabella who, however, as to worldly prudence was in general a very difcreet perfon, thought it proper to write a full account of this meeting, to her Henry, and at the fame time to

to expedite a billet to Mr. Peter Perkins, telling him that as fhe was now married, fhe never could defire to fee his face again.

It was now the anniverfary of little Tommy's birth-day, the darling of Henry and Arabella. He had attained his fourth year, and was the delight of the whole village. The prattling innocence of that age of beautiful fimplicity, renders a child inexpreffibly engaging. This lovely boy was particularly fo. His delighted mother had written to her beloved Henry to conjure him to return home on that day. ' My dear it is our Tommy's birth-day'.

Arabella

Arabella dreffed the fweet boy in a new little green veft, fhe had made on purpofe for this day. ' It is your birth-day, my lovely Tommy.' Having faid this fhe kiffed him, and fent him out to play on a fmall green plat before the door, and then began to bufy herfelf in preparing dinner.

Tommy for once had tranfgreffed his bounds, and with another little boy about his own age had run after a beautiful goldfinch, which flew directly to a rofe-bufh, that hung over a running brook at the bottom of the garden. The lovely boy now attempted to climb the fmall twigs of a willow tree, whofe branches were united with thofe of the rofe-bufh; but

164

but Ah gentle reader! how fhall I relate the miferable event? The branch of the tree, too feeble for his weight, gave way, and he fell at once into the brook, which was wide and rapid, and the poor babe was funk in a moment! By the rapidity of the ftream the body was carried down to a fmall bridge, a few yards diftant from where the accident had happened. The particulars of this unhappy event were afterwards gathered from his little play-fellow afore-mentioned.

Here I muft lay down my pen to give vent to the tears of facred pity, which fill my eye, when I reflect on the piteous fate of this fweet innocent.

But

165

But alas! what language can I find to defcribe the following afflicting circumftance? the tender father was now returning home, with joyful hafte to partake of the chearful repaft which Arabella had promifed to prepare for their darling Tommy's birth-day; when in paffing over the bridge, which led to his garden, he efpied floating on the brook, the garment, the little green *veft* of his dear child. Breathlefs with affright, he plunged into the ftream, and drew the poor babe from the rufhes and fedge: But ah! cruel, miferable event! he faw his lovely eyes were now clofed in death! he faw he was deprived of life! a pallid hue had already taken poffeffion of thofe coral lips!

His

166

His cheeks which wore the bloom of the opening rofe, were now changed to the livid tints of death! Where now were thofe fweet fmiles, which never failed of conveying tranfport to the delighted parents? Alas! gone, gone, gone!

' Gracious Heaven!' faid the diftracted father, ' what do I fee! My Tommy! Is it, can it be poffible? Ah, yes! O ye Powers fupport me! He clafped the breathlefs infant to his bofom in all the agonies of frenzy and defpair.

O reader! I cannot proceed.—A few moments juft to wipe away the gufhing tear, and then I will go on.

Mr. Lambert

167

Mr. Lambert whofe agonies for what his beloved wife would feel on this dreadful occafion, was diftracted how he fhould break the fatal ftory to her; and what ftill made it the more dangerous, the doating mother of this fweet babe, was now very far advanced in a fecond pregnancy; every precaution was therefore neceffary.

He wrapped the breathlefs little corpfe under his coat, and with almoft frantic fteps, conveyed it by a private ftaircafe up into a remote chamber, in the further part of the houfe. He laid him on the bed, and once more kiffed his pallid lips. Then in an agony of defpair, which no language

guage can defcribe, with hafty fteps, on hearing his beloved Arabella call him to dinner, he ran down ftairs. His agonies were ftill increafed, when he faw the chearful innocence, the fweet fmiles of that lovely woman, who had learnt his arrival from Margaret Grimes who had feen him enter.

' My Henry (fhe faid with the moft lively joy, and with an angel's fweetnefs) welcome, thrice welcome home. But where is our dear boy, where is Tommy? He is playing I imagine, on the green plat before the houfe. Call him my love to dinner. See, I have fpread the table with our fmall repaft, fee his little new knife you fent him from London. I have laid it ready for him.'

Poor

Poor Mr. Lambert fuffered at this dreadful period the utmoft agonies. How loth was the tender hufband, the affectionate parent, to difclofe the horrid tale! How unwilling to difturb the tranquillity of his beloved wife, which was founded on an ignorance of the dreadful event.

Arabella with her ufual fweetnefs, grew ftill more importunate.

' Say, my love, where is my Tommy?—Why my Henry will you not fetch the little truant to his dinner?' Henry could not ftand this: he flung himfelf into a chair with an air of frantic wildnefs, and now began to weep aloud.

Vol. II.   I   But

But here I muft clofe the melancholy, heartfelt defcription. It will eafily be imagined, the fond mother's anxious enquiries foon made her acquainted with the fhocking fact. For feveral hours fhe remained in a ftate of abfolute diftraction. Her neighbours teftified their kind affection by watching and attending her with the utmoft care. The violence of her fits at length brought on the pangs of childbirth, and fhe was delivered a little before the ufual time of another boy, even more beautiful than her Tommy.

Fortunately in a few hours little Tommy began to breathe again, and on the following morning was as merry

ry and playful as ever. Mrs. Lambert alfo fpeedily recovered and before the expiration of three days was as well as could be expected. So that the happinefs of this fond couple was reftored to them with the *additional joy* of having another fon.

I 2   Chapter

Chapter 19.

A CONVERSATION.

IT is a juſt obſervation of an author who well knew the human heart, that there is in *perfect beauty*, an attractive charm which is irriſiſtible. Old Mrs. Mandrake turned pale, and ſickened at the ſight of ſo much innocent ſweetneſs, and for once in her life, the well-bred aſſurance of a fine Lady forſook her for a moment only. She was heard to exclaim ſoftly —' O Heavens! what bloom! what features!'—Two of the gentlemen by an involuntary impulſe, roſe from their ſeats, and with a kind of homage

I 3   to

174

to ſo much beauty, were going to lead Arabella to a ſeat next the fire; but Mrs. Mandrake, who had by this time recovered again her former inſolence, cried ' Sit ſtill Gentlemen, I beſeech you,' then in a kind of ſcornful half whiſper, ' Poor thing, ſhe was a reputed orphan, but ſhe has thought proper to marry a Gentleman forſooth!'

Arabella juſt heard the laſt ſyllable, and bluſhed a deeper dye, which ſtill added to her beauty, ſhe had been in tears too, and the luſtre of her piercing eye, had now yielded to the ſofteſt languor. Well ſays the Poet,

' When

175

' When beauty ſorrow's livery wears,
  We fondly take the fair one's part;
But when love's ſhafts are dipt in tears,
  They pierce directly to the heart,'

' Sit down Madam!' ſaid Mrs. Mandrake. Arabella modeſtly obeyed her, and ſeated herſelf at the bottom of the room, and after a ſhort time finding her Henry did not appear, ſhe quitted the company.

The Gentlemen inſtantly exclaimed ' Good Heavens! what a charming woman!' ' Such eyes!' ſaid another. ' What an enchanting form!' another. not one but was in raptures.

' Why I cannot ſay,' ſaid Mrs.
I 4   Mandrake,

Mandrake, affecting to yawn with in-difference, ' I cannot fay I am fo vi-olently charmed with her perfon. I grant fhe has bloom, but it is the red and white of a milk-maid. She is, I think rather a *gawky* figure. Her arms are too long, and her eyes are horrid; fhe is tall I allow, and the picture of health, but fhe wants fafhion, fhe wants elegance.

Arabella tripped up ftairs like a young roe, and taking her children alternately in her arms, cried, ' O how much has a mother to anfwer, who vain and proud, is above per-forming the fweeteft of all duties, the improvement of her children's mind !

' Delightful

' Delightful tafk—
To teach the young idea how to fhoot,
To rear the tender thought,
To pour the frefh inftruction o'er the mind,
To breathe th' enliv'ning fpirit ; to implant
The generous purpofe in the glowing breaft !'

The next morning as Arabella was reading Euclid to amufe her infant progeny, and eating at the fame time a buttered crumpit. Mifs Slipfhod rufhed into the nurfery, ' O Mrs. Lambert, what a difcovery !' ' For Heaven's fake my dear,' faid Ara-bella, half fainting, ' what is the mat-ter?' ' My lovely friend,' replied the other, ' what do you think ? A Mr. Ireland has difcovered a trunk full of original manufcripts of the immortal Shakefpere himfelf; it is as true as

I 5   any

any thing; and there are befides two tragedies all written in blank verfe, with old fafhioned fpelling, with dou-ble dds and double ees—and then there are I don't know how many love-letters in Willie's own hand writ-ing, and a deed of gift to the finder of all that was in the trunk. Is not he a lucky man ?' ' I think he is in-deed,' returned Arabella; but my amiable friend, you cannot conceive how you alarmed me, I had nearly fallen into a fit, for by the hafty man-ner in which you expreffed yourfelf, I really fuppofed, my valuable huf-band had broke his collar bone.

Chapter

Chapter 20.

FINE DISCRIMINATION OF CHA-RACTER.

IT is one of the eafieft things in nature to begin a novel the author as you may fay ' Has the world before him where to chufe'—but as the work proceeds, then comes the difficulty—

' Aye, there's the rub
Muft give us paufe.'

Characters grow out of characters, frefh perfons muft neceffarily be brought forward to heighten the in-tereft, and as it approaches towards a conclufion, the plague is how to get

I 6   rid

rid of the good folks with decency—
Some muſt be *married*, ſome muſt be
KILLED OFF, and all muſt be properly diſpoſed of. Never did any
human being wiſh to get to the end
of a journey with more impatience,
than I (*my* Lady Harriet Marlow) do
to finiſh this elaborate performance—
I ' have taken arms againſt a ſea of
troubles' and hardly know how to
fight the waves any longer, for as my
prime boaſt is preciſion, and my *ſecond* conſiſtency, ſo the ignorant reader can have no idea of the painful
predicament in which I ſtand. ' AL-
LONS DONC,' as they ſay in France,
there is now no retreat to be made—
I muſt fight it out to the laſt, and
ſo I will.

I truſt,

I truſt, however, the ſpeculative
reader will pardon this digreſſion, for
in good truth *my Ladyſhip* does hate
digreſſing, as it is flying from the
ſubjeɛt, and of no uſe whatever, but
to lengthen out the performance, for
why ſhould any body digreſs, unleſs
he finds it of the greateſt utility? *Intellect* like *bread* is every day getting
more and more ſcarce, therefore we
ſhould make all poſſible ſhifts not to
deſtroy the ſtock in hand. But to
proceed.

Henry Lambert was a gentleman—
that is, he had wit, manners and money,
—by the bye, he had a fine houſe and
park with all dignified appurtenances
in Glouceſterſhire—but he preferred

to

to live in Arabella's cottage, becauſe
it was ſo ſnug, and becauſe Arabella
was particularly fond of honeyſuckles.
I mention this to juſtify the meanneſs
of his mode of living, for had he choſe
an eſtabliſhment equal to GEORGE
ROSE's he could have afforded it,
but never having held any office under government, he did not think it
decent.

Mr. Mandrake was a worthy man,
many years older than his wife, had
the misfortune to have a hump-back,
and was uſually laid up half the year
with the gout. Mrs. Mandrake had
been a very celebrated beauty in her
youthful days, and was even ſtill what
might be called a fine woman; but

one

one of her charaɛters was (for moſt
people have *two*) that of being proud
and imperious to the utmoſt degree,
beſides which ſhe was inordinately
fond of oyſters. Her worthy hufband who ſtill doated on her, and
who feared her frowns ſo much, that
he could hardly call his ſoul his own,
indulged her in every faſhionable ex-
ceſs. I mean ſo far as was conſiſtent
with the charaɛter of a woman of honour; for Mrs. Mandrake was, with
all her faults, a woman of unblem-
iſhed reputation; but ſhe was ty-
rannical, proud and capricious to the
laſt degree; what ſhe liked to-day,
ſhe diſliked to-morrow :—in ſhort, ſhe
was quite a fine lady. She aimed at
being thought a *wit* as well as a

beauty;

beauty; for which purpofe her houfe, which was one of the moft elegant in London, was the refort only of fuch as were celebrated for that character; and fhe was equally fond of fpeeches made to her *perfon*, as to her *under-ftanding*. She had two daughters, whom, though nearly of the age of Arabella, fhe ftill kept upon the footing of children, as the very idea of having a daughter attending her to public places, and rivalling her in beauty, made her ficken with the dreadful apprehenfion of approaching old age. That celebrated obfervation of Monfieur St. Evremond might juftly be applied to her, that ‘ the fighs of a fine woman at the hour of her departure, are more for the

the lofs of her beauty than the lofs of her life.’

It was a lucky circumftance for this unnatural mother (and too many there are in the great metropolis of the fame caft) that her two poor daughters (who were extremely to be pitied) were remarkably fmall of their age: they had the appearance of girls about thirteen. Mrs. Mandrake taking the advantage of their fize, ufed to call them at all times the *children*, and her *little ones*; fo that a byeftander would have imagined they had not reached even the above-mentioned age. They were clofely confined to their nurfery, in white frocks, and were never fo much as permitted to fit

fit with her, or dine at the fame table; fhe would have fainted had girls of their age called her *mother*, before any of her fine gentlemen vifitants.

Poor Mr. Mandrake loved his daughters, but was abfolutely afraid to fhew his affection, and had long fince loft his authority in the family. Mrs. Mandrake's invitation to Emily Smithfon, and notice of poor Mr. Grogram, proceeded from no benevolent principle. That worthy man, who was himfelf all truth and fincerity, had not the leaft idea of the falfe politenefs of a fafhionable fine lady. When fhe invited Emily to come to her, fhe had no notion the old man, as fhe called Mr. Grogram, would part

part with her; therefore thought fhe ran no rifque in afking her: befides the truth is, *pride* was at the bottom; as fhe, like many other fine ladies, took no fmall pleafure (though the miftaken would imagine it a *benevolent* principle) in having a poor dependent at her beck: to have one to *fcold*, juft when fhe pleafed; and as a witty author remarks,

‘ To keep a girl to fret upon.’

Monfieur Rochefoucault's admirable maxim, that ‘ we do not always do charitable *actions*, from charitable *motives*’ was never more verified than in this inftance of Mrs. Mandrake. She had no real defign of advancing poor

poor Mr. Grogram's fortune, and while that worthy but miſtaken man, was rejoicing, that his dear niece was now on the road to London to a rich and benevolent friend, this ſtrange woman would have ſickened to death, if ſhe had imagined that the little Welch girl, as ſhe called her, was perhaps, that day, the moſt beautiful young woman in England, adorned with every virtue, and poſſeſſed of the choiceſt accompliſhments. The friendſhip ſhe had in former days pro-feſſed for the amiable Mrs. Smithſon had been long ſince obliterated; ſo much does the diſſipation of this age of pleaſures entirely eradicate from the heart every ſentiment of honour and ſincerity.

But

But it is now time to return to Henry Lambert, who having fully diſcuſſed the above-drawn charaĉters, to Arabella—ordered his curricle, and arrived at the bull-baiting, with-out one ſingle adventure, or ' hair-breadth ſcape' on the road.

Chapter

Chapter 21.

A CRITICAL MOMENT.

FARMER GREEN'S cow had broke into Arabella's garden during the night, and had played the very devil—the peaſe were all trodden down, the onions rooted up, the ſpinnage annihilated, the turnips, carrots, and potatoes deſtroyed; in ſhort, there was a ' careleſs deſolation' in every part. ' What muſt we do?' ſaid Margaret Grimes, the big round tear trembling in her eye. ' I am ſure,' replied Arabella with violent emotion, ' I know not how to aĉt in this emergency; how unlucky, that

ſuch

fuch a *cataftrophe* fhould have happened in my beloved Henry's abfence. He is gone to the *bull baiting*, and the *cow* has *baited* us in revenge. I know but one meafure to adopt and that is to bear the misfortune with becoming fortitude. Complaint is ufelefs, we muft therefore fupport what we cannot rectify.' To the truth of this obfervation Margaret Grimes affented, with engaging modefty, and the children were called down, to whom the whole affair was properly explained. Mr Peter Perkins, who had never loft fight of his object, but whofe love for Arabella encreafed even to madnefs by the difficulties which had attended its progrefs, now approached the cottage

of

of Arabella and fent a fervant to offer any affiftance in his power. A tranfient blufh pervaded her cheek at this tender proof of his affection, but her duty to Henry triumphed over the tendernefs of her heart, and fhe requefted him to take fome refrefhment after his fatigue, making at the fame time every proper acknowledgment for the intended favour.

Arabella now requefted Margaret Grimes to examine minutely the depredations of the cow, and the good woman taking the hint, immediately retired.

No fooner did Mr. Perkins find himfelf alone with the dear idol of

VOL. II.   K   his

his foul, than he burft forth into a torrent of the moft enthufiaftic adoration. He kiffed her hand with fervor, a thoufand and a thoufand times, which fhe endeavoured to withdraw in vain, he entreated her to promife him, that, in cafe any accident fhould happen to Henry, fhe would take him for her fecond hufband. To this, his earneft requeft, fhe faintly replied, while her bright eyes were bathed in tears. ' O Mr. Perkins urge me no further, I fcarce dare think upon the fubject, but fhould the melancholy event you allude to ever take place, which may Heaven avert, I know not any perfon who poffeffes fo large a portion of my efteem as Mr. Peter Perkins.'

He

He now imprinted numberlefs kiffes on her vermillion lips, and fondly entwining his arms round her lovely waift, called her his *future bride*, his good genius, his protecting angel. In fhort, he appeared half frantic with extacy of joy, when Henry's voice was heard in the hall, which in fome degree moderated his tranfports, ' I wifh,' faid Mr. Lambert as he entered the room, ' that Farmer Green would take better care of his cow.' There was a comicality in the allufion that occafioned a general laugh, when Henry fhaking Mr. Peter Perkins by the hand, faid he was heartily glad to fee him, and kindly afked him if there was any news? ' None in the world,' replied Mr.

K 2   Peter

Peter Perkins with fomewhat of an embarreffed air, ' None upon earth, none at all that I hear of, the papers are quite barren of late.—The cow I find has done a deal of mifchief—Had you much fport at the bull baiting— Was parfon Chefnut there—I meant to have been there myfelf, but was prevented going—but I fancy it grows late—I am after my time, I muft be off, good day to you Mr. Lambert, good day to you Madam, I hope you will favour me with a vifit the firft opportunity—do—I fhall take it kind, I fhall indeed.' Having made his oration, he difappeared.

The fond and faithful Arabella now threw her fnowy arms round Henry's neck,

neck, and welcomed him home with that winning tendernefs which artifice can never feign. When dinner was over, and the children were brought in, Henry and Arabella gave way to thofe fine feelings which connubial tendernefs alone can experience. At length Mrs. Lambert took her harp and gazing on her hufband with fond delight in a moft enchanting manner fung the following

Air.

When you are abfent all looks *dreary*,
When you are abfent I am fad,
Becaufe I love my Henry dearly,
When he is with me I am glad.

K 3   O then,

O then, unlefs you wifh to grieve me,
No more defert my circling arms;
It breaks my heart that you fhould leave me,
The lord, the mafter of my charms.

Henry was fo enraptured by this extemporary proof of Arabella's attachment and regard, that he jumped from his chair, played a thoufand antics, rolled the children on the floor, drank a bottle of burgundy, and fung ' God fave the king.'

Chapter

Chapter 22.

CONCLUSION.

AFTER feveral months paffed in the retired pleafures of Arabella's cottage, Henry propofed going to London, that they might live in a ftyle fuitable to their fortune. Mrs. Lambert gave her confent, and in confequence his houfe in Grofvenor Square was ordered to be prepared for their reception. A fervice of plate was bought upon the occafion, a great number of fervants were hired, and every thing was eftablifhed on the moft expenfive footing. At half paft eleven one Monday the Lambert

K 4   family

family quitted their rural abode and proceeded in a coach and fix to the metropolis, where they arrived in perfeɛ health and fafety on the Thurfday following.

Their houfe foon became the refort of all the rich wits and fafhionable company of high life. They gave dinners, fuppers, balls, affemblies and concerts to the amufement, gratification, and edification of all their acqaintance; Henry and Arabella became amazingly fond of deep play, and being remarkably lucky, won immenfe fums of money which raifed them very much in the good opinion of the great. The children were educated in the utmoft

moft refinement, and with the moft falutary delicacy, and difcovered uncommon penetration and acutenefs in all their ftudies. Dr. Grampus, their tutor, pronounced them to be the two moft aftonifhingly clever boys, he had ever met with, and as he made it a rule never to reftrain them in any of their little defires, fo he became a wonderful favourite with them both, as well as with Papa and Mamma.

Arabella whofe exquifite beauty was the admiration of all the young men of rank aɛted on every occafion with fuch guarded circumfpeɛion, that though fome envious ladies of her acquaintance thought, or pretended

K 5   to

to think, that fhe was rather *too particular* with Lord Kiffville, yet they could not throw the flighteft imputation on her charaɛer.

Mr. Peter Perkins followed the enchanting Arabella to town, and for fome time frequented her affemblies ' fighing like furnace' but as he was little acquainted with the forms and appearances of high life, he foon became contemptible in her eyes, in a fhort time, therefore, fhe fo completely cut him, that he quitted the purfuit in anguifh and difmay, execrating in the bitternefs of his heart, the follies and vices of Ariftocracy.

Amongft

Amongft the number of elegant acquaintance which Mrs. Lambert had formed, was Lady Maria Jones, who though more advanced in life, treated Arabella with the utmoft intimacy. One day Lady Maria was particularly melancholy; the frequent fighs fhe heaved, and the tears which bedewed her languid cheeks, affeɛted the tender fenfibility of Arabella in the greateft degree. She wept from the ' mere virtue of compaffion,' and gently afked, ' I hope my dear Madam no frefh affliɛion is the caufe of thefe precious tears?' ' No, my Arabella, none, I have long been inured to mifery;—my forrows cannot be relieved but by death alone.' ' Would not,' faid the amiable

K 6   able

204

able Mrs. Lambert, a participation of your griefs tend to leffen their weight? for when the heart is abforbed in affliction, and has long been accuftomed to devour in fecret its own griefs, it feeks not for relief, but gains ftrength by feeding on its own melancholy.'

' Alas my fweet friend,' replied Lady Maria, ' my forrows are of a nature never to be redreffed. You know, I imagine that I am married, that I am a mother, (though my dear little angel my Dicky is taken from me) that my hufband, the hufband of my tender youth (for I was early married) is now wandering in a foreign land with an infamous courtezan. All this perhaps

205

perhaps you have heard, but methinks I read in my Arabella's eyes a kind curiofity to be further informed; a tender concern for the particulars of my unhappy ftory. I will gratify your defire, my Arabella I will relate them to you, in hopes the recital may prove a warning to you in future life.—To begin then,

' I was left at the age of nineteen with a large fortune, when I became acquainted with Mr. Jones. His fine figure enchanted my fight, whilft the excellent qualities (as I imagined) of his heart merited my utmoft regard: in fine I loved him to diftraction. His paffion for *me* appeared no lefs. No objection could poffibly be made to

206

to the alliance, as his family was refpectable though mine was noble, and his character was then good. But alas! it foon appeared his fole motive for marriage was my fortune only. The firft three months of our union were fpent happily; at leaft we were furrounded with fo much company, and fo many new fcenes of diffipation prefented themfelves, that I faw not, what very foon was *too vifible*, that the moft perfect indifference had taken place where I had ' treafured up my foul.' This firft began to appear, by his affecting to treat my underftanding with much contempt, becaufe I was a *woman*. If I ever in company gave my opinion on any reigning topic of difcourfe,

207

courfe, he would cut me fhort with ' Good Heaven, my dear! how fhould a *woman* know any thing of thefe matters?' He very early began to launch into many extravagancies, particularly that of keeping race-horfes. This I was acquainted with one day by feeing a beautiful horfe exercifing before the windows. On my afking him the occafion, he with a carelefs yawn replied, ' he intended him to run for the King's plate at Newmarket: but why,' added he peevifhly, ' do I tell a *woman* of this?'

But I was particularly hurt by his cruel behaviour to my aunt, a moft worthy old Lady, who had bred me up from my infancy. From a hundred

208

dred repeated flights, he at length absolutely forbid her the house, telling her the society of old women was intolerable. Soon after this, my dear boy was born. I wept in secret, I prest my innocent babe to my unhappy bosom, and was indulging a fond mother's hopes, that this little pledge of affection might touch his heart, when alas! that heart (but this I then knew not) was mine no longer.

I tenderly loved my husband, notwithstanding these proofs of his indifference. We had then an elegant villa at Richmond, where I had lately become acquainted with a most agreeable young Lady, a widow. She had lodgings very near me, and her company

209

pany was so peculiarly pleasing to me, that I in some measure forgot my griefs ; nay I even fancied my husband still loved me in his heart. I was perfectly charmed with Mrs. Ormsby, and found her cheerful conversation a great relief to my spirits. She had now been at Richmond near a month; Mr. Jones had been in London all that time. On his accidentally once or twice seeing her with me, and my expressing how much I esteemed her, he said he wondered greatly at my taste, for that he never saw a more disagreeable woman in his life; adding, whenever she is with you, I beg to know it, for her company I abominate. That afternoon he went with me to drink tea

210

tea with a family in the neighbourhood. I was in uncommon good spirits, as I fancied my dear Mr. Jones looked on me with more kindness than usual. Alas! how are we deceived! Mistaken mortals! About six o'clock we sat down to whist, all but Mr. Jones, who complained of a violent head-ach, and of a sudden recollected he had two letters to write, which he must send he said by the post that very evening.—' But my dear Maria', he added (O how delighted was I with the kind epithet!) ' you will stay I hope the evening, I will order the coach for you at eleven; as to myself, when I have finished my letters, I shall retire to bed, for I feel myself somewhat out of order.'

' After

211

' After he was gone I was extremely uneasy; I fancied (such was my tenderness for him) that he was more ill than perhaps he confessed, and as soon as the rubber was over, I told the Lady where I was, my fears, and that I would then go home, which was only in the next street. It was then about eight o'clock, and the season of the year delightful for walking at that hour. Accordingly I left the company, and was tripping home with great haste, when as I passed by Mrs. Ormsby's lodgings, I recollected a few words I had to say to her on a particular affair. I ran up stairs with my usual freedom, and seeing nobody in her dining-room, I at once opened her bed-chamber door;

when,

when, gracious Heaven! what was my amazement! I was almoſt petrified with aſtoniſhment. The firſt objeƈt I ſaw was my huſband in bed with Mrs. Ormſby. I ſcreamed with terror, and ſaw enough to be convinced ſhe muſt be the moſt abandoned of women. She inſtantly, as indeed they both did, jumped out of bed, and eſcaped into an adjoining cloſet. My cries brought up the maid who gave me water and drops; and from her I gathered (for now all ſecrecy was at an end) that Mr. Jones had privately kept this baſe woman above a twelve month in London; that he had taken this lodging for her at Richmond, and that ſhe paſſed for the widow of a late officer in the navy.'

As

As this *proſing* Lady was proceeding with her long ſtory, Henry Lambert ruſhed into the room in a delirium of joy—' O my Arabella, my angel, my life! what do you think has happened, the greateſt good fortune has come to us, we ſhall no longer wither in plebeian vulgarity—no my deareſt wife— we are now *noble*—my uncle the Earl of Frolicsfun is dead, he is upon my ſoul, and I inherit the ancient barony of the family—I am now, *my Lord*, and you are, *your Ladyſhip*—we ſhall have a coronet on our coach, and we ſhall have precedence, O what a glorious advantage it is to be a Lord, to ſit in the Houſe of Peers in one's robes, and to make fine ſpeeches, and to be called the *Nubble Lud*—I think I ſhall run mad with pleaſure.'

Arabella

Arabella ſmiled with ineffable ſweetneſs, and turning to her dear female friend, ſaid ' well Madam is not this good news?' to which the Lady anſwered by a low courteſy and by politely congratulating their *ſhips* on their newly acquired honors, after which ſhe took her leave with the moſt high-bred ceremony.

For the next fortnight their houſe was full from morning till night of perſons of diſtinƈtion, who came to pay their compliments to Henry and Arabella—both he and ſhe were allowed to be remarkably *affable*, at the ſame time, that they knew how to ſupport their *dignity* with propriety.

It

It was now announced in all the public prints that the Right Hon. the Earl of FROLICSFUN having died without iſſue, the earldom was extinƈt, but that the ancient barony of LAUGHABLE had deſcended to HENRY LAMBERT, ESQ. in right of his mother.

When the due period of external mourning was at an end, Lord and Lady Laughable were preſented to their Majeſties at St. James's, and were moſt gracionſly received.

To conclude, Lord and Lady Laughable continued to live together many years, taſting even greater happineſs in each other, from the contraſt which
they

216

they had formerly experienced, efteemed and beloved by all who knew them and dealing out bleffings all around them; and when death at laft called them to regions of eternal blifs, they left behind them in their children, faithful reprefentatives of their virtue and felicity.

AN

HUMBLE ADDRESS

TO THE DOERS OF THAT EXCELLENT AND

Impartial Review,

CALLED

THE BRITISH CRITIC.

LADIES AND GENTLEMEN,

As I am well affured that your invaluable criticifms on the various literary productions of the prefent day, proceed from the joint labours of many ingenious men, and refpectable old women, fo I feel myfelf deeply interefted in your dicifion on the merits of the foregoing work. It is therefore my moft ardent wifh to deprecate your vengeance, it is my

L   moft

218

moft anxious hope to obtain your praife.

" O do not break a fly upon a wheel ! "

But furely I fhall not be deemed too vain, or unpardonably prefumptuous, when I exprefs a lively confidence in your approbation of this my firft effay as a novelift—I am certain I have fpared no pains in the compofition, and I have carefully avoided all thofe allufions and remarks which might tend to produce an overflow of your bile, or excite your laudable indignation. As I well know your noble natures never can forgive thofe fcandalous fentiments of obfolete liberty, which our ridiculous anceftors were fo eager to diffeminate, but

219

but which all moderate, honorable, and enlightened perfons now hold in juft execration and contempt; fo my principal care has been to keep clear of all fuch fubjects, as could give the flighteft umbrage to your ingenuous minds, and extenfive underftandings. You alfo may conclude, that as far as filence gives confent, I perfectly approve of the two reftraining bills which have lately paffed into laws, that I am a decided enemy to all improvement in political fcience, and wifh to hear in the courfe of the enfuing campaign, that the Britifh grenadiers fhall have marched triumphantly into Paris.

L 2   But

220

But to return to my novel, I will be bold to say, that there is great precision and a pure moral tendency throughout the whole, with so inviolate a consistency of character, that I think I may challenge a fair comparison with any of my most celebrated competitors in the same line. The story you will allow to be plain, simple, interesting, well-connected, and full of pathos; and I doubt not but you will think it worthy of your generous protection; nay, I even trust, that the wisest and most patriotic associators of the immaculate Mr. Reeves, will be inclined to applaud its loyalty, and promote its circulation. Besides, as I have had the honor to inform you that it is the offspring

221

offspring of a female pen, I can rely with perfect satisfaction on the acknowledged gallantry of your gentlemen, and the tender sympathy of your ladies—indeed the more so, as I have the good fortune to be personally known to several very valuable members of your illustrious body, from whom I have already received many striking proofs of justice, liberality and good will towards me.

Being convinced that you possess the most exquisitely refined taste in poetry, I have been particularly attentive to this article, which I trust will be deemed of prime quality, calculated for general benefit and im-

L 3   mediate

222

mediate use, such as will neither clog your stomachs, nor produce that nausea, to which you are subject, upon taking any quantity of pungent, strong or stimulative rhimes.

If it should appear that I have occasionally borrowed a sentence or a thought from some of our most admired modern writers, I trust you will graciously forgive so venial an offence, as I am ready to affirm that any passages I may thus have selected, and transplanted, which shew to disadvantage in their new situations, were not inserted with a design of depreciating their excellence, but merely to display that happy intricacy of style and sentiment, without which no

223

no novel can have a just claim to your notice and approbation. With all humility therefore I am free to assert, that some of those extracts which unfortunately in my little work may seem ludicrous and absurd, possess great beauty and propriety as connected with their original combinations. If you should suppose that I have wished to excite a laugh at the expence of their respective authors, your high mightinesses are mistaken, my sole intention having been, by a happy mixture of discordant parts, to produce a pleasing regularity, with a lively and captivating variety.

" Thus from dissentions concords rise,
And beauties from deformities,
And happiness from woe."

L 4   I dare

I dare fay your imperial majefties will pronounce this quotation to be inapplicable; but if you fhould, I can only fay, that you do not comprehend me, and are not fo clear-fighted as you ought to be, and as hitherto I have always been inclined to think you.

Do me the favor to erect your magnificent ears with attention while I recite to you a fable that fhall fafcinate you.

A fcreech Owl, an Afs, a Peacock, and a Boar, formed themfelves into a critical Junto to decide upon the harmony of the groves, and the modulations of the foreft. The roaring of the

the Lion was voted *nem. con.* to be bombaft, the neighing of the Horfe vapid and jejune, the fong of the Nightingale miferable affectation, and the notes of the Linnet, the Goldfinch, and the Lark, namby-pamby nonfenfe. In fhort, they unanimoufly agreed that, (not including themfelves) no living creature poffeffed any genius, mufical powers, or natural melody, but THE MULE; his voice and abilities, therefore, they candidly acknowledged to be capital. Thefe four animals now endeavoured to convince all the beafts and birds that their decifion was a juft one, and that in confequence, the mule ought to be the hero of the day.

With

With your permiffion "moft potent, grave, and reverend Signors!" I will defer the moral, and the application, to fome more favorable opportunity.

But to lay afide all levity, it is impoffible to deny that you wafte your midnight oil, to fave the prefent race from the horrors of licentioufnefs and the encroachments of philofophy, and when it is confidered that

" The evil which men do, lives after them:
The good oft lies interred with their bones."

Your difintereftednefs muft be moft ftriking, for pofterity, perhaps, may not pay to the pious memories of you or your employers, thofe honors which

which you have fo affiduoufly ftruggled to deferve. You will, however, during your lives, find fufficient confolation from the idea, that you have fupported to the beft of your abilities, the good caufe of GENERAL RESTRAINT and that you have laboured in your vocation with unabated ardor. If indeed the reflections of the fallen Adam fhould occafionally crofs your minds, who on contemplating the miferies he had prepared for his defcendants exclaimed,

" Who of all ages to fucceed, but feeling
The evil on him brought by me, fhall curfe
My head, ill fare our anceftor impure
For this we may thank Adam."

Yet

228

Yet a proper fenfe of the immediate good enjoyed, muft ftiffle every fenfation of remorfe, while you rank in public opinion with the PITTS, the WINDHAMS, the DUNDASSES, the GRENVILLES, and the REEVESES of the day.

Go on then great and generous arbitrators of national tafte! in your glorious and fplendid career, direct the thunderbolts of your rage at the heads of thofe infamous and audacious libellers, who degrade literature by their free difcuffions, and philofophical remonftrances; and who even infult religion by their pernicious doctrines of toleration. Be it yours " to ftand in the gap" between error

229

error and truth, between vice and virtue, be it yours to fhake a flaming fcourge, and to chaftize thofe literary monfters who dare to pufh their refearches beyond the facred line of demarcation you have drawn.

To your virtues, liberality, and candour, the whole nation can bear teftimony, for I defy the moft impudent of your detractors to fhew a fingle inftance amongft all your writings, where you have fpoken favorably of any work that was bafe enough to vindicate the hoggifh herd of the people, that was mean enough to object to any meafures of the prefent wife and incorruptible adminiftration, or that was cowardly enough to cenfure

230

fure the juft and neceffary war in which the nation is now fo fortunately engaged. No, ye worthy magiftrates of the mind! you have exerted your civil jurifdiction with meritorious perfeverance, and if at any time you have ftepped forth as warriors to defend the exclufive privileges of the FEW, againft the vulgar attacks of the MANY, your demeanour has been truly gallant, you have thrown your lances with a grace, becoming the moft renowned knights of chivalry, and have hurled your anathemas at the murmuring multitude with a dignified fury that would have done honour to Peter the Hermit, or to the chief of the Holy Inquifition.

231

Owing to your animated exertions, and the vigorous meafures of your *patrons*, you may foon hope to fee the happy inhabitants of this profperous ifland exprefs but one opinion, and act with one accord, the rich and the powerful fhall be tranquilly triumphant, the low and the wretched patiently fubmiffive, great men fhall eat white bread in peace, and the poor feed on barley cakes in filence. Every perfon in the kingdom fhall acknowledge the bleffings of a ftrong regular government; while the abfurd doctrine of the Rights of Man, fhall be no more thought of, or refpected, than the rights of horfes, affes, dogs, and dromedaries.

Owing

That

232

That your enemies may ſpeedily
be caſt into dungeons, or ſent to
Botany Bay, and that yourſelves may
become placemen, penſioners, peer-
eſſes, loan-mongers, biſhops and contractors, is the conſtant wiſh and
earneſt prayer of,

Ladies and Gentlemen,

Your devoted humble ſervant,

HARRIET MARLOW.

THE END.

AZEMIA:

A DESCRIPTIVE AND SENTIMENTAL

NOVEL.

INTERSPERSED WITH PIECES OF POETRY.

By JACQUETTA AGNETA MARIANA JENKS,

OF BELLEGROVE PRIORY IN WALES.

DEDICATED TO

THE RIGHT HONORABLE LADY HARRIET MARLOW.

TO WHICH ARE ADDED,

CRITICISMS ANTICIPATED.

IN TWO VOLUMES.

VOL. I.

Fair views and beauteous profpects I invent,
Pines, poplars, ruins, rocks, and fentiment;
Fond lovers figh beneath my vines and larches,
While ghofts glide grimly grave through glimmering arches.

London:

PRINTED BY AND FOR

SAMPSON LOW, NO. 7, BERWICK STREET, SOHO.

1797.

DEDICATION

TO THE

RIGHT HONOURABLE

LADY HARRIET MARLOW.

DEAR MADAM,

WHILE with reverence and delight I reflect on the admirable performance with which you have favoured the Novel-reading World (and who in the world reads any thing elfe?), I tremble at the temerity with which I thus venture

VOL. I.   a 3   to

to lay at your Ladyship's feet my humble, my inferior production.

Despairing as I do to give to these pages the acumen, brilliance, consistency, delicacy, elevation, fancy, genius, humour, judgment, illumination, knowledge, luxuriance, merriment, naïveté, omniscience, pathos, quickness, raillery, suavity, tenderness, urbanity, vivacity, wit, 'xcellence, youthfulness, and zest, which corruscate from the *etincellant* pen of your Ladyship, I yet venture to flatter myself that this *debut* in literature, which I have thus the honour to place under your protective kindness; may, rather owing to your smiling approbation

approbation (dear to literary spirits), than to any individual merit, serve to amuse, not unacceptably, the elegant leisure of the amiable fair, in that superior region of the British atmosphere where your Ladyship sparkles a benignant and irradiating planet.

Sure I am, that if any of the pathetic scenes with which I have, perhaps, too much indulged the trepidating tenderness of a too sensible imagination, should beguile your Ladyship of your tears, or if the lighter disquisitions should emblazon your animated countenance with a soul-insinuating smile, my purpose will be fully answered.

However

However that may be, it is something to have an opportunity of declaring to the world, that I boast the ineffable felicity of being known to you; and that I dare thus speak publicly of the very profound veneration, esteem, respect, admiration, and regard, with which I have the honour and satisfaction to be,

MADAM,

Your Ladyship's

Most obliged,

Most obedient,

And most devoted Servant,

J. A. M. JENKS.

Belle Grove Priory,
March 1st, 1797.

Exordium

Exordium Extraordinary

THE narrator of the adventures of juvenile humanity finds less of labyrinthine involutions in the eccentricities of accumulated improbabilities, less of indescribability in the multifarious camelionity of terraqueous variety, or in the revolutionary scenery of planetary evolution, than dismaying-incomprehensibility in the enfoldings and vicissitudes of the involucrums of the pericardic

pericardic region. The wildeft wonder of imagination, the aftonifhing agglomeration of concatenated rotation, fade into imperceptible invifibility, when oppofed to the prevaricating pertinacity, which inoculates perfpective projects on what is prohibited, and launches with extended velocity on a chaotic vaguofity of oceanic indiftinction, unfathomable, ungovernable, and uncontrolable: its capability bounds over all limitations; its indefinition mocks the refrigitating operation of prudential precaution: inveftigation is baffled—penetration is annihilated; we can neither fathom futility, or appreciate abfurdity

abfurdity—*It* forbears to palpitate, and we lofe ere we can analyfe it. The vacuity is infcrutable unilluminated profundity, and conjectural fenfibility waves over it her many-fcintillating banner in vain !

Who at this æra of felicitous luminofity fhall adventure on the perilous undertaking of fuperadding, with due ratiocination, to the accumulation of vernacular entertainment ?—Who hazardoufly proceed in their aëronautic career in the accretion of fabulaftic hiftory ?......
With tremulous timidity, and retiring trepidation, the unexperienced female adventurefs in the literary

terary atmofphere, ventures her enrolment among the promulgatreffes of noveliftic narrative; and if in longiquity fhe fhould linger, or in loquacity lethargicife, fhe eventually avoids licentuoufity, and in the precifion of the precurfive picturefque prohibits her pen from perfonality.

AZEMIA.

~~~

CHAPTER I.

One True Briton and two Turks.

IN the bofom of the refpectable haram of Hamet-beig her father, and in the imperial city of Conftantinople, was born and nurtured the beauteous Azemia—educated would be an improper

Vol. I.   B   word,

word, for the advantages of education are to the Turkiſh virgin denied: but Nature had denied none of her moſt attractive gifts to Azemia; and ſuch inſtruction as an haram affords, ſhe received under the eye of the ſenſible and judicious Birkabeba, her paternal grandmother, who, though originally a Georgian ſlave, had a mind of ſingular ſtrength and lucidity. Azemia was the forty-fifth daughter of Hamet-beig, who had beſides nineteen ſons; ſo that the portion of parental tendernefs that fell to the ſhare of each of his numerous progeny could be but ſmall. The ſolicitous vigilance however of Birkabeba ſupplied to her infant charge every other deficiency; and in the lighter accompliſhments, ſuch as are taught in the ſeraglios of the Eaſt to adorn the perſon

perſon of females, taught only to ſpeak to the voluptuous eyes of their domeſtic tyrants, ſhe was amply and early inſtructed—ſhe danced to a miracle—ſhe ſung tender airs in the voice of a little ſyren, and with admirable expreſſion. Already with her fairy fingers ſhe had embroidered two handkerchiefs of ſky-tinctured gauze in ſilver flowers; and as ſhe occaſionally ſat before her ſtill lovely *grandmother* * Birkabeba, on a ſmall green ſatin cuſhion trimmed with gold fringe, engaged in ſewing ſeed pearl on a pale purple ſatin pincuſhion, there was ſo much pertinacity in the

* That a Grandmother may be not merely, but ſuperlatively lovely, is a poſition which, however it may have been difputed in preceding ages, is beyond a doubt afcertained in this.

queſtions ſhe aſked, ſo much intelligence in her countenance while ſhe ſpoke, that Birkabeba involuntarily enquired how it was poſſible that ſuch a creature ſhould be abſolutely without a ſoul. The word *ſoul*, or *alma*, made grievous work in the head of Birkabeba; ſhe had never heard it *defined*; ſhe had never thought about it till ſhe became a grandmother; ſhe had never read one of thoſe luminous lucubrations that have immortalized the names of their authors in Italy, Spain, Portugal, Germany, and particularly in Great Britain: in a word, ſhe knew nothing of the matter.

Her ſon, Hamet-beig, was remarkable for nothing ſo much as for a magnificent pair of muſtachios of a peculiar curl and colour: his ideas were not more numerous

numerous than his caftans, but like them they were uſeful, and he was not without living knowledge; not merely as it related to himſelf, but as it looked forward to poſterity—a concern with which the Turks, from the nature of their government, trouble themſelves very little: but Hamet-beig had that ſort of prévoyance about him, and was ſo well thought of by Peſtilenti Azem*, who was then vizir, that no man was more proſperous or likely to riſe. Had Hamet-beig been an Engliſhman, there is no doubt that he would have aſpired to, and poſſeſſed, ſome very eminent

* *Azem* means a Prime Miniſter, a Vizir:— *Peſtilenti*, however ungrateful it ſounds, is a *proper*, though not a Chriſtian name:—as we ſay, Pitt, Chancellor of the Exchequer, &c. &c.

post under Government, and, in due time, have retired upon a considerable sinecure, or a pension on the Irish Establishment; while, in all probability, his nineteen sons would, following the same career, have obtained peerages with the prettiest of all imaginable names.

Unfortunately all this could not happen: but the care and praise-worthy attention of Hamet-beig was directed towards providing for his children in the best manner he could; and, among other arrangements, Azemia had, at a very early age, been betrothed to Oglow Muley, a rich merchant, who of course was also a Mahometan. He traded very largely to Leghorn and Marseilles, where he saw among the Christian traders

ders with whom he dealt, so much integrity, goodness, humanity, charity, and other virtues peculiar to the Christian world, and super-eminently evident among *them*, that nothing could so strongly shew the force of the ridiculous prejudice in which Oglow Muley had been educated, as his not embracing the faith of the Nazarenes.

Liberality of enquiry, however, is little known among the Mussulmen; and indeed it begins to be altogether a thing, which in other countries it is much safer, and not less satisfactory, to have nothing to do with: it has assuredly many ill effects; it lessens the gross amount of acquiescent ignorance, and makes men very foolishly discontented with their various lots, which

B 4 are

are undoubtedly cast for them with every possible regard to the fitness of things, and the eternal rule of right. It occasions very impertinent remarks on the conduct and capacity of those whose elevation should lift them above the short-sighted politics of the undistinguishing multitude: it causes those who indulge it to yield incontinently to improper suggestions, that things *might* be better; whereas there is not an eminent statesman, basking in the radiating sunshine of royal and imperial favour, who *knows* not, and is not ready to *prove*, that all is absolutely and positively for the *best*; and that poverty and rags, starving and nakedness, drowning, dying by the plague, or perishing with wounds, together with other common incidents too numerous to mention, and

too

too insignificant to be attended to, are *no evils*, nor arise from any thing but one invariable scheme of inexplicable wisdom, which will sooner or later bring good out of evil, and make even the small and merely apparent inconveniences which the querulous enquirer murmurs at, turn eventually to the aggrandisement, prosperity, and power and glory, of this our dear country, which is, without dispute, the best of all imaginary countries in this superexcellent arrangement, and is governed by the most humane, benevolent, sapient, and magnanimous monarch, directing the wisest, most philanthropic, disinterested, and successful ministers that sovereign ever trusted. For these reasons (and they appear to me to be incontrovertible), let every loyal and

B 5 worthy

140

worthy Englifhman avoid all wafte of
time in fpeculative enquiries.——To
return to Oglow Muley, who, Turk
as he was, never made any.

Oglow Muley, or, as he is fometimes
called, Muley Oglow, hearing from the
report of Muzzled-Abib, governor of
his haram, that his betrothed wife Azemia was fair as the youngeft of the
Houris; that her eyes were as the eyes
of the Antelope, and her cheeks as the
Rofe of Geferat, commanded Muzzled-
Abib to bring her forthwith to Mar-
feilles, where his bufinefs unavoidably
detained him.

In obedience to this order, Muzzled
fought a fhip of his own nation bound
to that port; but it happening that none
then

then lay at the Sublime Port, Muzzled
caufed carpets and cufhions, and
other commodious accommodations, to
be placed in the cabin of a French
merchant fhip, Citizen Moutard commander, laden with figs, coffee, raw
filk, and other productions of the Levant, and took the paffage of Azemia
in it.

It would affect the fenfibility of my
readers too much, were I to relate the
parting between Birkabeba and her
darling Azemia, though fhe hoped their
feparation was to be fhort. Hamet-
beig faw her embark with more phleg-
matic philofophy, recommending her
however to the fcrupulous fidelity of
the Moorifh guard, Muzzled. The
veffel left the beautiful bay; its *mina-*
B 6 *rets*

rets and *mofques* were no longer vifible
—Azemia retired in tears to her cabin;
precious tears! Alas! they were the
firft fhe ever fhed; but of how many
were they not the *avant couriers!*

The wind was fair, and the voyage,
for two days, profperous. Ah! faithlefs flattering illufion! on the third a
ftrange fail appeared in fight—it was
foon perceived to be a fhip of great
force: it approached—efcape became
impoffible; and after receiving one
broadfide, which killed four men and a
boy, and wounded fix others, Citizen
Moutard ftruck to the glorious fuperiority of Britifh valour, and became
prize to the Amputator, of forty-four
guns, Captain Jofiah Wappingfhot
commander, who took poffeffion of the
veffel

veffel and her furviving crew, as well
as of her cargo of figs, coffee, raw filk,
and the fair Azemia.

The next day Captain Wappingfhot
announced his fuccefs in a very eloquent billet, addreffed to the Lords
Commiffioners of the Admiralty—but,
notwithftanding, purfued his voyage
homewards, whither he was fteering
at the time he made this fortunate
capture; and he landed in due courfe
of failing at the Point at Portfmouth.

CHAP.

CHAP. II.

An Hero.

THE brave Captain Wappingſhot, to whoſe fortunate lot it had fallen to be maſter of the liberty of the fair, young, and innocent Azemia, was a man far advanced in life—old, weather-beaten, and in almoſt all reſpects might have ſat to any artiſt employed to make deſigns for Peregrine Pickle, ſo nearly did he reſemble Commodore Trunnion. His mother, a dealer in geneva at Gravel-end,

end, had ſent him early to ſea, where, during above ſixty years, he had ſeen a great deal of ſervice; but, as he often ſaid himſelf, he had come off pretty well conſidering, for none of his main timbers were materially damaged, though in the war which terminated ſoon after the beginning of the preſent reign he had loſt an eye, the dexter ſide of his noſe, and the ſiniſter ear. In our fortunate conteſt with America he left three fingers off Sandy Hook; but in the preſent ſtill more glorious war he had not had the honour of ſuf-fering at all in his perſon—though he had loſt in various ways, by drowning, diſeaſe, or otherwiſe, five out of ſeven ſons with which Heaven had bleſſed him; but they ſlept in the bed of ho-nour, and he was content. Nevertheleſs, ſo

ſo ſlowly does merit riſe (dear as it is to our governors), from the nature of the ſervice, that Captain Wappingſhot owed his command rather to the friend-ſhip of the honourable Commodore, of whoſe ſquadron he was in the laſt cruize, than to his long ſervices and heavy loſſes. This noble commander, a man of high birth, had frequently had oc-caſion to experience other good quali-ties in the veteran Wappingſhot, beſides thoſe of bravery and ſeamanſhip. Wap-pingſhot had not the common indif-ference of ſailors, as to the main chance: on the contrary, he had it always in view, and had diſcovered that the attainment of money was in no way ſo eaſy as by flattering the foi-bles, and contributing to the accommo-dation, of his ſuperiors. To the noble Com-

Commodore he had been frequently uſeful; and therefore the very firſt oc-caſion was ſeized by that honourable perſon to *make him*, as the term is, by giving him the command of the Am-putator.

It may ſeem to favour of ingratitude towards his benefactor, that Wapping-ſhot did not (knowing his predilection for youth and beauty) immediately im-part to him the acquiſition made in the capture of Azemia; but the ſhip was then actually, as was before ob-ſerved, under ſailing orders for Eng-land, and Captain Wappingſhot had reaſons of his own which prevented his making, in this inſtance, the leaſt deviation from the inſtructions he had received.

In

In paffing the Straits, it occurred to him, that Muzzled-Abib would be a very troublefome and ufelefs perfonage in England; and after many debates with himfelf, whether it would not be better to fend him quietly overboard fome fine evening, his humanity had been at length fo far heard, that he ordered him to be fet on fhore on the Barbary coaft, where he doubted not but the old black dog would do well enough; nor did any reflections on the fate of poor Muzzled Abib ever after difturb his tranquillity.

*   *   *

And now, reader! thou haft perhaps feen the agile Gardel, or the immortal Veftris; thou mayeft, peradventure, have

have beheld the celebrated Didelot of the prefent day; or, if thou art a lover of the beauties of Grecian fculpture, thou mayeft have gazed with fcientific eyes on the Apollo, or contemplated the proportions of the Farnefian Hercules. If, in a lefs elevated fphere of life, where thefe examples of grace may never have been prefented to thee, thou haft, peradventure, turned with taftelefs indignation from the reed-like and flender figure of Lord Fritterville, eldeft fon of the Marquis of Maccaroon, and furveyed with more Britifh approbation the nervous ftrength and gigantic form of the Ruffian or Big Ben; be that as it may, and to whatever clafs of focial life thou belongeft, equally muft thy imagination be called upon to embody a form to which no defcription can

can do juftice. It is, gentle reader! my hero whom I am about to prefent to thee—A youth fo amiable in manners, fo unexceptionable in morals, in perfon fo beauteous, as fancy hardly ever formed, unlefs in the early dreams of fome fair vifionary virgin by the fide of a murmuring fountain on a fopha of mofs and flowers, and overfhadowed by myrtle and mimofa—when, after the perufal of fome foul diffolving tale of tender fympathy (printed at the Minerva prefs), and overcome by the languors of a fummer's day, fhe half indulges the fweet illufions of elegant imagination, and dreams unutterable things!

I will try however, for fuch as have lefs facility at this ideal painting, to

to tell what he was. Aid me, ye gentle generous mufes of Britain! ye, who know fo well and have fo often defcribed—" Youths as they ought to be!" Some lines of the *Swan of Lichfield* prefent themfelves, which are glowingly imitatively defcriptive, fuch as ever flow from the energetic pen of that celebrated young lady:

O'er his fair brows, the fairer of their fhade,
Locks of the richeft brown luxuriant play'd.

And again of his height:

* Tall as the pine amid inferior trees,
With all the bending ofier's pliant eafe!

Here then I muft reft my defcription of the figure of this infinuating youth.
But

* This is furely much more claffically elegant than the following lines from the pen of another female

But I muſt not omit his face: he had, then, full eyes of indeſcribable colour, beaming with ſweetneſs, ſparkling with intelligence, and ſurmounted by full dark eye brows. As to his noſe! if a connoiſſeur in noſes had made on purpoſe a voyage of diſcovery to the Promontory, and under the immediate direƈtions of Don Diego himſelf, a more exquiſitely-formed noſe could not have been imported. His lips emulated the Kentiſh cherry; of courſe his teeth rivalled mother-of-pearl, and he had the moſt intereſting beard in the world. Such

female author, whoſe *imputed* ſimplicity has ſurely more credit than it deſerves: ſhe ſays of a hero, that he is——

Graceful as Dutchmen in the aƈt of ſkaiting,
Yet upright as the wand of Lord in waiting;
Now agile bends, as Sportſman ſhooting Dottrell,
Now ſteps majeſtic—like Sir Clement Cottrell.

was

was the perſon of Charles Arnold, a midſhipman; alas! he was *only* a midſhipman on board the Amputator.

The father of this young man, a country gentleman of ſmall fortune, had left him and a younger brother in their early youth to the care of their mother, to whom he left alſo the diſpoſal of all his fortune during her life, not doubting her tenderneſs for her ſons: but in proceſs of time it appeared that this good lady, emulating the heroiſm of the Spartan mothers, or perhaps ſtimulated by the fame of the female patriots of modern Gaul, determined to dedicate both her ſons to the ſervice of her country; and as ſoon as Charles, the eldeſt, was of a proper age, ſhe had procured him a birth on board the Amputator, while the

the youngeſt was diſpatched as a cadet to gather laurels in the Eaſt Indies.

To ſay the truth, Mrs. Arnold was one of thoſe ſprightly matrons who hold it ſinful as well as fooliſh to waſte the rich ſummer of their days in pining widowhood: ſhe was a fine woman, of a portly and commanding preſence, of gay ſpirits, and high health; her eyes were of thoſe that mark high claims and expeƈtations, and ſhe thought it vaſtly abſurd to dedicate her life to raiſing poultry and regiſtering ſmall beer in a country village; ſhe quitted it therefore as ſoon as her two ſons were fairly diſpoſed of, and reſided in a ſmall but elegant houſe in the pariſh of Maryle-Bone.

Her

Her ſon, who had been by the kindneſs of an uncle particularly recommended to his commanding officer, had found means to attach all his meſſmates to him, as well as to be a great favourite with Captain Wappingſhot. Impatient therefore to ſee his mother, or for ſome other reaſon, he had entreated and obtained leave to go on ſhore; and it was, ſeated in the Royal Admiral long coach, with this youth on one ſide of her, and the one-eyed veteran on the other, that our heroine began her journey.

Now once more, all ye Muſes that ſip the Caſtalian ſpring, or play on the biforked hill! once more I invoke you— and you, ye Graces! whether ye wanton amid the flaxen ringlets (poſtiche or otherwiſe) of Lady Seraphina, or beam

from the eyes of the Countefs of .... *
whether ye wait on the Farren, or lurk
in the arch fmile of the Jordan—whether ye attend on Parifot or Hilligfberg
— a moment, a little moment, prefide
on my pen!——But where fhall I begin?
how venture to delineate one bright
feature? Let thofe who have ever per-
ufed the ponderous romances of former
ages, endeavour to imagine what muft
be the attractions of thofe inimitable
fair ones who could fecure their con-
quefts for years amidft the rigors of difdain: or, if fuch have never been your
ftudy, imagine what muft have been the
concentrated beauties of the moft celebrated charmer of antiquity; collect,
" in thy mind's eye," all that may have

* Whatever Countefs the reader prefers.

been

been related of Helen or Polydamna—
of Dido—of Thaïs, Laïs, or the Thra-
cian Rhodope—of Lucretia— of the
lovelieft of the Roman empreffes: in
more modern times, of Fair Rofamond,
Diana de Poitiers, Agnes Sorel, or the
fair Gabrielle—of the Geraldine of the
Earl of Surrey, Petrarch's Laura, or
Louife de Kerouaille — the Hampton-
Court Beauties, and " each bright
Churchill of the Galaxy:"—or, if all
thefe are infufficient, take fomething
from the Mifs Byron, the Clariffa, the
Pamela of Richardfon: borrow a little
from the Sophia of Fielding, and the
Narciffa of Smollet; and a feature, a
look, an air, from what thou canft
imagine of the favourite heroines of
the inferior and more modern fchools:
and having done fo, and compofed a

C 2 figure

figure and face (as little like thy wife, if
thou happeneft to be a married man, as
thy confcience will let thee; as much
like thyfelf, if thou art a woman, as thy
humility will permit), thou mayeft then,
peradventure, furnifh thyfelf with fome
refemblance of my attractive Mufful-
woman, my charming Azemia, and have
an incomplete conception of the truth
of that lovelinefs with which, breathing
fweetnefs from her rofy lips, and darting brightnefs from her fparkling eyes,
fhe fat — fhe who was worthy of a
throne — in a ftage — a common ftage
coach, as it moved between Portfmouth
and the Swan with two Necks in Lad
Lane.

CHAP.

CHAP. III.

A Declaration and a *feline* Favourite.

IT is impoffible to exprefs the *millionth*
part of the furprife with which our fair
Azemia faw herfelf carried along! no
words can defcribe what paffed *on that
occafion.* She, who had never been out
of the haram till her unfortunate em-
barkation, what muft fhe have thought?
She had never learned to difcriminate
her cogitations: fhe thought in the Arabefque, her native tongue, in which if

C 3 fhe

fhe had fpoken nobody would have underftood her: and the remarks fhe
made during this journey are not preferved; for, before her extreme aptitude
of acquirement had enabled her to exprefs herfelf in Englifh, the emotions
prefent to her then had faded from the
tablet where memory had engraved
them: as the white thorn of March is
remembered no more, while we watch
the golden progrefs of the daffodil, or
elevate our eyes to the fun-flower.

But what was her aftonifhment when
they were fet down at the Swan with
two Necks! The two gentlemen ordered a flight refrefhment; they drank
porter and ate cold mutton with pickled
onions; Azemia could not tafte any of
it. As foon as their repaft was finifhed,
a hackney

a hackney coach was called; and Azemia, being handed into it, was foon in
the houfe Mrs. Periwinkle, who kept a
flop fhop in Ratcliffe-Highway.

It was to the care of this refpeftable
gentlewoman that the Captain chofe to
confide, at leaft for the prefent, his
beauteous prize. His reafons may
hereafter appear for preferring the ma-
tronage of Mrs. Periwinkle to that
of his own wife.

Refiding at this time with Mrs. Periwinkle was her unmarried daughter,
Mifs Sally, a fair, fat, and facetious
damfel about thirty, who was a great
favourite of our brave commander's:
fhe was indeed a young woman of fome
pretenfions, confidering her obfcure
C 4 origin;

origin; for fhe had an aunt, houfekeeper
to a man of fafhion, and with her fhe
occafionally refided. The elegancies
of fuch a houfe, and the *polifhed manners*
of even the fecond table, very naturally
infpired Mifs Sally with ineffable contempt for all thofe who refided in the
vicinity of her mother's abode.

Her friendfhip however for Captain Wappingfhot was confiderably increafed now that he was commander of
a man of war: with her and her mother
the gallant veteran began to confult on
the difpofition of poor Azemia, while
the maid of the houfe conduéted her
to the room that had been prepared for
her. The unhappy Charles faw her
difappear with inexpreffible anguifh.
Till now he had fed his infant paffion
by

by gazing on her; and of the language
of his eyes — the eloquent and only
language in which he could convey his
fentiments—he had not been fparing.
He had told her—all that exquifite
fenfibility could diélate! Every glance
was a proteftation—every ogle a note of
admiration! And when at length, three
days afterwards, in the back fhop of
Mrs. Periwinkle he was compelled to
bid her a long adieu; when the fatal
conviélion that he muft leave her
preffed upon his heart; his too feeling
mind, agitated by this cruel certainty,
almoft funk under it. Yet while the Captain and the ladies were converfing in
the other fhop, he wholly withdrew his
attention from them, and fixing his melancholy eyes on Azemia, who leaned
penfively on the window-feat, the idea
C 5 of

of the firſt poetry he had ever written darted into his mind, and afterwards took the form of the following ſea ſong, which he determined to preſent to her the firſt opportunity :——

When on a clear and cloudleſs night
The moon ſhall pour her level light,
    And tremble on the ſilver ſea ;
I then ſhall watch her cheering rays,
And ſighing aſk, if thou doſt gaze
    On her bright orb—and think of me ?

When raving fierce through every ſhroud
The wild careering wind is loud,
    And I on the mid watch ſhall be ;
My heart will aſk, as tempeſts riſe,
If thou doſt hear ?—and gentle ſighs
    Heave thy ſoft heart, while pitying me ?

If

If deſtin'd in the bloody fight
To cloſe theſe eyes in endleſs night,
    That now ſo fondly gaze on thee ;
Even then, as life ſhall ebb away,
My lateſt lingering breath ſhall ſay,
    My only love !—remember me !——

But the cruel moment came when he muſt go : he *wriggled** (for extreme reluctance would not ſuffer him to walk) out of the houſe ; and juſt as he entered the ſtreet, a hackney coach full of ſmuggled goods, with a landlady from Wapping well known to our hero, happened to paſs.   Charles vaulted into it

* If any faſtidious critic ſhould object to the uſe of this word, I beg leave to refer him to the moſt reſpectable authority—the very words of a woman of faſhion in her moſt elaborate performance. I am indebted to the ſame elegant ſource for what follows to the end of the chapter.

C 6   with.

with the alacrity of a ſkipper ; while the coach, as if the horſes were inſpired by his deſire of volition, darted down the ſtreet like ſons of Eclipſe or Potoooooooo.

Converſation ſuch as Charles Arnold now enjoyed with his old acquaintance Mrs. Ginger, on this memorable evening, may be called the drawing out and diſciplining the whole ſtrength of his internal force : the more he ſpoke to Mrs. Ginger on the ſubject of his love, the more were his ideas inſpired, and his paſſion ſupported by freſh reinforcements. In the language of confidence there are many ſalutary hints, which, like the colliſion of hard bodies, make the ſoul take fire and the imagination corruſcate !

Now

Now am I well aware, that many of my female readers will *abuſe* me, and cry out,—" Bleſs us, Oh ! Lord ! Lord ! here is our friend Miſs Jacquetta A. M. Jenks writing about ſailors and bumboat women !—*people* of whom *people* that have lived among *us,* as ſhe *has* done, can know nothing in the world !"

Fair and friendly critics ! — ye who have with the ſweeteſt patience read ſuch an immenſity of nonſenſe, do not, oh ! do not tire, juſt when *I* entreat your attention to mine. Let us never, my kind-hearted female Mentorias ! let us never forget that friendſhip is an *ecſtatic compoſition of intellectual harmony,* grand in its tones as a trumpet — great in its effects as a chorus ! It *relieves,*
ſoothes,

foothes, abates, doubles, divides, fuspends,
and *accelerates*; and by fpeaking of our
misfortunes to a true friend we leave
part of our griefs behind us!

CHAP.

CHAP. IV.

It comes in fuch a queftionable fhape!
SHAKESPEARE.

Nay—never fhake thy hairlefs head at *me !*
SHAKESPEARE.

THE weather was extremely warm; and
Azemia, who had been in habits of enjoying the cool air of the fountained
quadrangles of the haram, overfhadowed
with the palm and the cedar, and *deci-
duous cyprefs*, alfo larches and poplars,
now languifhed for a little frefh air,
and determined to attempt finding her
way to the garden, as a fcene *interefting
to her imagination.* Having *wound down*
the

the only ftaircafe (which was rather narrow), and entered a paffage rather old
(of which the white-wafh had fallen
from the walls), fhe found herfelf in a
narrow paffage, terminated by two large
bucking-tubs, and a broken queen's-
ware bafon of uncommon dimenfions.
The garden, or rather court, then appeared: fhe defcended three fteps, and
entered a walk, formed of native earth,
but bordered with offifications of fheep,
and fhells of cockle and oyfter, which
gave this eaftern part of the inclofure
rather a marine appearance; while the
more elevated borders enclofed an old
oil-jar, in which had once grown a root
of Angelica, but it was now no longer
verdant. To the weft, however, were
fcattered feveral fmall tufts of turnips,
intermingled with mint and marjoram:
nor

nor was ornament wholly negle&ed; for
in a more remote quarter grew a flourifhing plant of the Canterbury bell.
—The view beyond the garden was
crowned with the awful fummits of the
neighbouring cheminées *, and beyond,
through a wicket in the wall, *the eye
caught* a part of the wild fhores of the
Thames, with wharfs and ozier grounds,
the whole terminating in a remote pro-
fpe& of the gloomy remains of two
frefh-water pirates fufpended fome years
before at Cuckhold's Point.

The contraft between this view and
thofe fhe had been accuftomed to,

* *Cheminées.* Some little variation of fpelling
may be allowed where dignity is to be given to a
fubje&—Cheminées is certainly better than chimneys, as being more like Pyrenées.

ftruck

ftruck forcibly on the fufceptible mind of Azemia; fhe felt it beat upon her heart, and a heavy figh efcaped her.

Then, traverfing flowly the quadrangle, fhe gathered a fmall fprig of the Canterbury bell, and returned filent and fad to her own apartment; and when fhe arrived there, the big drops that had long quivered in her eye fell into one of the cups of the flower.

This circumftance difturbed a folitary ear-wig that lay concealed there — it languidly crawled forth! The mind of Azemia, uncultivated as it was, was tremblingly fenfible of the fofteft pity for all animated nature. As fhe gazed on this lone infect, fhe thought it looked unfortunate : —" Perhaps," faid fhe, " this

" this poor *Forficula-Auricularis* is like me, a folitary and deferted being—far from its beloved relatives — banifhed perhaps for ever from its dear native flower—a wanderer in the world, and liable to be crufhed by every carelefs or inhuman paffenger ! ! !

The idea affected her; and yielding to the penfive influence, fhe followed this train of reflection, till it infenfibly affumed a poetical form, in the following lines :

THE FORFICULA AURICULARIS, OR EAR-WIGGE, TO HER LOVE.

In what fmall leaf of verdant fold
Art thou, my wandering love, enroll'd ?
Where lurk'ft thou, in what lily's bell,
My wanton rover, prithee, tell ?

Ah !

Ah ! what attracts thy vagrant fancy ?
The crimfon clove, or velvet panfy ?
Where keep'ft thou, love, thy flowery ftate ?
In three-lobed leaves, or leaves ferrate ?

Doft thou now pierce, with forceps keen,
Some rafpberry's hirfute globes between ?
Haft thou a bower luxurious got
In golden pulp of apricot ?

Or doft thou find a lodging fpacious
In pea's fweet bloom papilionaceous;
And, fnug as prieft in ample rectory,
Neftle in honey-flowing nectary ?

Say where thy agile form is curling,
In flower that nods o'er ftreamlet purling ;
Where, as in odorous barrack hollow,
Thou fill'ft a tuberous corolla !

Hid'ft thou in bloffom of geranium,
Like pictur'd nymph in Herculaneum ?
Tak'ft thou, perchance, thy quarters humble
Beneath the white bean's fpotted umbel ?

Soft

Soft doft thou dream in thick fweet-william,
Or perch on lupine's bright vexillum ?
Where'er thou art, oh ! quickly fcud
O'er powder'd bloom, or fpicy bud !

Thou com'ft !—Thy coat of polifh'd mail,
Thy biform antlers, crefcent tail,
Thy diamond eye fo fmall and fhiny,
Thy many twinkling feet, fo tiny—

I fee !—and, Wigling, hail the fight :
My foft horns tremble with delight :
Ah ! let us now, my love, refort
Where rich Vertumnus keeps his court !

There, in the hautboy deeply bury,
Or make our bride-bed in the cherry ;
O'er pearly grapes luxurious twine,
And raife young ear-wigs in the nectarine *.

* Let not my readers object to the probability of Azemia's writing Englifh verfes ; or, if they fhould, let them recollect, that fome of our celebrated heroines, though born in another country, and two or three centuries ago, write moft pathetic and polifhed poetry in very pretty modern Englifh.

Scarce

Scarce had fhe finifhed this fimple ef-fufion, and committed it to paper, ere *footfteps were heard* on the ftairs: they were as of one who attempted *lightly* and *foftly* to afcend.—Azemia liftened; the door opened—and fhe beheld—Charles Arnold! " I come," faid he, as he threw himfelf on his knees before her, " I come to put my life into your hands—I love you; to diftraction I love you!—Tell me, Oh! beauteous Azemia, can you, will you, pity me?"

Azemia, ignorant of the meaning of his words, yet perfectly aware of the fignification of his moving attitudes, felt extremely difpofed to return his tender-nefs; nor did fhe know any poffible reafon why fhe fhould not. She made figns, therefore, that he fhould rife, and

feat

feat himfelf by her: fhe gave him her hand, which he devoured with kiffes; but, determining to command himfelf, he endeavoured to explain to her, that he was forbidden by the people fhe was with from feeing her, and that it was by ftratagem only he gained one fhort mo-ment to throw himfelf at her feet.

But, alas! the innocent Azemia was totally unable to devife any means by which they might in future elude the vigilance of her mercenary guardians.

" What will become of me?" faid he. " The fhip to which I belong is in the Downs—we are under orders for the North Sea—I muft tear myfelf away! Captain Wappingfhot fufpects my at-tachment;

tachment; I fhall never, no never be permitted to fee you more!"

While he thus fpoke, a cat, which had of late become a great favourite of Azemia's, came purring towards her: it had been a kitten nurfed by Charles Arnold on board the Amputator:—the fight of it affected him even to tears.

" This little puffy," faid he, after an affecting paufe, and ftroking the cat with his left hand, " this happy animal *I* firft conducted to you! I faw you as you fondled it—I faw you fur-rounded by attractions too powerful for my heart: that moment is now prefent to my memory, and the creature comes even now, to witnefs the fad one of my departure!"

Grief

Grief interrupted his utterance!——When he recovered his voice, he faid—" Oh, Azemia! Azemia! when hereafter you carefs, you ftroke your furry favourite—when of an evening its emerald eyes glow with amber fa-tisfaction;—remember, ah! remember your unhappy Arnold, who will then, alas! be far from you.—Do not deny me the poor fatisfaction of believing, that the purrings of this happy indi-vidual of the feline fpecies, as it rubs round and round you, bring to your re-collection the mournful remembrance of my unhappy love!"

Azemia comprehended only half of what the interefting youth uttered—but it was enough; fhe fmiled on him with ineffable fweetnefs: he could bear no

more,

more, but, forcing himſelf away, ran
down ſtairs, mounted a horſe he had
hired, and hardly knowing, and not at
all caring, whither he went, *galloped* *
as faſt as poſſible to Deal.

By this time evening came on; and
when the vague ſenſations that had flut-
tered in the innocent breaſt of Azemia
had a little ſubſided, ſhe went in a penſive way into a neighbouring lumber-
room: it was old, ſpacious, and dark.
Azemia imagined that her cat, now
dearer to her than ever, had kittened
there; and in the preſent moment it
offered ſomething like a ſolace to her
mind, to reflect on the tender offices
ſhe might engage in, in nurſing. the

* All the perſonages in ſome novels gallop.

infant

infant progeny. She advanced therefore into the lumber-room; and ſlowly,
and with difficulty, making her way
among old ſea cheſts, hammocks, and
tables, coils of rope, remnants of carpets, and damaged pictures (for the immediate anceſtor of Mrs. Periwinkle
had been a broker), ſhe at length
reached the weſt ſide of this gloomy
apartment.

There was a dreary ſolemnity about
it; it was ſilent and ſolitary—the ſet-
ting ſun had almoſt ſunk beneath the
horizon, and his oblique rays, obſcured
by the neighbouring warehouſe of an
eminent dry-ſalter, were almoſt entirely
obfuſcated by the ſuccedaneums placed
in the dilapidated caſements, which
conſiſted of a piece of a mariner's

D 2   check

check habiliment, and a wad of faded
plaid that had compoſed the phillibeg
of a Highlander in the year 1745.
Azemia, who had never during her
early youth been in ſo *queer* a place,
looked round her ſomewhat diſmayed,
and for a moment her fears ſuſpended
her benevolent purpoſe. At length, recollecting the helpleſs family of her cat,
ſhe ſighed, and began to ſearch for
them: ſhe liſtened, but nothing was
heard, ſave only the wind, that whiſ-
pered in the waving of a harra-
teen bed, ſuſpended to a dyer's pole
on the adjoining roof. It was terrific!—Azemia ſhuddered—and as no
gentle purring, no ſoft ſalutation of
feline ſolicitation ſaluted her ear, and
the wind howled with redoubled violence, moving the Scotch plaid to and
fro,

fro, ſhe found her reſolution unequal
to a further progreſs in this forlorn
building; and was retreating, when a
cloſet door creaking on its hinges
ſlowly opened, and at the ſame moment
ſome looſe boards, on which ſhe ſtood,
cracked: Azemia ſtarted — ſhe looked
up, and beheld the figure of an old
man, bald and ſqualid, ſitting in a long
dark robe reaching to his feet: his
beard was as white as ſnow—his throat
bare and wrinkled—and his withered
hands, with long nails, appeared beneath
the cuffs of his garment. Azemia looked
at him with terror and aſtoniſhment: he
nodded to her; yet there was ſomething
of an air about him that intereſted her,
and a paralytic tremor agitated his head—
but he did not ſpeak. Azemia had ne-

D 3   ver

ver heard of a ghoſt* (in Turkey
they are but little in uſe ; but terror, of
ſhe knew not what, poſſeſſed her; ſtill
ſhe could not move from the ſpot. The
figure nodded; again and Azemia, in
extreme apprehenſion, haſtened back to
her apartment, and ſhut the lumber-
room door, by placing a joint ſtool
againſt it. For the preſent, the exceſſive agitation of her ſpirits baniſhed the
idea both of her fond lover and her favourite animal.

* Leſt another opportunity ſhould not offer to
explain in the ſequel of my widely-wandering hiſtory, this ghaſtly and terrific appearance, I let my
readers underſtand, that it was *not a real ghoſt*, or
even a *wax-work figure*, but a large Chineſe Man-
darin, damaged in its voyage to Europe, and which
had nodded ever ſince in the muſeum of Mrs. Periwinkle.

CHAP.

CHAP. V.

In which the Hiſtory is for a while ſtationary.

I SHALL now put in a few words whilſt
my hiſtory pauſes, touching *my* opinion
of the nature of that ſpecies of literature called Novels: and here, novice
as I am, let me venture (as I cannot do
wrong while I follow the example of
a reſpeĉtable veteran, grown gray in
amuſing and edifying the world) to anticipate with my readers the favour
which I expeĉt hereafter to deſerve

D 4   from

from them, by the number and variety
of elegant produĉtions with which I
purpoſe to oblige my country. Pre-
ſuming then on this, and making a ſort
of poſt obit on their indulgence, let
me, whilſt I apologize for thoſe imper-
feĉtions to which every human work is
liable, give them my *notion* of what a
novel ought to be.

" If puerilities are pleaſing," quoth
one of the venerable fathers of our
craft, "men (and of courſe women)
will write ' ut pueris placeant." Whether it is on this ground that he has
himſelf told us a long and ſtrange hiſtory, in which his heroes preach, and
his heroines *love*, one and all (with even
more voluntary and genial kindneſs
than the ladies of the South-Sea Iſlands);

or

or whether he does not think ſuch matters trifling licences, I am not well
read enough in his works to underſtand:
but in many points I entirely agree with
him, and ſhall be charmed if this public avowal of my being his humble diſ-
ciple, ſhould engage him to wave in *my*
favour his violent antipathy to female
underſtanding ; and ſince, perhaps, neceſſity as well as choice may have ſomething to do in my taking up this " idle
trade," to ſhew *me* ſome mercy, among
thoſe whoſe caſes he is " *well aware
ought to be exceptions*," when he draweth
his tranchant quill againſt noveliſts.—
Reſpeĉtable Sir ! ſince in your laſt great
work *in the novel way*, you have conde-
ſcended to ſuppoſe yourſelf ſpeaking to
a young author *ſitting down for the firſt
time to his maiden work*, let a *virgin*

D 5   *muſe*

muſe avail herſelf of your precepts. I ſtop, however, and tremble as I continue to peruſe the reſt of the page from whence I have extracted the above line; for you ſay, the firſt thing neceſſary, is, for a man *to underſtand himſelf*. Alas! Sir, how may a feeble and a *young woman* hope to achieve this, when one is every day convinced that *men*, and even *old men*, miſtake themſelves entirely?

But however this ſtumbling-block may lie in my way, I recover a little courage, while I promiſe to adhere as nearly as I can to the rules you have ſo generouſly given us. As my heroine is a Turkiſh girl, ſhe has never been *ſpoiled by* a modern education, and perhaps, inſtead *of libelling nature, as edu-cated*

cated women do with the pen or the pencil, may be as tenderly ſuſceptible as *Suſan May*, or as *fiercely loving as Fanny Clay-pole.* Here then I hope I ſhall meet your approbation; and I further aſſure you, that in my repreſentations I will not caricature or libel human nature. By no means—every body I repreſent ſhall be people who have, as you recommend, ſome dark ſpecks on their bright ſide; and ſome bright ſpecks on their black ſide, which I hope will give them that *middle tint*, which, (without a piebald appearance), is the very ſoul of keeping in a picture. I will not bring their black ſides too near the eye; they ſhall be ſoftened down, till the whole is moſt harmoniouſly blended and ſtibbled together; truſting that the bold relief and infinite variety of my characters and

D 6 ſtyle,

ſtyle, will prevent obſcurity and confuſion. I will not ſay a word more *touching* negroes or negro ſlavery; and I am almoſt tempted to eraſe what I have written about Muzzled-Abib; for on reading, for the fifteenth time, your admirable work above mentioned, I obſerve, that you give it as your opinion, that the horrors that have happened, or have been ſaid to happen, in the Weſt-India *blood-beſprinkled iſlands*, have been ſolely owing to the *breath of others!* i. e. of poets and noveliſts. I ſuppoſe, worthy Sir! you have ſome very good reaſon for ſaying ſo. For my part, I ſhould not, had I heard it from leſs authority, have imagined that *any breath*, however *tune-ful*, could have reached ſo far; ſtill leſs the ſoft *condolences of ladies* ſung to the lutes and lyres of modern conſtruction.

And

And I ſtill cannot comprehend how theſe effuſions of falſe pity and affected compaſſion have found their way into the circulating libraries of negro towns, or rather the aſſemblage of huts, where they are allowed to remain ſo few hours out of four-and-twenty. However, warned by *this terrible example*, I will not hazard a word that may perchance inflame with inordinate and unreaſonable thirſt of freedom theſe naſty black fellows and impudent wenches. No, Sir: be aſſured that I will carefully avoid calling forth *your bluſhes* on the occaſion; and pardon ſo abrupt a tranſition, as from the loweſt being in the rank and file of human creatures (the link that immediately connects us with the ouran outang), to that higheſt and brighteſt ring of the chain, which has only

royalty

royalty between it and heaven!— I mean the Nobles of this, and every other land where there are any of that fublime defcription remaining. I fay, Sir, that I will *religioufly abftain*, " or at leaft as far as I can," not from coots, didappers, and water hens, (my fentence ran fo like one of Sterne's, that I was unawares going on with it), but from touching, in the way of reflection, on, firft, any of the Blood Royal, male or female, for whom I have the moft decided and profound veneration and refpect; next, on any Duke, Duchefs, or their firft, fecond, third, fourth, fifth, fixth, or feventh fons and fo on to all and every fon they may happen to have— or any of their graces' daughters, whether married or fingle; nor will I reflect upon any Marquis or Marchionefs,

their

their fons and daughters, uncles, aunts, nieces, nephews, and coufins; nor on any Earl or Countefs, their progeny, or relatives; or any Vifcount or Vifcountefs, Baron or Baronefs, Englifh or Irifh; nor will I fay any thing reflecting on the good name of any Baronet, whether ancient or modern, or the dames their fpoufes, (for I really think this equeftrian order have been worked too hard by all novelifts); nor will I hint at the leaft difrefpectful thing of the Knights of the Bath, Knights Bannerets, or even Knights of the City; for I really do opine with you, that the little reverence fhewn to titled people is as much a caufe of the vile levelling principle that is got among us, as the poet's lamentations over the fufferings

of

of negroes have caufed the flaves to revolt in the iflands. But, my very good Sir! deign to confider what a very great diminution all this muft make of the ftock an unfortunate novelift has to work with; and if you thus fhut me out from thefe realities, may I not be allowed a few extraordinaries — a little rambling in the woods, my dear Sir!—a caftle or two, or an abbey — a few ghofts, provided I make out afterwards that they were not ghofts, but wax-work and pafteboard; and a little fprinkling of banditti, juft to excite a fmall emotion of terror!—and then I may be able to fill up my little book without a word of politics, revolutions or counter-revolutions, and prattle through my volumes as prettily,

and

and beat up my literary *pap* with as innoxious ingredients as the moft ftraight-laced matrons, or rigid elders, can recommend for their babes and fucklings.

CHAP.

CHAP. VI.

═══

An alteration—and fcenes in fuperior life.

═══

THE reader may remember that Mifs Sally, the daughter of Mrs. Periwinkle, was not only the friend and confidante of Captain Wappingfhot, but alfo in the efteem of other perfonages of yet more confiderable confequence: among thefe the noble Duke, with whom her aunt lived as houfekeeper, was the moft illuftrious. Eminent for his attachment to all that were young and

and handfome, and for his boundlefs generofity to indigent beauty, Mifs Sally, probably in the pure benevolence of her nature, imagined that fhe could not do a more friendly action towards the young ftranger than to introduce her to this great man. In this view, three or four days after the final departure of her captor, Azemia, dreffed in her Turkifh habit, and made to avail herfelf of all her charms, was conveyed in one of the Duke's private coaches to his houfe in a part of the town very remote from Ratcliffe Highway.

It happened by a very ftrange contretems, that his Grace, who was on this day to have been in town by appointment, was overtaken in the morning with fo fevere a fit of the gout, that he was

was confined to his bed at a villa twelve miles from it. Nothing could be fo unfortunate !—What could be done ?—Sundry domeftics were difpatched for his phyficians, and another confidential fervant ordered to direct the houfekeeper, and her amiable and confcientious niece, to retain the young Turk at the town houfe, and fuffer no one to fee her. With thefe orders the good ladies of courfe were ready to comply ; while the innocent Azemia, totally unconfcious of the fate to which fhe was deftined, was extremely glad to find herfelf in a place fo much more comfortable than her former abode, which, as well as her journey, had given her no very delightful idea of England.

The

The fpacious manfion of the noble Duke was uninhabited in his abfence, except by his fervants, for he had at prefent no *arrangement* within its walls. Azemia, therefore, was placed in a very handfome apartment, where fhe feemed fo well contented, that her governeffes imagined there was no occafion to prohibit her leaving it, while they fet forth on fome fcheme of their own which was likely to detain them the whole morning.

But among the many fair ones to whom this veteran in gallant achievements had occafionally paid his court, was a woman of fafhion, *un peu fur le retour* indeed, but ftill, as fhe herfelf was willing to believe, eminently graceful and accomplifhed. That fhe was ftill fingle single was certainly a moſt extraordinary circumſtance; but ſhe aſſured the world, as plainly as ſhe could without directly ſaying ſo, that it was owing to her long but moſt purely Platonic affection for the noble Duke: and on his part, whether his regard was Platonic or no, he certainly encouraged ſuch a degree of intimacy, that the lady was viſited, and viſited him, at all times, with the ſoothing, and doubtleſs the innocent, familiarity of a ſiſter.

This lady, whom we will call Lady Belinda, knew that the Duke was expected in town, and, as he had been abſent near three weeks, flew on the feathered feet of friendſhip to ſee him.

With

With conſternation ſhe heard that he was ſeized with the gout and confined to his bed. Summoning the only footman that was to be found, ſhe enquired when any meſſenger was to be ſent; and hearing that a ſervant was to go off in two hours with a ſupply of various elegances and medicinal accommodations, which his Grace would never be in the hazard of miſſing, ſhe bade the man open the coach door, ſaying, ſhe would get out and write a few words to be ſent by this conveyance. The footman obeyed — conducted her into a boudior at the end of the houſe, where there were materials for writing, and left her.

Lady Belinda then, ſighing deeply, took up her pen, and began to expreſs,

in

in terms the moſt energetic, her tender grief for the illneſs of her dear friend; hinting in very delicate, yet forcible terms, how delightful a taſk it would be to her, would the paltry prudery of peeviſh preciſeneſs allow her to attend him as a friend and ſiſter, to ſoften his pain, and mitigate the wearineſs of confinement, by the gentle offices of diſintereſted attachment!

Then, to prove (as if any doubts could have remained!) her powers of amuſement, even at a diſtance, ſhe entered on a detail of what had paſſed the preceding day in a large and illuſtrious circle where ſhe had been, which ſhe did in theſe words, among much other entertaining matter.

PART

PART OF LADY BELINDA'S LETTER.

" The Duke was quite in ſpirits, ſo was the Ducheſs: dear Lady Anne was immenſely entertaining, and Lady Rebecca delightfully gay! I never remember ſeeing the Biſhop ſo *ſprightly* as while he converſed with Sir Pertinax and young Jenkingbury, whoſe converſation, you know, his lordſhip declares is in a *ſuperior ſtyle.* A number of admirable things paſſed, and ſeveral excellent bons mots on Mr. Jackall's ſpectacles: Lord Robert and the Marchioneſs had, I thought, leſs of hilarity than uſual. The faculties of our poor Viſcount were ſomehow ſtrangely in *a ſtate of ſuſpenſion,* and even Lady Anne's charade produced no ſenſible emotion.

tion. Alicia Kindlefide, however, (fhe and her fifter came with Lady Rebecca) was wonderfully amufing; fhe is really clever—though not at all handfome in opinion. Her natural vivacity was heightened by the arrival of the Baron Van Gormagon, who had juft left the Stadtholder, and was going to Ranelagh. The attention of the company was infenfibly attracted by a narrative that Alicia was giving the Baron of her prefentation at Court—it was truly characteriftic: ' My heart,' faid fhe, ' my heart did not lie ftill, or my fight return to any lucidity of perception, till I had gone through the whole ceremony; but the obliging and gracious enquiries their Majefties had the infinite goodnefs to make after the tooth-ache I had, you know, that day, entirely removed

moved all my diffidence, and gave me a freedom of breathing which I had not felt before, ever fince the time that the maccaroni at the Marquis's difagreed with me."

Hardly had Lady Belinda finifhed the fentence, and was confidering in a reflecting pofture, her cheek leaning on her hand, what next to fay, when hearing a flight noife fhe lifted up her eyes, and looking through the door of the antiroom, which had been left open on account of the heat, beheld a figure moving flowly at the other end of it, which ftruck her with amazement!—The drefs in which it appeared did not greatly differ from that of our fair countrywomen; but Lady Belinda thought it rather fome angelic emanation of heaven

than a mere mortal compofition, fo much did the beauty fhe beheld exceed all fhe had imagined, and certainly all that fhe had feen. The fair phantom approached without regarding her — Lady Belinda arofe—and then Azemia perceiving her, was retiring, when, determining to know who this extraordinary perfon was, fhe fpoke to her.

Her extreme youth, and evident ignorance of the Englifh or any of the other languages in which Lady Belinda addreffed her, now gave rife to the moft uneafy conjectures in the mind of the latter. She gueffed the truth, and, in the fafcinating object before her faw the deftruction of all thofe hopes fhe had long been cherifhing, of feeing a ducal coronet illumine her fummer brow.

brow. To dread, and to determine on removing the caufe of her dread, was with her but the bufinefs of a moment: how fhe contrived it is not material: fuffice it to fay, that by the affiftance of the footman, the only perfon that had feen Lady Belinda enter, Azemia and her pacquet of clothes were removed from the dangerous fituation where the cupidity of thofe into whofe power fhe had fallen had placed her, and was conveyed to a very retired houfe, eleven miles from London, on the contrary way to the Duke's villa, where, as it was inhabited only by the old Countefs of Killicranky, Lady Belinda's fuperannuated mother, and feveral trufty fervants, who were directed how to behave to her, Azemia found herfelf per-

fectly at eafe, and extremely glad to
be removed out of the blacknefs and
fmoke of London, at liberty to breathe
the frefh air in a large walled garden,
and delivered, fhe hoped for ever, from
the prefence of Mifs Sally, from whom,
though fhe knew nothing of her de-
figns, fhe had taken a mortal averfion.
With the fimplicity of an uneducated
child, fhe amufed herfelf with the flowers fhe faw around her, and with the
birds in a fmall net-work aviary adjoining to a confervatory; and fometimes fhe thought of Charles Arnold
with a fort of tender regret: he was indeed the only perfon among all thofe
fhe had feen in England whom fhe ever
defired to fee again.

In

In the mean time, the houfekeeper
and her niece, Mifs Sally, were furious:
the former anticipated with difmay the
lofs of her place; the latter, the lofs of
that poft which has often been poffeffed by very great men, as a preli-
minary to thofe of more honour. It
had been long the employment of Mifs
Sally to find out indigent beauty in
very early youth in obfcure parts of
the town, and among the poor, whofe
neceffities compelled them to wave any
nicety as to the deftination of their
daughters. Never had fhe met with
fo fair a creature as Azemia — never
did fhe fo anxioufly anticipate the profits of her difcovery; and when they
were thus unexpectedly fnatched from
her fhe became outrageous; while Lady

E 4   Belinda,

Belinda, having perfuaded herfelf that
in what fhe had done fhe had acted
upon the moft virtuous principles, confidered her own work with the utmoft
complacency.

CHAP.

CHAP. VII.

====

Schemes and the man I fing who tills the foil,
And ferves his country with—his tongue of oil.

====

LADY Belinda, however folicitous to
preferve the lovely Turk from the evil
machinations of the Duke, was by no
means rich enough to undertake the
fole care of providing for her, and foon
began to confider that fhe had brought
herfelf into a very untoward predicament; fhe was however fertile in refources, and imagined that a friend of
hers, whom in various exigencies fhe
had

E 5

had found ftill more fo, might be confulted with advantage on this occafion.

This gentleman, whofe name was
Wildcodger, was one of thofe perfonages who live at good tables—go about
to great houfes in the country—are liftened to by the gentlemen in their con-
fultations on improvements, and make
rebuffes and write verfes for the ladies—help them to quiz the chaplain,
and bear with admirable patience, and
even pleafantry, to be quizzed themfelves. He had the reputation of underftanding every thing, and would
either value an eftate or prefcribe
for a lap-dog. Sometimes he was
an author — yet oftener a critic —
wrote in the newfpapers—had a mortal
averfion

averfion to the impertinence of all re-
formers—was an optimift from principle, and could argue for a whole day to
prove that nothing could be otherwife,
of courfe nothing more eligible than it
is: his chief forte, however, lay in
fchemes to make that better which
he already afferted was beft. He
now and then got into a paradox, but
prefently efcaped from it by dint of
his former profound ftudies in the fchool
of Martinus Scriblerus.

Thus, when he had found a fuccedaneum for bread in a time of national
diftrefs approaching to famine, owing
to the beft conducted and moft neceffary of all poffible wars, and, boafting
of his admirable difcovery, was defired
to explain how, in a world fo wifely

     conftructed

conftructed as ours, and under the very
beft government that the wit and wifdom of man could, in that excellent
ftructure, devife, it happened that nine-
tenths of the people had nothing *but*
bread, and now by no means *enough* of
that; he would, with impreffive folemnity, begin, ftanding with his back
to the fire, and waving one hand with
great dignity, to fay,—

" Sir, in all matters of this fort there
are feveral things to be confidered.
The queftion, Sir, is not, whether the
people fhould have bread enough—No,
Sir: the queftion is, whether they cannot, and to their own advantage, be
taught to do with lefs: I am perfuaded
it might be brought about, and that the
people of England, naturally a grofs
and

and heavy race, would be more alert—
more animated—make better artifans,
labourers, and particularly foldiers.

" When I confider that neceffity is
the mother of invention, and reflect on
the numberlefs inventions which have
of late done honour to this age and nation, how can I regret the neceffity
that may incite to new difcoveries?
No, Sir: when I fay, whatever is is
right, I maintain my pofition, by ad-
ducing, that the urgency is a good one
which is productive of exertion in human intellects, which might otherwife
lie inert and torpid. If we want bread,
well—be it fo; we find with a little reflection a fuccedaneum, and when the
fcarcity ceafes, what is the refult? Why,
an admirable one—inftead of one ftaff
of

of life we have two : from thence I
draw my conclufion, that a fcarcity is
a good thing ultimately, and that a nation is better after it than if it had never happened. You may *depend* upon
it, my dear Sir, you may *depend* upon
it, that every thing in this well-regu-
lated country of ours, is fo conftructed
upon unalienable and fundamental principles, that, good Sir, good and happinefs always come out of evil, whatever blindnefs and ignorance may fay
to the contrary. Befides the real advantages, of which I have given you
an example, grant me leave to lay fome
ftrefs on the higher intellectual grati-
fications, fuch as are alone worthy
the confideration of reafonable beings.
When we are of neceffity denied what
we are unwilling to deny ourfelves, the
full

full fruition of fenfual indulgences,
with what happy pliability the mind goes
forth in fearch of vifionary felicity,
creating as it were new worlds of its
own !

" It may be alleged, perhaps, that this
mental blifs can be attained only by
thofe who from cultivation have acquired this facility of indulging in intellectual and ideal pleafures : but that
I deny ; by applying to their groffer
fenfes, the *Gentium Colluvio*, the very
Civitatis Sordes, might be taught to
find fatisfaction in imaginary enjoy-
ments.

"A very fenfible and intelligent author
has proved beyond a doubt, that much
may be effected by a proper application
to

to the optic nerves of the vulgar orders. Thus he afferts, that by looking
at a well-painted reprefentation of fire,
a man, or any number of men, may
be made to believe themfelves warm ;
and fo on of eatables and drinkables.
This fact being afcertained (as to me it
appears incontrovertibly to be), I have,
in my late memoir addreffed to the
Agricultural Society, propofed a plan to
that honourable and refpectable body,
which they moft judicioufly intend
adopting : it is what I am going to relate.

" I have propofed, then, that a fub-
fcription fhall be raifed for the purchafe of feveral excellent paintings on
large canvafs (the moft philanthropic
members of the Royal Academy will
undoubtedly

undoubtedly contribute their affiftance
gratis) : thefe, by means of the Poly-
graphic art, may be multiplied in proportion to the demand. They are to
reprefent good coal fires, with various
articles of food roafting, ftewing, and
boiling ; thefe fhall be fent to the Lord
Lieutenants of the different counties, to
be diffeminated at his difcretion among
the parifhes, according to the neceffities
of the people, and as the Deputy Lieutenants and Juftices of the Peace under
him fhall direct. For very extenfive
and widely-fcattered parifhes, reprefentations will be furnifhed of a Lord
Mayor's feaft, or, what is yet more fa-
tisfactory, a Treafury dinner; then, proper glaffes or fpeculums being provided, the men, women, and children
will be fummoned immediately after
divine

divine fervice every Sabbath—and no doubts are entertained but that this meafure will amply fuffice for their comfortable fuftenance and fupport for the feven enfuing days. To make the benefit of this happy illufion more extenfive, it is propofed, in order to accommodate the houfelefs, if any fuch there are (which however is their own fault), to have, on the fame principle, various views painted of houfes and feats, after the manner of Mr. Repton, and in the moft picturefque point of view—fuch as Mr. Pitt's feat at Holwood, Mr. Dundas's at Wimbledon, Mr. Rofe's at Cuffnells, &c. &c. &c. and in contemplating in thefe reprefentations, the great affluence and flourifhing ftate of their country, the wretched animals whofe own folly and

indifcretion

indifcretion have not left them forty fhillings a year (which is the average price of a cottage), muft furely (at leaft they ought to do it) forget all *their* trifling inconveniences in the great and patriotic fentiment of rejoicing in the profperity of their country. I am fure the fans culottes of England, by a little of this management, may become the moft *docile* and contented race under the heavens.

" I own to you, my dear Sir," would Mr. Wildcodger continue, " I own to you, that not doubting the efficacy of this fcheme of mine, added to the proper and feafonable reftraints lately laid on the mutinous, feditious, and jacobinical, I am fure of receiving the thanks of my country as foon as it fhall

be

be completely underftood. Indeed, I know nothing equal to it fince the introduction of the Mangel Wurzel, or *root of fcarcity*, into this happy ifland.

" Perhaps you may not have read Dr. Lettfom's admirable treatife on this root; and a knowledge of its virtues it may never have been in your way to acquire. I will, if you pleafe, juft explain it to you.

" The root of fcarcity then, at this time fo much known in England, was originally introduced into this country from Germany, about the time of the happy fucceffion of the moft illuftrious houfe of Brunfwick. It was but partially known, however, during the reigns of the two laft kings, who gave but

little

little encouragement to difcoveries of any kind: but at this moment it is *very widely diffufed*. Since the two very fortunate wars which have illuftrated the happinefs of the prefent reign, it has been almoft the only root tafted by the mafs of *common people*, and it has made very confiderable progrefs towards being in general ufe among the fomewhat fuperior and even middling claffes; nor have I a doubt but that in a year or two more, our affairs being ftill conducted by our Heaven-born Minifter, the Mangel Wurzel *, or root of

* It is fuppofed that the words Mangel Wurzel mean, to eat worfe and worfe. However difagreeable the found may be, faftidious people ought to confider that there is no reafon why we fhould live better than our Saxon anceftors.

fcarcity,

fcarcity, will be the only one with which the Englifh will "be familiar."

If this be not a fufficient fpecimen to give my readers an idea of this able and intelligent man, it is poffible they may hear more of him as we go along. At prefent, let me merely inform them, that the inftant he underftood Lady Belinda's views, he propofed taking Azemia into his own houfe, where he already had two other ladies as boarders, who, together with his wife, a very good fort of woman, refided at a village within twenty miles of London, where Mr. Wildcodger rented an experimental farm.

The Duke was one of his particular friends; but as he piqued himfelf on his

his virtuous propenfities, and talked a great deal about them, it is probable Lady Belinda's pure intentions, affifted as they were by other cogent arguments, over-ruled every other confideration. Of this arrangement, however, *we* have no means of knowing the minute particulars.

CHAP.

CHAP. VIII.

———

In maiden meditation, fancy free!

———

A ZEMIA, every where a ftranger, had no objection to a removal at the pleafure of Lady Belinda, and was foon, by a new viciffitude of fortune, fituated in the houfe of Mr. Wildcodger, at his experimental farm in Hertfordfhire.

Mrs. Wildcodger was one of thofe ufeful little women who feem to be fent into

into the world for the exprefs purpofe of making cheefecakes and puddings, and producing children to eat them. Of the few, the very few ideas that were innate in her mind (and of acquired ideas fhe had none), the chief was the neceffity of providing for the future tarts and cheefecakes of her family: and as her hufband had told her that he was to be paid very handfomely for Azemia's refidence with them, and that by receiving her he fhould oblige a perfon of high rank, who could be eminently ufeful to him in his purfuits, his obedient and pains-taking helpmate received Azemia with the utmoft placability, and put her into a very decent apartment. The fortunate poco curanteifm fhe poffeffed prevented her afking any queftions whatever; but when fhe

162

understood that the young lady was a
foreigner, and could speak no English,
she concluded she was a French woman,
it never having occurred to her that
there were more than the two nations
upon earth of which she heard the most.
Her husband never took the pains to
explain any thing to her, which was,
he found, for the most part, labour
thrown away: he left the mystery of
Azemia to explain itself, and returned
to London.

In the next room to our fair wanderer lived a maiden lady, whose disposition was as great for the acquisition
of all information, as that of her hostess
was indifferent to it. This lady, who
was called Miss Grifelda Ursula Ironfide, was of a very ancient and respectable

able family in the bishopric of Durham:
she had formerly had that extreme sensibility so dangerous to youth and
beauty; and even now, when, though
certainly not old (for she was born only
in the year 1733), she no longer felt
the indiscreet ardours of early youth—
there was a trembling tenderness about
her, which neither falsehood nor neglect (and she had suffered from both),
could subdue. It was unfortunate that
her benevolence, which was ever willing
to exert itself in correcting the errors
of her acquaintance, and of mankind
in general, was limited at present to
what she could do in a small village,
where her efforts to reform and polish
were by no means received with the
gratitude they deserved. The young
had the impertinence to despise her,
F 2   because

because they thought (however erro-
neously) that she was old; and the up-
start rich, of which there are numbers
within twenty miles of London, looked
upon her with contempt, because they
thought her poor: none of them cared
a farthing for her remarks or admoni-
tions; which was the most unaccountable thing in the world, considering the
proofs she continually gave of her disinterested philanthropy.

Sometimes, in that languor which re-
sults from goodness counteracted and
friendship rejected, Miss Grifelda Ursula
Ironfide shut herself up in her apartment for several days together. It was
during one of these periods of melancholy seclusion that Azemia became
an inmate of the house: but Miss Ironfide,

fide, hearing she was a French woman,
and being then in a fit of justifiable
spleen against all the ci-devant inhabitants of Gaul, refused to hold any
converse whatever with her. In a few
days an accident cleared up the mistake:
Miss Ironfide discovered that the young
stranger was only a Turk, and her natural benevolence instantly re-assumed
its wonted influence. Actuated by so
pure, so graceful a principle as the desire of instructing, and perhaps of
rescuing from infidelity and the Koran,
a very young creature, who there was
every reason to believe would be tracta-
ble and grateful, Miss Ironfide soon
made an acquaintance with our beautiful
heroine; and forgetting that she was
uncommonly lovely (for there was no
man in the way with his impertinent
F 3   admiration

admiration painfully to remind her of
it), she really set about cultivating by
European instruction the admirable natural disposition of the fair Oriental
damsel.

And here let me pause in my narrative, to contradict most solemnly, on the
faith of an author, an invidious report,
which I know has been disseminated by
the enemies of the amiable Griselda,
that, instead of pure and graceful motives
of genuine benevolence, this respectable
member of the sisterhood of spinsters
was in reality urged to what she did by
a latent hope of procuring from this
Eastern beauty a small quantity of the
balm of Mecca, so celebrated for the
preservation or restoration of the beauty
of the fair ones of the Levant; or, if
not

not the balm itself, the nature of the
materials of which it was composed.—
Against such malignant misrepresenta-
tions of the best actions, how shall
benignant purity defend itself?

For some weeks the active attention
of Miss Ironside to her engaging pupil
was unremitted: she taught her some
English, though with extreme difficulty,
because she had no medium but visible
signs through which to convey the
meanings she would impress. Azemia,
however, had a comprehension the most
lucid, and the graceful assiduity with
which she attended to her lessons was
equalled only by the affectionate attention of her zealous and well-informed
instructress.

F 4 Azemia

Azemia sang Turkish airs divinely.—
Miss Ironside was a proficient in music—
she listened, and learned to play on the
piano forte these singular airs—she made
a bass to them with scientific exactness—
they were delightful! Every body who
heard them was in raptures!—and Miss
Ironside saw herself more attractive at
her piano forte than she had ever been
at fifteen. It was enchanting! all the
neighbourhood crowded to her; those
who loved music, those who cared nothing about it, and those who would
rather have heard a concert of cats on
the house-top; for it was the fashion,
and there was not a creature among les
gens comme il faut, under the rank of
a Baroness, but who made interest to see
the beautiful infidel who sang Turkish
airs. Miss Ironside put at least two-
thirds

thirds down to her own account, and
grew so good-humoured, so bloomingly
serene on the occasion, that one would
have asserted that she had really obtained from her engaging pupil the
secret of the balm of Mecca.

What pity! that so sweet and interesting a connection, an attachment so
consonant to the pure pleasures of the
female heart, should be broken!—With
reluctance we are now to relate how the
deprecated event that dissolved this
graceful and affectionate union was ac-
complished.

Miss Griselda Ursula Ironside had a
nephew—a young man, as she termed
him, who, still a member of the Uni-
F 5 versity

verfity of Cambridge, refided there, and who feldom failed to call upon her for a day or two as he paffed and re-paffed from London thither.—He was ftill, it is true, a young man, not being above five-and-thirty; but as being aunt to any grown-up gentleman, or clergy-man, may give infenfibly a notion of old age, which Mifs Ironfide did not tho-roughly delight to think of, fhe took care, whenever her nephew was men-tioned, to inform the company, that he was quite a young man—though being the fon of her eldeft fifter, a great many years, almoft twenty years indeed, older than herfelf, it was lefs furprifing to hear him call her aunt; a liberty, how-ever, in which all her fondnefs for him did not induce her to indulge him, when

fhe

fhe could prevail upon him to recolle& the properer appellation of Mifs Iron-fide.

With all thefe dedu&ions made by perfonal vanity in the fear of being thought old, our amiable fpinfter really was proud of her nephew, and loved him as well as it was in her nature to love any thing.

Her pride was well founded.—The Reverend Solomon Sheeppen was a poet, and had acquired fame, and, what was better, profit, by his poefy.—He had written feveral admirable pieces in the very fonorous meafure called blank verfe; and by thefe blanks had carried off prizes. He never paffed a day in his tranfit from London to the banks of

F 6 the

the ofier-crowned Cam, without fhew-ing her fomething exciting her admira-tion and applaufe. Once it was a happy effufion, in this favourite meafure, called Timothy Tickle, or The Firft of April; at another time, a moft beautiful nar-rative, all in Miltonic verfe, of " moving accident by flood and field," which had befallen a certain Anthoniano, a coun-try divine; and Chloe, Sylvia, Corinna, and Daphne, his four coufins; together with Petronia, his aunt's daughter-in-law; and Jeremy, or Jeremio, a young gentleman of their acquaintance.

This laft tale was that which Mr. Sheeppen put into his cloak-bag to fhew his aunt Grifelda before he had it print-ed in London, whither he was haften-ing.

Before

Before he faw Azemia, or knew that his refpe&able relation had fo fair and attra&ive an inmate, he began, as was his ufual pra&ice, to read in a calm, yet fonorous tone, this moft recent pro-du&ion of his mufe; and here, as it is the only opportunity I may have, I can-not deny myfelf and my readers the high gratification of tranfcribing fome of the moft touching paffages, in which his fublime, though defultory mufe, happily imitates, and, as fome opine, rivals, in graceful and dignified familiarity, the Bard of the Oufe.

He thus defcribes an affray in which his hero young Jeremy defeats an im-pertinent fellow, who wanted to behave very rudely indeed to a dormant beauty.

" Hear

" Hear what befel : I in a hackney coach
Was overturn'd that night near Tothill-fields,
And in a black ditch fell.—To the fnug houfe
Of the coach driver and his fon I went,
For I was dripping wet. They lent me clothes;
And as I came along near Palace-yard
I met this lovely damfel in a chair :
Her chairmen flept, for they had drank of porter:
She too (for lately fhe had loft a friend),
Was likewife much difpos'd to fall afleep *.
I *faw and was refrefh'd* †; but had not gaz'd
A moment's fpace, ere yonder villain came.
Thy friend and I retir'd, and unperceiv'd
Beheld the devilifh antic tricks he play'd.—

---

* This way, *i. e.* fending all the parties to fleep
is the manner in which this celebrated poet difpofes
of his favourite charaéters when in great affliétion—
perhaps he may have a view to the mitigation of
his readers' painful fympathy, too keenly awakened,
and generoufly mean to fend them to fleep alfo.

† The fight of fleeping beauty is refrefhing.

Then,

Then, fudden fpringing forth, the kennel near,
Into that pool I trundled him :—had it
By chance been even yourfelf, the very fame
Sauce I'd have given you !"

The anfwer of Timothy, or, as he is
elfewhere called, Timotheus, is worthy
of his name, full of fpirit and poetry.

" Who knows," cried Timothy, " his friend thus
  tumbled
Into a muddy ftream, and not refents it,
I hold is bafe.—I'll in a fharp account
The tumbler punifh, refcue the tum*blee*,
And you fhall know."—" Nay, hold," faid Jeremy."

Thefe morceaux cannot fail to give
my readers a moft elevated idea of the
poetic talents of the Reverend Solomon
Sheeppen. The books are out of print,
from the extraordinary demand for
them, or I would enrich my memoirs
with

with fome more copious extraéts: as it
is, I am obliged to reftriét myfelf to the
fcanty fpecimens I have from the de-
tached MSS. of Mifs Ironfide. I cannot forbear the following defcription
of a bench on which a nymph was
feated, who was deteéted by Jeremy
in the very faét of trying to compofe
a fonnet :

Lonely fhe fat upon a painted bench,
Green with white nobs 'twas painted; honeft Tom,
Inftruéted by young Jeremy his mafter,
Had at his fummer leifure painted it.

We will defcribe anon the nymph,
and re-print the very fonnet that excited the indignation of the Reverend
Solomon Sheeppen, D. D. and P. P. to
which, with the noble indignation of
offended orthodoxy, he gives vent in
the

the charaéter of his hero, Jeremy or
Jeremio ! of whofe talents at confolation, when people in great forrow happen unfortunately to keep awake, I
think the following lines an admirable
fpecimen:

——————— Generous fympathy
Paus'd in his heart—and quiver'd in his eye :
So, taking up his hat, he faid—Good bye !
Open'd the door and walk'd out—with a figh.

A farther account of the talents of
this great genius, and of the nymph he
admonifhed, a fifter mufe, is of a length
fuch as precludes their relation till the
enfuing chapter.

CHAP.

CHAP. IX.

He writes an infinite deal of nothing,
More than any man in Cambridge!

BEFORE we pursue our history of Azemia, we feel it incumbent upon us to make our readers more acquainted with the Reverend Solomon Sheeppen, and some of those to whom he occasionally had addressed poetry admonitory, to which he was on most occasions supposed to be more inclined than to the *amatory line*.

The

The lady, to whom he in most sententious blank verse preaches against sonnets and suicide, was, and perhaps is still, a muse. " The daughter of the sun, whose soul was made of fire," had once been a dear friend of Miss Ironside's; and their great intimacy, carried on under the names of Iphanissa and Ultramarina, (because the latter had once a lover in the East Indies, and had said her heart was there) had only been dissolved since the Reverend Solomon Sheeppen had taken to poetize himself with such success, that Iphanissa, who hated every body that was successful, began to hate her friend for being his relation. They had, besides, a personal pique—Mr. Sheeppen abhorred sonnets and sonnettesses — the lady detested blank verse, which (following very great authority)

authority) she insisted was no verse at all.

To this animated and animating daughter of the muses, and to two or three less obtrusive sisters of the shell (the small sonnetteering shell was theirs; Iphanissa possessed an immense and sonorous bivalve of her own), the following lines, or something like them, were addressed :

Oh! all ye powers—(in case such powers there be,
And if there be not, I am sorry for it)—
Ye powers that day by day, and all night too,
Smile on poetic parsons, and professors,
Come, and, link'd close in virtuous harmony,
Assist me.—This day is St. Valentine ;
Up jump the maids—quick from their drowsy
        pillows,
And to the window all agog they run
To know what happy swain the fates provide

As

As mate* for life.—Then follows vast discharge
Of true-love knots, and sonnets nicely penn'd.
But to the learned critic's eye no verse,
But prose distracted trotting it away
All helter skelter, truly feminine,
Like yelping cur with kettle at his queue !
Forgive me, gentle maids of poesy,
Maria, and Jemima, Susan, Anne,
And Dorothea—A man I mean
May laugh, yet love—and much I do admire,
Fair ones, your skill, though it perchance is short
Of excellence itself. I love a maid †

---

* It is hoped this is a mere mistake, and that the poet was not such a Turk in principle, (though he denies the existence of female intellect) to mean that all the maids *who were agog* should have only one mate among them.

† When some less fortunate author declared he loved a maid, the Monthly Reviewers remarked, that he might have loved a widow. From such criticism, equally invidious and puerile, the superior merit of Thomson and the Rev. Solomon Sheeppen exempt them.

Who

Who is ambitious—not imitative;
Who knows to do much more than flirt
Her fan, or make charades; or paint a pink,
Or dance the Scottish or the Irish step,
Or pen a sonnet, that fantastic folly,
Scum of false taste, and bubble of the day.
Shall Iphaniffa, she whose round black eye
Glancing from heaven to earth, from earth to
    heaven,
In a fine phrenfy rolling—shall Iphaniffa
Write puerilities which every Miss
At boarding-school can do as well as she ?

Iphaniffa, however, loved a sonnet
if it was *legitimate,* joining issue with
. the Reverend Solomon Sheeppen in afferting, that fourteen lines rhyming un-
lawfully together, in quartrains, or al-
ternate rhymes, was a *nullus filius* in
poetry, begotten and born between licentioufnefs and incapacity, had no
claim to the support and countenance
of

of the orthodox and chafte poets and
poeteffes of the prefent day, and of
courfe fhould be banifhed from all decent fociety, fuch as from that of Milton (Shakefpeare was a dreadful en-
courager of illegitimacy), Mifs Seward and Mrs. Mary Robinfon, otherwife Laura Maria. Mr. Sheeppen held
in abhorrence all fonnets whatever;
and the breach between thefe tuneful
friends infenfibly became wider and
wider, till the poetefs, like a prieftefs
of Apollo in the moment of infpiration,
one day fnatched up the pen, and (which
made the difference irremediable) fent
to the Gentleman's Magazine the following fonnet :

Ill-earn'd applaufe ! how bitter is thy fmart
To thofe who praife exclufive only love !
How light, compar'd, all other forrows prove !
                                        Thou

Thou fhedd'ft a night of woe, from whence depart
The poeteffes patience ; and the heart
'Mid leffer ills illume : fhall Sheeppen rove,
On the high fummit of Parnaffian grove,
Blank *Versificator ?*—Alas ! thy dart
Kills more than life poetic—all that's dear,
Till we, fo mortified and pain'd, would change
For phrenfy that forgets malicious tear,
Or wifh in non-poetic fit to range
Where moon-revolving Fafhion loves to fip
Her mawkifh draught, or fkims with flirting trip.

From the moment this effufion of the
angry mufe was publifhed in the admirable mifcellany of Sylvanus Urban,
all hopes of peace were at an end between thefe two irafcible fpecimens of
the *genus irritabile.* A paper war of
effays and letters, fatire and fonnet,
began in that excellent and impartial
periodical mifcellany, the Gentleman's
Magazine; and the acrimonious con-
                                        troverfy

troverfy had already continued fome
months, and greatly impeded by its length
and frequency Mr. Urban's moft important antiquarian refearches, in fo
much that he had not yet had room
fully to elucidate the very material
point which he had long been endeavouring, with the moft praife-worthy
induftry, to afcertain. It was as follows:

In the parifh church of Puddlemarfh,
co. Effex, on the left as you go from
the very antique font of pudding ftone,
(which by the bye is a very curious monument of antiquity) towards the aifle
leading to the altar, and about the height
of a man's fhoulder, is a fmall horizon-
tal fepulchral ftone, which feems to be
part of a farcophagus, and is fuppofed,
from the ftyle of its workmanfhip, to

have been erected A. D. 1667, or there-
abouts; the letters visible on it are,
Da......is......pot........r.—
Now the question is, whether it was not
raised in memory of *Dame* Elizabeth
Pottinger, third wife of Sir Peter Pottinger, Kt. of Pottinger Hall, co. Ess.
and daughter of Stephen Stickler, Gent.
of Stump Court, co. Suffolk, by Patience, daughter and co-heiress of Francis
Fiddleford of Quizbury, co. Norfolk:
—" To this opinion," says Mr. Sylvanus Urban, " I am myself strongly inclined; though willing to give every
praise to the ingenious conjecture of my
obliging correspondent P. Q. who, on
the information of certain old persons
in the neighbourhood, thinks himself
authorised in maintaining that it is a
memorial of one Daniel Purvis, a potter,
who

who was a notorious republican in that
village, and died so justly execrated by
his neighbours, that, after his relations
had erected this stone, it was immediately defaced by the zeal and loyalty
of the inhabitants of that quarter of the
hundred; an example which, whether
true or false, ought to be held up *in
terrorem* at the present alarming crisis.
Which of these opinions is founded on
fact, I mean, with the unwearied perse-
verance such an enquiry merits, to in-
vestigate more fully in the course of the
next ten years."

Now the controversy between Iphanissa and the Reverend Solomon Sheeppen had taken up so many pages of the
Gentleman's Magazine, that among all
the information worthy of the most in-
G 2   genious

genious and enlightened F. A. S's, with
which that respectable work has teemed,
the most important point above mentioned has never to this hour been exactly and precisely ascertained.

In this posture were affairs when Mr.
Sheeppen visited Miss Ironside.

Scarce had he finished one movement of his spirited poem above mentioned, ending with this animated line—

" So out he went, and wink'd, and bang'd the door,"

when, without any banging at all —
light as the breeze that floats over the
thistle-feathered down, and like the embodied rosy vapour of a half-evaporated
rainbow, Azemia entered.

Down

Down dropped the book from the
hands of Mr. Sheeppen—he had never
on any occasion so entirely lost his
presence of mind—all the calm dignity
of the divine, the respectable phlegm
of the Englishman, were for a moment
forgotten!

With inexpressible dismay Miss Ironside beheld this unexpected effect.

G 3   CHAP.

CHAP. X.

A very long chapter, including an epifode, which has as much to do with the principal action as epifodes generally have.

THE diftrefs and anxiety occafioned by the paffion of the Reverend Poet for the fair Turk, were fo dreadful to poor Mifs Ironfide, that her pity, her tendernefs, her fentiment, all feemed annihilated; fo that even after the departure of her nephew fhe became fo uneafy, that fhe could not bear the fight of the innocent object of her apprehenfions; and

and Azemia, without knowing why, found herfelf a fad and folitary being, fubject to the cold and fupercilious looks of Mrs. Wildcodger, who, from the infinuations of Mifs Ironfide, began to doubt whether her hufband's loyalty to herfelf might not be endangered by the beauty of this outlandifh girl, whom Mifs Ironfide had difcarded from her friendfhip for having, as fhe declared, meditated the ruin of her nephew, the firft of all writers in blank verfe, and the moft promifing genius of the age.

This eminent luminary had in the mean time travelled to London, publifhed his poem, and, returning to Cambridge without calling on his aunt, began to confult with fome very learned and venerable men whether he could, confiftently

G 4

fiftently with his fpiritual and temporal welfare, marry a Turk. Various and curious were the opinions given on this matter; but that to which the lover feemed with the moft pleafure to liften, was the decifion of the Reverend Doctor Squably, who opined, that, if he firft converted his intended fpoufe, he would do an action worthy of all rewards, both temporal and eternal. He talked of the joy over a ftray lamb till the tears were in his eyes. Mr. Sheeppen wept with him—never was any thing half fo pathetic: it would have converted the whole French Directory, could they have witneffed the zeal of the Doctor, and the touching humility of the younger divine, who was too candid to recollect that Doctor Squably had a nephew, who anxioufly waited for a fellowfhip in the college

college of which he was member, and which his marriage would vacate.

Armed with the fanction of Doctor Squably, as with a fhield of adamant againft the remonftrances of his aunt, forth went the Reverend Solomon Sheeppen to reconcile her to his marriage, and to convert the beautiful infidel. Alas! when he got to Brambledown Farm (the name of the village where Wildcodger's houfe was fituated), it appeared that Mifs Ironfide had gone with a neighbouring family to Margate, and Mrs. Wildcodger abfolutely refufed to tell him what was become of Azemia. As much agitated at this news as he was capable of being at any thing, he attempted to perfuade the fervants to inform him; but failing of fuccefs,

G 5

cefs, he returned to Cambridge; and
while he called together all the confo-
latory fentiments he had ever heard, he
compofed at intervals a poem of three
thoufand nine hundred and ninety-fix
lines, in which he gave fo charming a
defcription of his fufferings, that all the
ladies who read long poems were enraptured.—It was talked of for above
three weeks by all the party who meet
at Mrs. Primly's and Mrs. Mufty's:
and though nobody elfe but thofe gentle
beings, and the bookfeller who publifhed
it (and of courfe puffed it in his own
Review), ever knew that fuch a book
exifted; he was convinced that nothing
but the ftate of the public mind, which
was uncongenial to the tender, the
fublime, and the ftark-ftaring phrenfy
of poetical enthufiafm, prevented its
having

having the moft rapid and extenfive fale
that had ever been experienced fince the
days of Pope.—While the Mufes were
thus healing the wounds inflicted by the
Graces, fhe who poffeffed the latter in
fo eminent a degree as to have endangered the heart and the orthodoxy of
Mr. Sheeppen, was far removed from
his fearch.

A widow of competent fortune, who
refided in the neighbourhood of Mifs
Ironfide, had buried at an early age an
only child, a daughter, of whom fhe
was paffionately fond.—Life had from
that moment loft all charms for her but
what fhe found in literary amufements,
and it was painful to her to mix in fociety: however, the entreaties of her
friends now and then drew her from her
G 6   folitude,

folitude, and in one of her vifits fhe
had feen Azemia with that tender compaffion which a good mind feels for
youth and beauty unprotected and defti-
tute. This excellent woman, whofe
name was Blandford, happened to call
one morning on Mifs Ironfide, at the
very moment when fhe was in one of
her paroxyfms of rage againft poor
Azemia, for having, as fhe faid, feduced
the heart of her nephew. Mrs. Blandford perfectly underftood the lady, and
the pity fhe had before felt for the
orphan ftranger now became the moft
active compaffion. Mrs. Blandford was
not one of thofe who are content with
declaring how forry they are for the
unhappy, and with crying, "Oh! very
fhocking! A melancholy affair indeed!
Well! I am exceeding forry." Mrs.
Blandford

Blandford faid but little, but fhe felt
much; and her feelings were all right,
for they originated in an upright and
excellent heart. "Why," faid fhe,
as fhe looked at Azemia, and afterwards
heard the cold and mercenary complaints of Mrs. Wildcodger, and the
fenfelefs and romantic rage of Mifs
Ironfide — "why fhould I not take this
poor young creature, thus defolate in a
ftrange land, under my protection?—
Surely it will be an action acceptable to
Heaven, which feems thus to have
thrown her in my way, under circumftances fo truly pitiable.—Alas! had my
poor Amelia been fpared to me, fhe
might have

"Refembled her in figure as in age.

"Her

" Her mind is yet like that of a child, innocent, and capable of being formed: the expence fhe will be to me I can well afford—*I* have now no ufe in laying by any part of my income, and in what greater act of charity can I employ it?"

Such were the reflections—in confequence of which Mrs. Blandford propofed to Mrs. Wildcodger to take Azemia home with her, and in future to provide for her. The offer was accepted with the greateft eagernefs; for that careful gentlewoman was not only apprehenfive left her hufband fhould take a fancy to his lodger, but doubted whether he had ever been paid by Lady Belinda for her board, and indeed whether he ever would be. Certain it was, that

that whenever in talking over their family affairs fhe had touched on this fubject, her hufband had efcaped from it with one of thofe fullen replies, which he well knew how to give when his notable moiety teafed him, and which generally put an end to any farther remonftrance on her part:—her fpoufe, though he had been in other times a prodigious advocate for liberty of all forts, being in his own family one of the moft overbearing tyrants that ever a poor meek and pains-taking wife was tied to.

This man of practical fcientific agricultural fame was now gone into the North to fee the progrefs made there by a celebrated breeder of Cape fheep, in improving the fize of their tails, and in the invention of light carts to carry them in;

in; an improvement that promifed the moft happy confequences to the lovers of, and dealers in, mutton fat.—This journey left the lady of the houfe at liberty to act as fhe thought proper about Azemia; who, with more pleafure than fhe had yet felt fince her unintentional vifit to England, packed up her fimple wardrobe as foon as fhe underftood whither fhe was to go; for the fweetnefs and fenfe of Mrs. Blandford's manners fpoke to all hearts, and Azemia had felt herfelf particularly attracted towards her the firft time fhe ever faw her.

In a few hours Azemia found herfelf perfectly at eafe with her new protectrefs; and in as many days Mrs. Blandford, an excellent judge of the human

human character, found much to be pleafed with in the innocent unadulterated mind of her protegée. No perfon, among all thofe through whofe hands fhe had paffed, had taken the leaft pains to inftruct her in any thing, and fhe yet hardly knew as much Englifh as fufficed to enable her to afk at table for what fhe had occafion for. Mrs. Blandford found infinite pleafure in making up for this omiffion; and fhe immediately began to teach Azemia Englifh by the help of an Arabic dictionary which fhe procured from Oxford, the very emporium of learning of all forts, and more particularly of the Oriental languages. Never was there a fcholar fo apt as Azemia: to learn any thing from Mrs. Blandford which fhe defired to teach her, was indeed to her " the labour

bour of love." Her capacity was naturally good, and she insensibly acquired, from her earnest desire to oblige her benefactress, the habit of application, which, in her earliest years, she had never been accustomed to: in a word, she could within a fortnight spell; in five weeks she could read and translate; and when Mrs. Blandford went from Cheltenham (whither she had gone as soon as Azemia became her companion), to pass the ensuing winter in London, the scholar was so far advanced as to be able to converse with ease, and to read any thing printed or written with perfect fluency—though still with a foreign accent—which rather added to, than took from, the charms of one of the sweetest feminine voices that ever was heard. The following narrative was one

one among those she was employed to read to Mrs. Blandford; it came from an intimate friend of hers, who, during a tour through the north-eastern counties of England, had promised Mrs. Blandford regularly to write to her. The story is so well authenticated, that it may serve, like that told by the admirable author of the Observer, Vol. III. No. LXXI. page 92, to substantiate the notion of ghosts and spectres, which, as readers seem tired of all representations of actual life, and going fast into the childish horrors, impressed by ignorance and superstition seventy or a hundred years ago, may possibly be very acceptable.

LETTER

LETTER TO MRS. BLANDFORD.

" YOU love descriptions; and therefore, as little else will sometimes occur, I shall not fear tiring you even by such very simple English landscapes as alone are likely to offer themselves. Sometimes I shall give you a figure in them, not of a nymph or a shepherd, but such as will correspond with the scenery. In that of to-day, and it will not be riante, I shall place my solitary friend, of whom you have so often heard me speak; and if I conclude with the miraculous, you, who have, in defiance of so good an understanding as you possess, read, and with pleasure, the ghostly novels that have of late increased the catalogues

catalogues of circulating libraries, will, perhaps, think the supernatural the most entertaining part of my letter.

" Mrs. Herbert, whose narrow income and tender solicitude for her sons, who depend entirely on her, determine her to a very retired manner of life, found even the rent of the cheapest house she could hire a very great charge on her slender fortune; and the very rapid increase of every necessary expence determined her to accept the offer a distant relation made her of a residence at his vicarage, where himself lives no longer than is necessary to receive his tithes, and the cure is served by a young clergyman, who resides at a town eight miles distant.

" I arrived,

" I arrived, on my long-promifed vifit to my fecluded friend, in the middle of November; and certainly her lonely abode never could appear to lefs advantage. The country in which it is fituated is as little interefting as any I have ever feen.—There are neither rifing grounds nor hedge-rows to relieve the wearifome uniformity of common fields on one fide; on another the eye turns with difguft from a dreary moor, interfected by fluggifh ftreams, and apparently the abode only of the otter and the heron : difcouraging as thefe appearances are, the general character of the country is that of fertility. It would have fuited the tafte of Dr. Johnfon; but the poet, the painter, or the enthufiaft in picturefque beauty, would undoubtedly travel through it as faft as they could.

" The

" The pleafure my friend expreffed at feeing me forbad every remark on the forlorn place where I found her; and in the power of giving even a tranfient fatisfaction to one I had fo long known and efteemed, I was myfelf confcious of more than I have felt for many months. It was three years fince we laft met; and though there was little of happinefs to be remembered on her part, fhe feemed to have pleafure in relating to me what had befallen her in that time, and dwelt with peculiar delight on the progrefs of her fons—one of whom is at Cambridge, and the other a cadet at Woolwich.

" When thefe narratives, interefting to the heart of a mother, were difcuffed, we had recourfe to books.—A few odd volumes of polemic divinity were all that

that the little dark and long-forfaken room, formerly called a library, afforded. Thefe offered us nothing that could beguile even one of thofe long evenings we were to pafs together. My friend, therefore, fent, by a weekly meffenger, to the neareft market town for a fupply of the neweft books of entertainment. I will not enumerate their titles, or the manufactories they came from : fuffice it to fay, that they were returned by the earlieft opportunity, and gave rife to a converfation, which perhaps I may relate at length another time.

" I wrote for a fmall cargo of reading better fuited to our tafte; and in the interim we amufed ourfelves by talking over the hiftories of many of our acquaintance who had entered the world at,

or

or nearly at, the fame time with ourfelves; Mrs. Chefterton taking occafion to fay, that it might not be an unentertaining or ufelefs tafk to enquire whether, among the ten or twelve perfons we had named, any one of them was really an object of envy even to us, who were both difpofed to believe that fortune had dealt by us unkindly.

" The refult of this enquiry will perhaps amufe you at fome future period. I am now going to relate our obfervations during one of our walks, which in a country fuch as I have defcribed, and at fuch a feafon, were not very frequent.

" But as the fupply of our table depended on the caprice of the wife of a

rich

rich farmer in the neighbourhood, who sometimes, to shew her consequence, sent all her goods to market, without consulting the convenience of Mrs. Chesterton; my friend, therefore, found it one day necessary to walk to another farmhouse in the neighbourhood to obtain sundry articles for our frugal repasts, and, ' on hospitable thoughts intent,' sallied forth. I accompanied her, though under that depression of spirits which, without any new cause, sometimes overwhelms a mind fatigued by anxiety, or unnerved by affliction.

" My friend was less cheerful than usual; and as we traversed a flat common field, which, whatever might be its appearance when covered with ripening corn, was now extremely dreary, we

we hardly exchanged half a dozen words.

" At length, trees terminating this extensive flat, we entered a long and gloomy lane, shaded on either side by high elms, whose last yellow and sapless leaves fell in our path. They were joined by a very thick old wall, almost strong enough for a fortification:—withered grass and weeds covered its top, and filled up the interstices from whence the mortar had fallen. It ceased, and the ancient house to which it had served as an inclosure appeared through the broken boards of an old gate or folding door, that opened into the court immediately before the dwelling. The house itself was built with pointed roofs, and massive clusters of

tall chimneys. The lower windows were half hid by some large variegated hollies, long suffered to escape from the sheers that had formerly shaped them. We passed the wall of the court, and entered by a common gate into the farm-yard (filled with straw, racks for cattle, and pigs and poultry), to the farmer's kitchen, to which we ascended by five or six worn stone steps. The housewifely mistress of it received us with courtesy, and, hearing our business, promised to my friend the supply she desired.—Declining the refreshments she offered us, we sat out on our return.

" As we repassed the front of the house, I remarked that I had never seen a more dismal-looking place. ' It seems,' said I, ' to have been formerly a manor house.'

house.'—' It is still so,' replied Mrs. Chesterton; ' the possessor of it has also the right over a very extensive domain. He is a banker in London, and comes down once a year to shoot; but he lodges in a cottage fitted up on another part of the estate; for it is not easy to prevail even on the farmer to inhabit any part of this old house on account of its bad reputation, being believed by all the neighbourhood to have been haunted by the most persevering ghost or ghosts that have ever been heard of in these parts.

" ' There is some such house in every neighbourhood,' said I: ' I recollect two or three about our former residence in Dorsetshire.'—' I assure you, however,' rejoined my friend, ' that the legend that belongs to this is no common ſtory. The laſt rector, who died a very old man in the houſe I now inhabit, took the pains to write out an authenticated narrative, given by his predeceſſor Mr. Jackſon (who was himſelf an actor in the ſcene), of the extraordinary appearances that had been ſeen in the old manſion we have paſſed, with a ſort of hiſtory of its inhabitant whoſe conduct gave riſe to theſe terrific viſions. My couſin, the preſent incumbent, read it to me when I came to ſettle in his houſe; I dare ſay he put it back into the drawer in the old book-room. When we get home I will look for it—it may ſerve to amuſe us this evening.'

" On ſearching in the drawer, where ſhe thought ſhe had ſeen it depoſited, in the

the deſerted ſtudy, Mrs. Cheſterton found an old manuſcript, written in a legible, but old-faſhioned hand.—It ran thus:

' ANOTHER BLUE-BEARD!

AN AUTHENTIC HISTORY WELL KNOWN IN LINCOLNSHIRE.

IN the year 1709, the manor-houſe of Marſh Barton was inhabited by a gentleman of the name of Grim-ſhaw, who poſſeſſed, beſides that eſtate, other conſiderable property in this and the next county. He was a man of violent temper, and rough harſh manners, but his money made him to be feared; yet he was very covetous, and kept but few ſervants for one of his eſtates. His mother lived to a good old

H 4　　　age

age in the houſe with him, but, being bed-ridden, knew nothing of what paſſed in his houſe more than he pleaſed to tell her; ſo that his marriage with a pretty young woman, named Mrs. Anne Lilburne, was kept a ſecret from her, under pretence that ſhe would be diſ-pleaſed thereat, inaſmuch as Mrs. Anne, being the daughter of an officer killed in Spain a few years before, had no portion but her beauty. The old lady at laſt died; but after that the 'Squire ſeemed no more deſirous of ſhewing his wife than he was before, ſo that hardly any of the neighbours or tenants that uſed to go to the houſe knew her by ſight; and none but a woman ſervant, of no good repute, that had lived with Mr. Grimſhaw before he was married, was allowed to be about her, although it

it was often given out that ſhe was ſickly and ailing.

' Strange ſuſpicions were ſometimes harboured by the people of the country, for Mr. Grimſhaw led an odd ſort of life. Sometimes he was gone away for a great many weeks together, none knew whither; and at other times he brought home with him, and generally in the middle of the night, certain ſtrangers, who, if by chance they were ſeen, ſeemed to the neighbours to be ſuſpicious perſons. They ſat up, it was ſaid, late, and ſometimes all night long, drinking hard, and were always waited upon by that woman ſervant that was in her maſter's confidence. As to the poor young lady, ſhe was leſs and leſs heard of, and nobody dared to ſay what

H 5　　　they

they thought; for all the parish belonged
to the 'Squire, and he would have
ruined any body that had talked against
him; for he was vindictive and revenge-
ful, and had put some poor men to
prison that had offended him about the
game, and others had been obliged to
quit the country on his account. The
then rector of the parish was of a quiet
and somewhat indolent temper, and the
fierce and violent lord of the manor was
not one with whom he chose to con-
tend.

' Some time about the year 1715 it
was given out that the young lady he
had married two or three years before was dead; and to all appearance
she was buried in the same vault where
his mother had been laid some eighteen

or

or twenty months before, and no more
questions were asked about her.

' The 'Squire went away soon afterwards, and staid some months. It was
always a joyous time for the people who
had any dealings with him when he was
absent; for he was of such a hard and
cruel nature, that his dependents trembled before him.

' After being absent eighteen or twenty months he came home with a lady,
quite a young creature, whom he had
married in London; and then it was
given out that he intended to live more
sociable among his neighbours, and that
his lady would keep such company as the
country afforded. But the man himself
was so hated and disliked, that none of

H 6   the

the better sort of people round would go
to see him. The Rector dined with him
twice, and saw the young lady, his new-
married wife. She was a very pretty
and agreeable person; but seemed so
low-spirited and dejected, that it made
his heart ache to see her. She looked,
while she sat at the head of the table,
like one who was suffering without
daring to complain; and every now and
then her husband seemed to fix his fierce
and angry eyes on her, as if he was not
willing her sorrowfulness should be remarked by the stranger.

' The Rector liking the ways of
Grimshaw less and less, went no more;
and the same gloomy silence and seclusion reigned about the house as was
seen there before. Hardly any body

ever

ever appeared in the family but the favourite housekeeper, who still governed
every thing; and whenever the 'Squire
was seen, it was only in some act of
tyranny, or in a storm of passion and
fury, and he seemed to grow worse and
worse every day; so that his house was
looked upon like the den of a wild beast,
which all people were afraid to enter.

' In 1715 was the rebellion, and it was
said that the 'Squire was gone out to
join one of the associations that were
made: there was not a soul in the
neighbourhood for twenty miles about,
but what would have been glad to have
heard that he had met the rebels, and
that they had knocked him on the head.
As to the poor lady, his wife, she appeared no more; and there were people

who

who fcrupled not to fay, that fhe was
unfairly dealt by, or fpirited away as the
other unhappy young gentlewoman had
been before.

' One dark night, towards the end of
November, Mr. Jackfon, rector, who
was going a journey the next day, went
to the window of his room at the rectory to
look at the weather, when he thought he
faw fomething white move among the trees
in the orchard :—he opened the cafement and fpoke : nobody anfwered : he
fpoke louder, faying, ' Who is there?'
A low murmuring voice was heard, as
of a perfon endeavouring in vain to
utter the complaints that pain or terror
would have extorted.   Mr. Jackfon
held the candle out of the window, and,
looking earneftly down thought he faw
                                a female

a female kneeling on the ground, with
lifted hands in the attitude of imploring
fuccour. He fpoke again, and the effort
to anfwer was repeated by the perfon
beneath him.

' Mr. Jackfon was a timid and retired man, an invalid for many years :
he had another living in a pleafanter
part of the country, near Lincoln, and
never refided here longer than he was
compelled to do, by the ill-natured attempts made by fome of his parifhioners
to deprive him of his benefice for non-
refidence. . . . . . His feeble fpirits were
ftrangely alarmed by the general appearance of the figure on which the
light fell ; but the features he could not
difcern : —he trembled—he hefitated—
and then he heard again a fort of ftifled
                                found

found of moaning ; and not having courage to open his door, though he hardly
knew of what he was afraid, he rang
the bell at the head of the bed, and at
the fame time knocked loudly againft
the wainfcot with a ftick. His only
fervants, a woman who had long had
the care of his houfe, and her hufband
who worked in the garden and took
care of the horfe, were prefently roufed
and came to the door, demanding to
know what was the matter ? Their
mafter, having let them in, directed them
to look from the window, where they
both faw the fame figure ; but now, inftead of its former attitude of fuppli-
cation, it feemed to have fallen againft
the wall of the houfe, where motion-
lefs it lay half ftretched on the ground.

                                ' 'Tis

' 'Tis a woman !' faid James Walling, the labourer, ' and, to my thinking, fhe is dead !'

' Some traveller, I warrant,' cried
his wife : ' there a been two or three to
our door to-day.'

' The man of peace and charity felt
for a moment that it was his duty, as a
clergyman and a chriftian, to fhelter
and relieve her whatever fhe might be ;
but fears, of he knew not what, among
which fome apprehenfions of expence
failed not to mingle themfelves, half
deterred him. The fervant man had
more bowels and fewer fcruples ; and
though his wife muttered fome half fentence againft it, he went down un-
bidden, and, approaching the unhappy
                                object

object on the ground, while Mr. Jack-
son and the woman looked at him from
the open window, he cried out to them,
that it was no traveller nor beggar, but
looked fomehow like a lady, but fhe
was quite cold and fenfelefs, and he
believed dead. However, without
ftaying for orders, which Mr. Jackfon
feemed ftill but half difpofed to give,
he took her up in his arms and carried
her into the kitchen, where he placed
her before the covered embers, on the
hearth. His mafter and the woman now
defcended; the care of the firft was
immediately directed to the door, which
he carefully faftened within fide, while
James faid to his wife, ' Why don't you
look at the poor young gentlewoman,
and fee what help you can give her if
fhe isn't quite dead? — How can you
have

have fuch a heart? I think I have feen
this poor woman before—I don't know
where—but be that how 'twill, don't let
her die without help.'

' This awakened fomething like humanity; and indeed, what little could
ever be produced in the half-petrified
bofom of the woman, could not but be
engaged on contemplating the piteous
object before her. She now began to
rub the palms of her hands, and, taking
fome brandy from a cupboard, chafed
her temples and applied it to her nofe.

After a while the young perfon
opened her eyes; and the firft ufe fhe
made of her fpeech was to conjure Mr.
Jackfon, in a feeble voice, not to let
her be carried back to Barton-Marfh
Houfe.

Houfe. It proved to be the poor young
lady, wife to 'Squire Grimfhaw, who,
in a dying condition, had efcaped from
the den of her mercilefs tyrant, and
entreated Mr. Jackfon to afford her his
protection; as the horrors fhe under-
went at the manor houfe (not only from
his cruelty and her extreme deteftation
of him, and from the infolence and inhumanity of the woman fet over her,
but from an apparition that continually
difturbed her and prevented her ever
fleeping, when her barbarous perfecutors left her any repofe), were fo great,
her mifery became fuch, that it was impoffible to endure it any longer. Mr.
Jackfon, timid and cautious in his nature, was, from habits of interefted
compliance, abjectly afraid of offending
any rich or powerful man; he therefore
hefitated

hefitated whether he fhould receive and
protect the unhappy young creature who
had thus thrown herfelf upon his mercy:
yet he could not look upon her, nor
liften to the plaintive and trembling
voice in which fhe attempted incohe-
rently to relate her wretched condition,
without feeling it to be his duty, as a
chriftian and a man, to defend her.
His natural cowardice, however, and
the extreme fear that Grimfhaw infpired
in the neighbourhood, would have prevented the good effects of thefe feelings,
if his fervant, who had more fpirit and
humanity than himfelf, and by whom
he was very much governed, had not declared, that ' while he had a drop of blood
left the poor gentlewoman fhould not be
forced back by no fuch hard-hearted
tyrant as the 'Squire.' His wife praifed
his

his refolution; and their mafter confidering that he was to go away in the morning, and of courfe might efcape being
any party in the bufinefs if Grimfhaw
fhould be troublefome, confented to let
the poor young woman be led by the
female fervant to a bed, where he left
her without farther enquiry, and at day-
break fet forward as he had intended
on his journey.

' The woman, though of a harfh,
cold, and covetous difpofition, was
moved by the wretched fituation of the
unfortunate young perfon: and her intereft came in aid of her compaffion,
when fhe learned that the family of Mrs.
Grimfhaw were rich tradefmen in London; and that though fhe had been facrificed to her wicked and cruel hufband,

band, in order to leave more money
at the difpofal of her father for a favourite fon; yet, her father being as
fhe believed dead, her mother and an
uncle, as well as that brother himfelf
to whofe advantage her father had made
her a victim, would now, fhe was fure,
not only receive and protect her, but
handfomely reward the humane people
who fhould be the means of her prefervation.

She wrote a few lines to her mother
as foon as fhe had ftrength to hold a
pen; but from long difufe and great
feeblenefs in her hands fhe could hardly
make what fhe wrote legible. Walling
fet out with the letter, and put it himfelf into the poft at the next market
town,

town, giving his wife a ftrict caution
not to fay a word to any of their few
neighbours, as to their having a ftranger
in their houfe; for he obferved, that
though the 'Squire was gone from the
Marfh-houfe, yet Madam Hannah, as
fhe was called, would foon fet out after
her miftrefs, and try to be fure to hinder
her from telling tales—perhaps by killing
her for good and all.—' I know well
enough,' faid the honeft clown, ' that
there have been defperate bad doings in
that there houfe, and I warrant they
wou'd not ftick at nothing. This poor
young gentlewoman is much to be
pitied, and if I can help it fhe fhall not
be delivered no more into fuch wicked
hands—for to be certain it is well known
that t'other pretty young creature did
not

not come fairly by her end, and I warrant the lady here knows that by more
tokens than one.'

" Mrs. Walling had an old grudge
againft the 'Squire for having deftroyed
a whole litter of her pigs with his hounds
in mere wantonnefs as he returned from
hunting, for which he had refufed to
make the leaft reparation: fhe affented,
therefore, to all her hufband faid, and
promifed to conceal from all her neighbours that Mrs. Grimfhaw had taken
refuge in their houfe.

" To this unhappy young lady fhe now
fet about adminiftering fuch relief as
was in her power: but fo great had been
her fufferings, her fmall and feeble
frame was fo emaciated from the effects

of terror, famine, and want of reft, that
fhe appeared unlikely ever to recover,
or even to live till her friends could
come to her.   Honeft Walling now
began to hope, that, fince three days were
paffed, her perfecutors were afraid of
making any enquiries after her; and as
fhe feemed to him, as well as to his wife,
to be in a dying condition, he determined not to wait for news from London, but to apply to fome of the neareft
gentlemen for their advice, and to fetch
an apothecary from the next town.
Regardlefs, therefore, of the cautious
fears of his wife, who recurred now and
then to her former apprehenfions of
their getting into trouble, he once more
fet forth on his benevolent purpofe of
procuring relief for the fick lady.

" The

" The firft gentleman to whom he applied, and who lived at the diftance of
eleven miles, was even more the enemy
of Mr. Grimfhaw than the other magiftrates and people of fortune in the
county; for he was quite of another
party, and a great fportfman, in both of
which charaêers the politics and purfuits of Grimfhaw grievoufly interfered
with him.   He liftened eagerly, therefore, to the melancholy tale told him
by Walling; and delighted with the occafion, which he thought prefented itfelf,
of crufhing a man he hated, he promifed Walling all the affiftance that
could be given to the lady : but, with
more prudence than he generally poffeffed, advifed, that another gentleman
who lived nine or ten miles the other
way, and who was remarkable for his

I 2   benevolence,

benevolence, as well as knowledge of
the law, might be applied to alfo.—
Walling again fet forth, and obtained
not only an hearing from this worthy
man, but an affurance of the moft immediate and effeêual fteps being taken
towards the relief of the poor lady—for
Mrs. Bargrove, the lady of this gentleman, propofed fetting out herfelf, and
bringing the unfortunate Mrs. Grimfhaw to her houfe; while Mr. Bargrove
himfelf took meafures for a proper enquiry into the ill-treatment fhe had received, to which he imputed the ftrange
converfation fhe had told; imagining,
as was indeed very probable, that weaknefs and terror had alienated her reafon.

" On the arrival of Mrs. Bargrove at
the parfonage houfe, attended by Walling,

ling, whom fhe had direêed to be
affifted by the loan of a horfe; the woman, Mrs. Walling, was found furrounded in the kitchen by all the goffips
in the neighbourhood, and four ftout
clowns, who, till they difcovered who
the party were, had refifted their ad-
miffion.   They no fooner faw the good
and benevolent Mrs. Bargrove was come
to direê them, than fhe was furrounded
by the ruftic group; and while fome of
the women buftled about to make a fire
in the beft room, and get the beft accommodations ready for Madam, Mrs.
Walling, who could not refift the pleafure of relating all fhe knew, began to
tell how (almoft as foon as her hufband
was gone) they were alarmed by a vifit
from Miftrefs Hannah from the great
houfe; ' who, firft of all, Madam,' faid

I 3   Mrs.

Mrs. Walling, ' came all at once upon me, as I was a ierning in our kitchen. Lord! when I fee her I was in fich a way, one mid have a knock'd me down wi a ftraw!—So up fhe comes, and fays fhe, " So, Dame Wallings, how do you?"—Says I, but I'm fure I was as white as that there wall, " Pretty well, thank you, Madam Hannah; how be all you?"—" Oh!" faid fhe, " much as one; mafter ben't at home."—" Thefe are troublefome times, Dame Wallings." —" Aye, Ma'am," faid I, " the be fo indeed—but the worfe luck's ours."— " So the 'Squire's at the wars, I fup-pofe."—" Yes; he's a Captain now, Dame," faid fhe, " and gone to fight the Scotch rebuls agin his king and country." So I took no notice, but went on ierning; and I minded that fhe looked

looked about the room, and about the room, and at laft fhe faid, " This here houfe feems to me to be a better houfe than I thoft; I fhould like to fee your bed-chambers, Dame."—" There's no-thing to fee, Mrs. Hannah," I anfwered, but I was read to drop, I was in fuch a fright; " and befide," faid I, " Mafter have guied me orders not to fhew nobody them rooms on no account."—" Never mind," cried the bold huffey; fo fhe flipped by me, and up fhe went, and without more ado popped into the room where the poor young lady was lying on the bed, in fome poor clothes of mine that I had lent her while her own were wafhed. O dear! if you had but feen her, poor young thing! fhe gave a fhriek, and then fell back dead on the bed, all one as if fhe had been fhot.

I 4 So

So with that I told Madam Hannah that fhe fhould not ftay there, let what would come of it; and our Sam and Jack Pil-cocks at Mill coming in juft then, which was lucky enough, I bid um come up; and giving them to underftand what was the matter, they turned the impudent woman down ftairs, and out of the houfe; and Pilcocks he was in fuch a paffion wi her, that he fwore if fhe did not tramp off he would roll her in the ditch without more ado: aye, and drag her through the horfe-pond—for he knew her, he faid, of old. Well! fo when we'd got her out of the houfe, and bolted all the doors, I went up again to the poor lady, who came by little and little out of her fit; but the minnut fhe opened her eyes fhe fcreamed out again—' Oh! fave me, fave me—Oh! there

there is Hannah'—Oh! cruel, cruel!— and fo fhe went on, and have gone on ever fince—quite gone and loft as one may fay; and every now and then fhe frights me fo that I think I fhall be as bad as fhe; for fhe cries out, that there's the fpectre of the murder'd fomebody and her child; and then fhe fpeaks to fomething fhe fancies fhe fees, and fays, ' No, no, poor Gertrude; I am not gone—I am coming to you—the mon-fter ftill holds me; Oh! don't help him! poor Gertrude!' And fo fhe goes on from time to time; but never has fhe fpoke one word reafonable, as one may fay, ever fince Hannah's vifit; and I'm certain, that if fhe was to fee her again, or if the 'Squire himfelf was to attempt for to fee her, fhe would die that very moment upon the fpot.

I 5 " From

"From this account, which, though it was very tedious, Mrs Bargrove patiently liftened to, fhe found it would be very difficult to introduce herfelf, a ftranger as fhe was, to the poor fufferer, without a great rifk of making her worfe.   However, by the help of a fkilful apothecary, and the great care and goodnefs of Mrs. Bargrove, who attended her with the utmoft care and humanity, fhe was well enough at the end of three days to be moved to Mr. Bargrove's houfe; and the fame day of her removal her brother came with two friends from London, determined to refcue her at all events from the hands of her wicked hufband, whofe conduct her furviving friends had always fufpected to be bad towards her, though they had no idea how bad it was, nor how

how much fhe had fuffered.   It was not before a confiderable time, and only by degrees, that Mrs. Bargrove heard the following account of all the terrors fhe had gone through; which, though fhe heard it only at intervals, as the poor young lady could relate it, fhe collected in a narrative:

"I am fure," faid the poor young woman, who was hardly nineteen, "that had my father known three years ago, when he married me to Mr. Grimfhaw, the wretchednefs to which he condemned me, nothing would have induced him to have fo facrificed me."

"Mrs. Bargrove tenderly enquired to what family fhe belonged?

I 6   "My

"My father, Madam," faid Mrs. Grimfhaw, "was a fubftantial tradefman in London—my mother, the daughter of a wealthy citizen.   I was well brought up; and we might all have lived in competence if my father had not thought proper to take up an opinion that his fon only muft be amply provided for, and that his daughters muft do as well as they could.   He hoped he faid to fee his fon Lord Mayor; his daughters muft marry whoever would have them. It was in purfuance of this plan that I was, I believe, fent to the houfe of the perfon who had married one of my fifters, when it was known Mr. Grimfhaw was to be there.   He paffed for a widower, and a country gentleman of large fortune.   Unhappily, he took a liking

liking to me; while I, the moment I faw him, felt myfelf tremble, and a deadly cold feemed to ftrike my heart.   I fhrunk from his civilities with terror and difguft; and when he was gone, my brother-in-law rallying me upon the conqueft, as he called it, that I had made, I burft into tears.   The next day, however, he came to my father's houfe, and again the fight of him made me fhudder, and his voice ftruck cold to my heart.

"Indeed, Madam, had I then dreamed that this man was to be my hufband, I muft I think have died; but our misfortunes come upon us by degrees, or elfe I fuppofe they could not be borne at all.

"In

"In three or four days he made his offer to my father, who accepted of him with eagerneſs as his ſon-in-law: the ſettlements were then agreed upon between them, and even the day was fixed without my being once conſulted:—my mother was ordered to tell me of it, and ſhe bade me not ſay one word of oppoſition, or even one word that might demand delay.—The fatal wedding was ſettled for that day ſe'nnight: it was in vain I knelt to my mother— it was in vain that, on the ground, proſtrate at his feet, I implored my father to have mercy upon me—nay, if they were determined to get rid of their poor Eleanor, to kill me, rather than to compel me to marry a man I could not help hating.

" They

" They both treated me as a ſilly child, that did not know what was for her own good; and my father, ſuſpecting that one of his ſhopmen had ſome regard for me, turned the poor young man away at a moment's notice; while my mother ſent me to my eldeſt ſiſter, who was as hard-hearted as herſelf, and had never loved me: there I was ordered to remain in an upper chamber, where I was teaſed all day during this ſad week, by my ſiſter and brother-in-law's advice; and my mother in the mean time got my wedding-clothes made for me, and, the day before the dreadful one of my marriage, came to tell me that the next was fixed for my becoming the wife of Mr. Grimſhaw. She then ſhewed me the clothes ſhe had prepared, in a way as if ſhe thought that ſuch things would reconcile

reconcile me to my lot—when ſhe told me that Polly Such-a-one, and Betſy Such-a-one, had neither of them half as much, or half as good clothes on their wedding as mine were; and that *they* were only married to tradesfolks, whereas my intended huſband was a gentleman of fortune, an Eſquire, and had a fine ſeat in the country.

" Never in my life had I been allowed the leaſt will of my own; for though I was the youngeſt, I was not a favourite, and had been uſed to be ordered by my brother and ſiſters, and all the family— I had nobody to help me to reſiſt this cruel tyranny.—Mr. Grimſhaw, I thought, when I dared to look in his face, liked me the better for not liking him, and ſeemed to ſurvey me, juſt

as

as I can fancy a wild beaſt looks at the prey he is ſure to have in his power.—Ah! Madam, the dreadful day came—I was carried to church more dead than alive; and though I never I believe moved my lips, for I was half inſenſible, yet I was congratulated on my marriage by my family, and put into an hired chariot and four, which Mr. Grimſhaw had provided, and, without any friend with me, brought to the manor houſe.

" As I entered it, I felt ſure that it would be my tomb: if it had been ſo directly, how many miſeries ſhould I have eſcaped from!

" The firſt perſon I ſaw when I entered the houſe, was Mrs. Hannah, who was dreſſed dreffed out to receive me, as if fhe had been the miftrefs of it, and I only an inferior vifitor.

" She furveyed me with fcrutinizing eyes; but I faw a great deal of malice and ill nature mixed with her curiofity, as fhe from time to time fpoke to her mafter in a fneering tone, and appeared hardly able to command herfelf from fpeaking the difpleafure her looks expreffed. Oh! Madam, when, in addition to fuch a reception, I confidered myfelf at fuch a diftance from my friends, and in the power of fuch a perfon as Mr. Grimfhaw, whom I had, during our journey, found to be the moft illtempered and fierce man I had ever feen (for he had fworn and fcolded the whole way like a lunatic), and in that difmal

difmal great houfe, it is impoffible to defcribe how my heart funk, and how earneftly I wifhed, that, young as I was, I might go to my death-bed rather than remain the wretch I was. But, bad as my condition then feemed to be, it was, even when I made the worft of it, far, far fhort of that I found it really to be afterwards.

" Mrs. Hannah, or, as I was defired to call her, Mrs. Pegham, was our companion at table, and directed every thing in the houfe, where I was never confulted; for both fhe and the man whom it was my mifery to call my hufband, treated me like a child too infignificant to be noticed. I was very glad of that; for I did not defire to interfere in Mr. Grimfhaw's family, and was obliged to

to them for letting me at any time efcape from the neceffity of hearing their voices, or ftaying in the room with them. Mrs. Pegham took upon her to treat me with great infolence: fhe ordered even what clothes I fhould wear, and locked up the reft, faying to me, ' that fuch a filly young thing was no judge of what was proper.' I did not complain, becaufe I knew it would have been ufelefs, or even worfe than ufelefs, becaufe Mr. Grimfhaw would only have laughed at me if he had been in a good humour, or fworn at me if he had been in a bad temper, which much oftener happened; and befides, I did not care for my appearance, and wifhed, that, except being clean, I might never look well in his eyes again: fo that, far from caring about the fineries that were taken

taken from me, I had no fatisfaction fo great as being fuffered to ftay up in a clofet at the end of the houfe, where I heard nothing of what was paffing; and there I ufed to remain and cry for hours together. My amufement, when I could take refolution to dry my eyes, was to write out of a bible, the only book I had for fome time, fuch fentences as feemed to fuit my fad condition; and this occupied more of my time than one would imagine, becaufe I had not had much learning, and wrote very flow: but by degrees, and as I took a pleafure in it, I began to make out a little better, and the firft want I found, was of materials for writing. I now and then took a fheet or two of paper out of an old leather cafe that lay about the parlour, when nobody faw me;

me; for I dared not afk for any, Mr. Grimfhaw having told me once, when I expreffed fome wifh to write to my mother, that he never fuffered goffiping letters to be fent out of his houfe—that my mother did not want to hear more of me than *he* told her—that I was very well—and he forbade my ever fending letters to any body. I faid nothing at the time, but felt a ftrong defire to write from that moment; and I was now fo much alone that I had plenty of time; for Mr. Grimfhaw, to my great fatisfaction, was fometimes abfent for a week, a fortnight, or even longer; and though when he came home he was generally in fuch a terrible humour that nobody but Mrs. Pegham could endure the houfe, my comfort was, that he feemed to care lefs and lefs

for

for this unfortunate perfon of mine which had occafioned all my misfortunes. Yet, when he had driven all his fervants away by ill humour (for he ufed to abufe and beat the men fo that he had actions brought againft him continually), he would come up into the room where I was allowed to fit, and afk me what I did there? And whatever anfwer I gave, it was all the fame :—he either ftood raving in the room till I fell fenfelefs with terror, or dragged me down to the room where he and Mrs. Pegham fat, and there he feemed to take an unaccountable pleafure in tormenting me; though, as I was fo patient, and he had no one fault to accufe me of, it required fome ingenuity to find topics of reproach and wrath. One of thefe however conftantly was, that I was

grown

grown ugly. Far from that making me uneafy, I rejoiced at it, and wifhed to be the moft odious and loathfome of human creatures, rather than ever appear in his eyes an object of what he called love. So paffed the firft wretched year of my marriage: at the beginning of that time I had been fometimes fhewn to the few people whom he could not avoid feeing, as his wife, and had fat at the head of the table. I thought that once or twice fome of the guefts looked upon me with pity and concern : but as foon as the table-cloth was removed, I always had a hint from Mr. Grimfhaw to retire; and I never had an opportunity of fpeaking a word to any of thefe good people, who, if I had, could not perhaps have done me any fervice.

" Autumn

" Autumn came on, and Mr. Grimfhaw. who affected to be very fond of field fports, went away into the North a-fhooting. I knew the time he was to go, for I was lucky enough then to fleep in a room by myfelf; and I remember, that in a dark morning in October I foftly opened the cafement, from which, over an old wall, I could fee into the ftable-yard; and when I heard him go out, fwearing at his fervants, my heart beat with apprehenfion, left, as it was a bad morning, he fhould delay his journey; for he was very capricious, and often took it into his head to return after he had fet out, or find fome excufe for not going.—He feemed always purfued by fome tormenting thoughts, that never fuffered him to reft contented any where many days together.

" However,

" However, this time he went—I heard him depart, followed by a fervant with his gun; and as the noife of their horfes' feet, and of the man whiftling to the dogs, became fainter and fainter, I felt quite relieved; fo great was the horror of his prefence, and, alas! fuch fort of negative comfort was all I could now ever hope to have.

" Mrs. Pegham, who perhaps hates him in her heart, was that day in a rather better humour than ufual. She had fome friends, fhe faid, out of York-fhire, who were to dine with her, and fhe defired I would dine in my own room, as I had often of late been fuf-fered to do. I was very glad to do fo now, and had not the leaft curiofity to fee her friends, or wifh to be a party in

in the merriment that feemed to go on in the beft parlour, which I heard as I ftepped acrofs the landing-place of the great ftairs, to go down as foon as I had dined to walk in what is called the lower garden — I had always chofen this place when I was allowed to go out, becaufe it was hid from the windows of the houfe by the great garden walls. On one fide of this fecond garden was a row of old fir trees, and a high cut holly hedge beyond them: the walk be-tween led up to a fort of bower or ar-bour made of yew, cut alfo, and a wooden table in the middle of it; and fhrubs, fuch as holly and lauruftinus, grew about it, fo that it was open no way but that which looked down a grafs walk, between the holly hedge and the fir trees. There were table vegetables

K 2   grew

grew in the middle of the plot of ground, and on the other fide was a long double row of filbert trees, fo old that they met at the top, and formed a fort of arbour all the length of the garden.

" The evening I fpeak of was cold and gloomy, though there was but little wind. I walked to the end of the fir-tree walk, and fat down in the yew arbour. It was nearly dufk and every thing was quite filent about the garden. I fell into reflections on the different fituation I was in now from that when I was in my father's cheerful houfe in the midft of a great city, with the buftle of commerce always about me, and where every body feemed fo bufy, that none had time to think themfelves un-happy. Now, in this cheerlefs folitude, the

the ceffation of the actual mifery I fuf-fered in Mr. Grimfhaw's prefence gave me but time to confider how dreadful my fate was.

" As I thus gave myfelf up to melan-choly thoughts, my eyes were infenfibly fixed on the end of the long dark walk that was before me—when a figure, not diftinctly feen through the gloom, ap-peared there, and I could juft difcern that it feemed to be a woman, and was clad in fome light colour. I felt no alarm, for I thought it was Mrs. Peg-ham, or one of the maids; I looked fteadily, and faw that fhe waved her hand as beckoning me towards her. My heart mifgave me—I feared that Mr. Grimfhaw was returned, and that I was fent for in. I arofe with this idea,

K 3   and

and walked towards the perfon, who
feemed to me to wait for me at the end
of the walk; but as I approached, the
form became more and more indiftinct,
till it feemed diffolved in air; and when
I found myfelf clofe to the fpot where I
had imagined it to be, there was nothing.
I looked round me in amaze, but ftill
without terror—I liftened.—It was, I
thought, furely my fight that deceived
me, or fome reflection of the trees in the
declining light. I felt rather relieved
than alarmed; for any thing was preferable in my opinion to what I had dreaded
as the caufe of this fummons, the return
of Mr. Grimfhaw. But the evening was
become very cold, and it was growing
dark. The leaves on the ground ruftled
mournfully as I paffed under two lime
trees

trees from which they had fallen, meaning to pafs through the filbert walk, to
reach a door that led through an orchard
the neareft way to the houfe. As I did
fo I looked down it, and fancied that
about the middle I faw the fame figure
that I had perceived before ftanding
quite ftill. The leaves were thin on
the filbert trees, and many had fallen.
I now fancied it the dairy-maid, a
young country girl, whom I was ordered
never to fpeak to, but whom I *had* fometimes talked to when I could do it un-
obferved: fhe had occafionally put me
upon my guard againft the ill-humour
of Mr. Grimfhaw, when he returned in
one of his frantic fits. She feemed to
pity me—I felt myfelf grateful for fuch
little acts of kindnefs as it was in her

K 4 power

power to fhew me. Perfuading myfelf
now that fhe waited there to give me
fome intelligence, I ftepped down the
walk. The figure appeared ftationary till
I was within twenty paces, and I difcerned it to be a woman; but when I
was almoft near enough to difcover the
features, the vifion again feemed to melt
into air; and when I reached the fpot
where I thought it had ftood, there was
nothing!

" A cold chill crept over me as I
ftood for a moment looking fearfully
round.—I liftened in breathlefs terror—
No found but the faint ruftling of the
half-faded leaves broke the dead filence
of the night, and it became almoft entirely dark before, with trembling fteps,
I got back to my own room.—I reached
it,

it, however, breathlefs, and fat down
fighing loud and deep. My terror was
not leffened when I heard the figh repeated from a clofet near the head of
the bed, where I ufed to hang my
clothes.

" Starting up, I was going on the
immediate impulfe of fear to open the
clofet, but a low murmuring noife I
heard in it deterred me. Faint dews
hung upon my face: I became fick,
and caught the poft of the bed to fave
myfelf from falling. As I had nobody
to liften to my terror, or by reafoning
to remove it, I knew it would be ufelefs
to call for affiftance, and I was a great
way from the inhabited part of the
houfe. I endeavoured, however, to
argue with myfelf, and to enquire what

K 5 I had

I had to fear? Stories enough I had heard of ghofts and ftrange appearances; but it had alfo been imprefled upon my mind, that thefe things never were feen but by the wicked.—An internal con-fcioufnefs of my own innocence, and at the fame time a full fenfe of my own wretchednefs, feemed fomewhat to re-ftore me. ' What have I done,' faid I, ' that ought to make me fear the dead?— Which way can mifery reach me from among the living? and how can I be more unhappy than I am?'

" By thefe arguments I acquired ftrength enough to open the door of my room, meaning to have gone down a narrow back ftairs at the end of a long paffage, that there joined another nar-row ftairs which led down to the cellars; and

and it was a way by which Rebecca, a woman of the village, who was fometimes employed in the houfe, ufed to come into my room, fometimes brought what I wanted; and I meant to call for a candle, which I fuppofed Mrs. Pegham's having company for her to wait upon might have occafioned her to forget. I was flowly defcending, when I thought I heard her coming up, and ftopped: fhe foon appeared; but the moment fhe faw me fhe gave a loud fhriek, let the candle fall, and I fuppofe, to fave herfelf from falling, threw herfelf forward on the ftairs.—Hardly knowing what I faid, I fpoke to her, and, though we were in total darknefs, tried to help her up. After a moment fhe was re-affured by the found of my voice, and by being con-vinced it was I who fpoke to her. I

took

took her hand; and though my words trembled on my lips, I entreated her to let me know what had fo alarmed her.— All the anfwer I could obtain was, ' Oh! Madam, you don't know! Such a fright! but it ferves me as I ought to be ferved.—I was told laft year how 'twould be.'

" I found it vain to afk an explana-tion of all this, the woman ftill con-tinuing to lament herfelf; I therefore defired fhe would try to rife and light the candle, for that I was extremely cold in my own room, and wifhed for a fire. At length I prevailed upon her to exert herfelf to go down, leaning on my arm; but as fhe went fhe continued to ex-claim, ' Cold! ah, well you may! Poor young thing! Who would be a great rich

rich lady to live in this houfe?—Not I, I am fure.' Of this and fimilar fpeeches I entreated an explanation, but in vain. Taken up entirely with herfelf, all I could obtain from the woman was, that when fhe faw me upon the ftairs fhe had taken me for the fpirit that walked in and about the houfe, and which the dairy-maid had declared fhe had feen ftanding againft the pales of the great granary. I fhuddered, and earneftly en-quired what was meant. ' Ah! poor young lady, you will know foon enough. was all the anfwer I could obtain from this perfon, who, as we approached the place where it was probable fhe might be heard by Mrs. Pegham, lowered her voice, and feemed to fubdue her fears by confidering her intereft. I could not prevail upon her to ftay even while I waited

I waited for the dairy-maid: but fhe haftened away, and left me alone in the kitchen; for the fervants now in the houfe, who were only two maids, and a fort of farming man, were all employed, as I fuppofed, in attending on the friends of the houfekeeper: the kitchen was entirely deferted.

" It was, however, comparatively cheerful; for there was a good fire, fupper feemed to be preparing, and feveral dogs lay round the hearth. I thought it would have been a confolation, and in fome fort a protection, if I could have prevailed on one of thefe to follow me to my room. There was an old water fpaniel that I had fometimes fondled and fed, and which had often followed me in my folitary walks. I now, fancying

ing I heard Mrs. Pegham's voice, haftened to retire; for the terror of her infults was as great as almoft any other, and I had been ordered by Mr. Grimfhaw never to be feen in the kitchen. I coaxed the fpaniel to follow me; and taking up a candle, with which I intended to light my fire, I crept flowly back to my own room, dreading to look up the ftairs, and fomewhat re-affured by hearing the found of my four-footed companion's fteps after me. Hardly, however, had I reached the door of my room before the dog began to howl in a ftrange manner, and ran away with fuch fpeed, that any attempts to ftop or overtake it would have been to no purpofe. I cannot defcribe the terror with which I entered the room; but perceiving nothing, and feeling half dead with fear

fear and cold, I lit the fire, and, when it burnt up, fat down and ate what had been fent me for my fupper, which Rebecca had left upon the ftairs. I found myfelf reftored to a little more courage, but on the apprehenfions of the evening I dared not think As foon, therefore, as I could, I haftened to my bed, having bolted the door of my chamber, and that of the clofet, into which I dared not look.

" I know not how, after fuch dread and apprehenfions, the more terrible for not being afcertained, my fpirits fubfided into compofure, fo as to allow me to fleep: but I had certainly forgot myfelf for fome time, when I ftarted fuddenly at fome fancied noife, and through the curtains of my bed, that were of old thin linen,

linen, I thought I faw a figure ftanding before the fire, which burnt brightly. Involuntarily I reached toward the foot of the bed, and undrew the curtain. I faw very plainly a female figure, leaning with her head againft the mantle piece, while her back was towards me. Immoveable with terror, I remained gazing at it fome moments, till turning towards me it approached the foot of the bed, where I fell in undefcribable horror on beholding what appeared to be a corpfe. It looked earneftly on me for fome time; then I heard the fame deep hollow figh as had before reached my ears from the clofet; and gliding towards that clofet the fpectre again melted way.

" I cannot well defcribe the ftate of mind in which I remained the reft of the night;

night; but the moment I faw day-light gleaming through the fhutters I opened them, and fat there till it became broad day, when I crept more dead than alive to the kitchen, where my appearance at that unufual hour, and the horror mark-ed on my countenance, were obferved by the old fervant who was moft in Mrs. Pegham's confidence, and who might well be called one of my keepers. She afked me fiercely and brutally what I did there, and why I looked fo white? I told her that I had been very much terrified during the night by fomething that had appeared in my room: to which fhe gave me only a harfh anfwer, faying, I had better fpeak to Mrs. Pegham, and hear what *fhe* would fay, forfooth, to my indulging fuch vagaries. Contrary, how-ever, to my expectation, Mrs. Pegham fent

fent for me to breakfaft with her; and the woman having told her what I had faid, fhe affected to laugh at my fears, and told me that fhe fuppofed I had takenfuch fancies into my head in con-fequence of fome nonfenfical ftories I had heard of the houfe being haunted; ' but fuch things are always faid in thefe lone villages,' added fhe, ' of old fafhion-ed houfes like this. I would not advife you to take any notice of thefe nonfen-fical ftories to Mr. Grimfhaw; for he will be very angry, and has often de-clared he fhould be tempted to fend any body to the other world to keep com-pany with ghofts, if they were fuch ideots as to talk of them in his houfe. I affure you he has turned three or four fervants out of doors for it already.'

" Ah!

" ' Ah!' thought I, ' how glad I fhould be, if he would turn *me* out of doors!—And how willingly I would beg my way to London, if he would but let me leave this houfe of horrors!'

" Mrs. Pegham, however, was more civil than ufual to me during the reft of the day: fhe kept me to dine with her in the parlour; when, juft as we were fitting down to table, a man's voice was heard in the hall. I turned pale with terror, concluding it to be Mr. Grimfhaw re-turned; when, to my great aftonifhment, I faw come into the room Mr. Au-berry, the young man who had lived fome time with my father, and who had fhewn fome partiality for me. He feemed in great confufion and diftrefs of mind; and as he addreffed himfelf to

to me, as the miftrefs of the houfe, I faw that he was ftruck with the change that had taken place in my appearance; while, as he turned to anfwer Mrs. Peg-ham's rude enquiry of what his bufinefs was, and what was his name? I per-ceived his eyes lighten, and his cheeks glow with indignation.—For my own part, I waited in breathlefs fear for the end of the dialogue between them, ex-pecting nothing but to hear that my father or mother was dead, or that fome great misfortune had happened to my family.

" When with a trembling voice I made the enquiry, he affured me that they were all well; but, he added, im-prudently enough, that my father had lately been much troubled in mind about

about me, from certain dreams he and
my mother had been afflicted with, and
that they neither of them were able to
reft till fomebody they could depend
upon had feen me: therefore, as he was
travelling into the north of England for
orders, being fhortly to be taken into
partnerfhip with my father, he had come
about forty miles out of his way to convince them I was alive and well.

" Mrs. Pegham heard him with great
impatience, and faid, now that he had
feen me, fhe fuppofed it was enough.
She had no authority to invite any-body
to the houfe, while Mr. Grimfhaw was
abroad, fo it was not in her power to
afk him to dinner; but if he chofe a
glafs of wine, or ale, or the like, he was
welcome. I then ventured to fpeak,
and

and told her that I hoped fhe would allow *me* to invite Mr. Auberry to dinner,
that I might have time to enquire after
my friends, whom I had not heard of
for fo long a time. Auberry refufed
eating any thing, but faid he hoped the
houfekeeper's permiffion was not neceffary to fpeak to me, which he defired
to do alone; but fhe pofitively refufed,
and told him, that if he came there only
to fet a young woman againft her hufband, and make unhappinefs and difcon-
tent in a family, the fooner he was gone
the better:—that fhe fhould let no
young fellows that came rambling
about talk to Mr. Grimfhaw's wife,
and fhe defired him to walk out, and
not give her the trouble of having
him turned out.

" Auberry,

" Auberry, convinced by my looks
that my fituation was dreadful, and
feeling all the infolence of Mrs.
Pegham's conduct, perfifted in faying,
he would fpeak to me. Mrs. Pegham haftened in a rage to the door to
call for the farming men, and I took
that opportunity to entreat of Auberry not to abandon me.—'Oh! for
God's fake,' faid I, ' fave me if you
can! I am the moft unhappy wretch
breathing.—You know not, nobody
can know, all I endure.'

" Mrs. Pegham by this time returned,
and again infolently ordered Mr. Auberry to leave the houfe. He again pe-
remptorily refufed. The woman, who
feemed to have affumed all the qualities
of a fury, then beckoned to two men,
who

who came in with pitchforks in their
hands, and turned Mr. Auberry by
force out of doors; while I, driven to
defpair in proportion as this hope of
deliverance feemed efcaping from me,
clung to him, till the woman, feizing
me by the arm, tore me away:—then
dragging me toward my own room,
while fhe loaded me with reproaches,
and protefted in the moft virulent terms
that fhe would inform Mr. Grimfhaw of
all that had happened, and take care it
never fhould be in my power to attempt
to go away again, fhe locked the
doors, barred the windows, and left me
to myfelf!

" I had a few hours before thought that
nothing could be fo dreadful as being
fhut up in that room; I now preferred
it

it to the dread I felt of Grimfhaw's return, and wifhed for nothing but to die, rather than be expofed again to meet him.

" Night came, and with it the recollection of thofe terrors I had undergone the night before—they were not lefs now. About midnight, the profound filence was broken by a ruftling and low moaning in the clofet: it was as of one confined there in pain and uneafinefs, and ftriving to get out. If I had had a light, I do not know that I fhould have had courage to have opened the clofet, though I had been endeavouring to obtain fufficient refolution, by repeating to myfelf the queftion—What have I to fear? and would not death be welcome?—As I had no light, I made that

that a fort of excufe to myfelf for not attempting to affure myfelf of the caufe of this extraordinary noife—to which I had not liftened, in increafed terror, above half an hour, before a pale difmal light gleamed through the room. I put back my curtain, and faw the fame figure I had feen the night before—it glided from the clofet-door, and placed itfelf again at the foot of the bed. I attempted in vain to fhriek, to fpeak— fear quite overcame me; yet I could not withdraw my eyes from the figure, which, after remaining immoveable fome time, waved its arm, and then paffed to the door of the chamber, ftill motioning for me to follow. A ftrange impulfe, which it feemed as if I could not refift, occafioned me to leave my bed, where I had thrown myfelf without being

L 2   undreffed.

undreffed. I ftood then within a fhort diftance of the object and to my aftonifhment I faw it pafs through the door, which I knew to be fhut; yet I ftill perceived it on the other fide gliding flowly through the long paffage that led to the back ftairs. I involuntarily feized the lock. It opened—I followed the fpectre along the paffage—it defcended the ftairs; on the top of which I continued to ftand half fenfelefs with amaze, and doubting my fenfes. When the figure had reached the place where one ftaircafe branched off toward the cellar, and the other toward the kitchen, it ftopped and turned—then pointed with one hand down one ftaircafe, while it feemed to beckon me with the other toward that which led to the kitchen; and then it became fainter and fainter, till, the femblance

blance of the human form being loft, only a blueifh and very feeble light remained—which flowly went on, while, without any afcertained purpofe, I followed it foftly, my knees trembling, and my breath oppreffed. It wavered through a great and almoft empty fpace behind the kitchen to a large door made for the bringing in wood and turf, which was in winter piled up there to dry for the ufe of the kitchen. Through this door, which flowly opened at its approach, the myfterious light moved, and in a few paces I found myfelf ftanding in the midft of a wood-yard. The light was no where vifible, but I faw a few ftars above my head. I felt the air blow refrefhing on my face—I breathed more freely— and the idea that I might now leave my hideous prifon for ever, and that Providence

L 3   vidence

vidence had interpofed for my deliverance, fuddenly occurred to me.

" Having once feized this hope, I feemed
to recover my ftrength. I looked round
the place, in which I had never been
above once before, for a door: I found
one, and feized the latch eagerly, dreading left it fhould be faftened. It was
open: but it led into the orchard; and
that was immediately under the windows
of the room where I knew Mrs. Pegham flept. I looked up and faw there
was a light in her room, and I ran trembling to hide myfelf among the trees,
though, as they were almoft leaflefs, they
did not afford me much fhelter; but I had
unfortunately difturbed a great houfe-
dog, whofe kennel was under her windows, and which I knew was very fierce.

He

He came raving and barking towards
me, while, entangling my feet in fome
boughs and loofe wood that was feat-
tered under them, I fell, and gave myfelf
up for loft. The dog, however, no fooner
approached me, than he ran howling
away as if he had been beaten. This
noife alarmed Mrs. Pegham.—Judge of
my terror when I plainly perceived her
open the cafement and look out! After
the other miracles I have feen, I will
not fay it was miraculous that fhe did
not fee me, for fhe did not; though,
when I faw her fhut the window, I expected nothing but that fhe was gone
to call the fervants to drag me to my
former prifon, where I was to fuffer yet
worfe treatment than had been exercifed
upon me already. But after remaining
fome moments, and hearing no noife,

L 4 and

and feeing no other light moving about
the houfe, I took courage, and, creeping
as much out of fight as I could, went
round under the pales, and found the
door that went into that lower garden
(which I have defcribed) a-jar. I hurried through it, fhutting it as foftly as
I could after me, and bolting it. I
thought now of nothing but my efcape,
for I believed I could get through the
hedge by the yew arbour. I croffed towards it among fome rows of French
beans that were ftill high, and came
into the walk. My heart beat almoft to
fuffocation as I looked towards the feat,
for I believed I fhould again fee the
fpectre: but figure to yourfelf how much
greater was my terror, when, being within a few paces of it, I faw (for the evening was clear, and the northern lights
were

were very ftrong and bright) a man, or
what appeared to be fuch, leaning on the
table! He perceived me at the fame
moment—ftarted out, and feized me by
the arm. I uttered an involuntary
fcream, and fell almoft fenfelefs to the
ground. Terror, however, had not fo
entirely deprived me of recollection but
that I knew, as foon as he fpoke, the
voice of Auberry.

" ' Eleanor! dear Eleanor!' faid he,
' by what miracle are you here? This
is beyond my hopes. Oh! try, try, to
recover yourfelf, and hear what I have
to fay.'

" I clung to him as one drowning catches
at an object that offers affiftance; but I
had only breath to fay, ' Oh! Auberry,

L 5 do

do not leave me!'—' I will not,' anfwered he; ' I will not quit you but
with my life; but cannot we efcape
from hence?'

" I endeavoured then to recall all my
recollection, and remembered that there
was a place in the yew-hedge, not far
from the fpot where we ftood, where
I had remarked people had paffed. I
led towards it, and he helped me over
a ditch that was on the other fide. We
were then on a wide marfh that fpreads
to a great diftance, and I looked round
with dread that there is no defcribing.
I had never been out of the houfe before, and I was fure Mr. Auberry could
know nothing of the country. However,
he bade me have courage, and led me,
as quick as terror allowed me to walk,
towards

towards that fide which he thought led
to the road he came. At an ale-
houfe on the fide of that road he had
left his horfe, and the nights were now
fo long that we hoped to reach it
before day fhould make my extraordinary appearance the fubject of remark to
fuch paffengers as we might meet. The
hope of efcaping for ever from my
wretched imprifonment lent me ftrength.
I walked with more eafe than I expected,
and we at laft found ourfelves on the
banks of a river; and to pafs farther
feemed impoffible, unlefs we could, pur-
fuing its courfe, meet with a bridge. I
ftill endeavoured to preferve my prefence of mind; but wearinefs quite overcame me, and I was compelled to entreat
my conductor to let me fit down on the
ground for a few moments.

L 6 " While

" While I fat, I entreated him to tell
me by what miracle he had thus been
fent to my prefervation. He related,
that my father and mother being rendered very uneafy, not only by dreams
that had tormented them on my account,
but by reports about Mr. Grimfhaw's
conduct to his firft wife, they had defired that he would fee me, and inform
them in what fituation I feemed to be,
and whether I was well treated. ' I accordingly,' faid he, ' came to the next
market-town; where, I am forry to fay,
that from the anfwers I received to my
enquiries, I had not much doubt but
that all the reports we had heard in
London were true. I learned that nobody ever faw you, and that the favourite houfekeeper, not you, was the
miftrefs of the houfe; and I befides
found

found that Mr. Grimfhaw was univer-
fally execrated as a favage and a tyrant. As I came nearer to his houfe, I
faw the people I fpoke to anfwered me
with mingled fear and deteftation, and
all I could gather of a certainty was,
that I fhould not be fuffered to fee you,
and that the only way that gave me any
chance of it, was to enter the houfe
unexpectedly while the mafter of it was
abfent, as he now was. I did fo, and
the event you know.

" ' After I was compelled to quit the
houfe, without having an opportunity of
fpeaking to you alone, I was returning
flowly to the little inn where I had left
my horfe, when I was overtaken by an
odd, wild-looking woman, who turned,
after fhe had paffed me, and eyed me
with

with an expreſſion that raiſed my cu-
rioſity. She continued to look at
me, and to mutter till ſhe entered a
poor cottage at the end of the village,
whither I followed her; and putting half
a crown into her hand (a ſum which ſhe
ſeemed to conſider as immenſe), I deſired
her to tell me if ſhe knew any thing of
the inhabitants of the manor houſe?

" ' And now, dear Madam," ſaid Auberry, ' have you courage enough to
hear what this woman related to me?'

" I aſſured him I had, and he thus
proceeded:

" ' She told me, then, that ſhe ſhould be
ruined, if ever what ſhe ſaid came to
the 'Squire's ears. It was well known
in

in the country, that his firſt wife did not
come fairly by her death, and that ſhe
was given out for dead long before ſhe
was ſo; becauſe ſhe was reduced by ill
uſage to ſuch a ſtate, that her wicked
huſband dared not let her be ſeen by
the relations that he was afraid would
enquire for her; and that inſtead of
her, a parcel of ſtones was buried, and
ſhe lingered in a wretched place under
ground, where at length ſhe died; though
even then it was believed her end was
haſtened by poiſon, or ſome ſuch wicked
means, which nobody could do more
than gueſs at, becauſe ſhe had never
been ſeen afterwards; but that it was
well known that every year about the
time ſhe had thus lingered and died,
her ghoſt appeared about the houſe, and
that ſeveral people had ſeen it.'

" O think

" O think what I felt at hearing all
this! and how great was my horror
when I reflected that I was the wife of
this wretch, and might again be in his
power. I could with difficulty command
myſelf to liſten to what followed.

" ' The woman told me," continued
Mr. Auberry, ' that ſhe had been hired
in the houſe occaſionally, and was juſt
come from thence, having been frightened by the report of the ſervants—that
this was the time the ſpirit walked, and
that there was more than one bad ſtory
of wicked actions done by the 'Squire
and his houſekeeper; for it was ſaid a
brother of the young lady, his firſt wife,
coming from beyond ſea, and landing
at Hull, croſſed the country to viſit his
ſiſter, whom he had never ſeen ſince
her

her marriage, and that he was ſcarce in
the houſe above one night before the
horrid man picked ſome quarel with
him, and ſtabbed him; and moreover,
added the woman, they ſay his body
was carried to a cloſet up ſtairs to hide
it, till they could make away with it;
and all the way from that cloſet acroſs
the room, and through the paſſage, folks
ſay there is drop of blood to be ſeen
on the floor. And that is true enough,
to my knowledge; for I've ſeen them
myſelf. I have heard ſay that the 'Squire
have had them floors planed ever ſo many
times, but the blood always appears
again; and moreover, that at laſt he
had the boards turned, and ſome of the
worſt on 'em changed, but that ſtill, do
what he will, the blood-ſpots came exactly in the ſame place again, as red as
if

if they had juſt ſprung from the murdered gentleman. I then remembered
that there were pieces of old tapeſtry
nailed down to the floor, quite from the
door of that fatal cloſet to the end of
the long paſſage, and that once I had
dropped a little ring my mother had given
me, and was trying to look under this
tapeſtry cloth to find it, when Mrs.
Pegham, coming into the room, put herſelf in a great paſſion, and ſaying, ſhe
had no notion of having the furniture
pulled and tore about in that manner,
puſhed me away, and nailed the carpet
down cloſer than before.'

" This dreadful narrative ſeemed to
renew the courage neceſſary for me to
attempt making my eſcape. I begged
Mr. Auberry inſtantly to proceed, and
again

again we walked on, I believe three
miles at leaſt, before we came to a
bridge, where it croſſed the river to a
ſolitary farm. It was not yet day-light:
therefore, after reſting again about a
quarter of an hour, I again proceeded—
though ſo very weary, that nothing but
the extreme dread I had of my tyrant
could have induced me to undergo ſuch
ſuffering.

" Soon after day-break we reached a
market-town, and I now hoped to find
ſhelter and repoſe in a ſmall inn. We
went under the gate-way, hoping at this
early hour to paſs unremarked, except
by the people that belonged to it, to
whom Mr. Auberry thought he could
account for my extraordinary appearance.

" Ah!

" Ah! think what became of me when,
ſtanding at a ſtable door in the inn-yard,
juſt ready to mount his horſe, I ſaw Mr.
Grimſhaw himſelf!

" He uttered a furious oath, ſprang
forward, and caught me by the arm.
I became inſtantly ſenſeleſs, and only
knew, by what I have heard ſince, that
he loudly accuſed me of being an adul-
treſs; and as Mr. Auberry did not deny
that I was his (Grimſhaw's) wife, nobody choſe to liſten to any thing he
had to ſay, as reaſons why I had left
his houſe; but rather aſſiſted, than
tried to prevent, Mr. Grimſhaw, when
he put me, ſenſeleſs and fainting as I was,
into the firſt carriage he could find, and
conveyed me back to this den of wick-
edneſs and murder, his houſe. When
I returned

I returned—(would I had never returned!) to my ſenſes, I found myſelf in total
darkneſs. Every thing that had paſſed
ſeemed like a dream, and I tried to recollect diſtinctly the ſtrange images con-
fuſedly impreſſed on my mind. As day
dawned through my ſhutters, I found
I was in the very ſame room from
whence I had been liberated (if I had
not really been dreaming) by ſupernatural means. Soon afterwards, however, I was too well convinced that the
miſeries of my fate were aggravated.
My jailoreſs, and the inhuman wretch,
her employer, ſoon appeared, and began, with the moſt barbarous inſults, to
inſiſt on my telling them how I eſcaped
from the room, where Mrs. Pegham
proteſted ſhe had locked me in. I was
deſperate; and without trying to ſoften
any

any part of what I had to relate, I told it
all, and repeated all the horrors Mr.
Auberry had heard, in addition to thofe
I had feen. I accufed them of a double murder—and added, that I had nothing to defire of them, but that they would
deftroy me at once, as they had done
the unfortunate young officer, and not
let me linger like the miferable victim,
whofe fate I was convinced would fooner
or later be mine.

" Never was feen furely fuch malignant
guilt, mingled with horror, as the countenance of Grimfhaw exhibited; while
that of his affociate expreffed the triumph of daring and confirmed cruelty
over every other fenfation. I was now
confined for fome time on bread and
water in a fort of cellar, which I had
reafon

reafon to believe was the place where
the poor young lady, my predeceffor,
had ended her miferable days; but I
feared neither darknefs nor confinement,
nor want, equal to the prefence of my
cruel perfecutor. Mrs. Pegham found
me tranquil—I complained not—I did
not afk for liberty. Nothing moved me
but the apprehenfion of feeing Mr.
Grimfhaw, or the fear of what might
have become of poor Auberry, who, I
fuppofed, muft have been murdered,
or elfe, that he would have informed
my friends of my fituation, who would,
I thought, have made fome enquiry
after me.

" When this wretched imprifonment
was found to make no impreffion upon
me, I was dragged back to the fatal
room

room ftained with blood, and the fcene
of former murders; and there I was
fhewn a fhirt-buckle and lock of hair,
which Mrs. Pegham told me infultingly
was fent by my paramour, as his laft gift,
for that he had been tried for I know
not what crime, of affociating with the
rebels, and was to be executed. At another time I was informed that my father
was a bankrupt, and my mother gone
into an alms-houfe. Every device was
ufed, during many months, to weaken and
deprefs my mind, which gradually funk
under fuch treatment. I was at the fame
time expofed to hunger from having only
difgufting food, and my clothes were often
infufficient to fave me from the rigours
of winter, or the intolerable diftrefs of
fqualid dirt, which was indeed the fevereft of my fufferings, except only
when

when Mr. Grimfhaw himfelf approached
me: then the only fenfation I was confcious
of was fomething like joy, that my appearance was fo wretched, that I muft be an
object of abhorrence to him, inftead of
his finding any attraction in the frame or
face which had been the caufe of his
hateful liking.

" I was fometimes neglected, and without food for two days, and I have reafon
to believe Mrs. Pegham and her mafter
were at thefe times out; I tried once or
twice to make my efcape, but in vain.
On her return, thefe attempts were
always difcovered, and then the cruel
woman ufed to beat and drag me about
the room, afking me why I did not get
the ghoft to come again and let me out?
Of the ghoft I was now no longer afraid.

Rendered almoſt callous by unexampled hardſhips, I ſometimes was nearly unconſcious of what paſſed, and I believe I have, more than once, lain for days on my bed in a ſtate of inſenſibility; then, as if my perſecutors were afraid of loſing their victim, they gave me more nouriſhing food, and relaxed in ſome degree their barbarity.

"No interference, either natural or ſupernatural, now ſeemed likely to ſave me. When I ventured to look forward, nothing appeared but a courſe of the moſt deplorable ſufferings terminating in the grave. If I looked backwards, the memory of former times overwhelmed me with vain and fruitleſs regret. I thought of the manner of my life in my father's houſe, where, though there

there was always a great diſpoſition to ſacrifice too much to the accumulation of wealth, I enjoyed the decencies of life; yet I had ſometimes thought myſelf unhappy, and ſhed childiſh tears over imaginary miſeries.—('How little,' ſaid Mrs. Blandford to Azemia, as ſhe read this part of the narrative! 'how little, my ſweet love, do we know in early youth the happineſs we enjoy, merely from ignorance of evil!—How few are there, who, if they could ſee what this ſubſequent life promiſes, would wiſh for maturity, for middle life—for old age!—But go on, my dear Azemia, my reflections will only make us more melancholy than the narrative we are reading.)'—Azemia proceeded.

M 2   "Winter

"Winter now again approached, and to other diſtreſſes were added thoſe of gloom and of cold —I had been long ſince removed into the room of blood, becauſe of that I ſeemed to have the greateſt terror, and I had often heard the low murmuring, as of a wretch confined in pain, in the cloſet, and behind the wainſcot of the room; but I dreaded the dead ſo much leſs than the living, that I conſidered this poor unquiet ſpirit as my friend; and ſuch was the deep and ſteady deſpair of my mind, that I wiſhed to converſe with this ſpectre, and to eſcape, as the form it once inhabited had eſcaped from the inſupportable evil of being in the power of Grimſhaw.

"Such was the ſtate of my mind, when late in the month of October I was

was one night awakened from diſturbed ſleep by ſome noiſe in my room. I liſtened; but then every thing was ſo ſtill about the houſe, that I diſtinctly heard the clock, which was at a conſiderable diſtance from my room, ſtrike twelve. After a few moments, the hollow undeſcribable noiſe that had ſtartled me was repeated: it came from the fatal cloſet. I looked towards the door— a figure with a bleeding wound in its breaſt glided to the feet of the bed, and ſtood immoveable: it did not reſemble that which I had ſeen before. I endeavoured, but in vain, to ſpeak: the ſpectre pointed to the place from whence it had appeared. I again looked thither, and ſaw a ſhade inſenſibly form, as it were, from a thin vapour into the ſame figure of a woman that I had before ſeen, holding an

M 3   infant

infant in her arms. This too was foon vifible at the foot of my bed: its ftony and ghaftly eyes were mournfully fixed upon me, who trembling with a fenfation I cannot define, but which was not fear, at length, cried—' Tell me what you are! tell me, if I can do any thing for your repofe?'

"A low fepulchral voice anfwered—'I am Gertrude!—The wretch deftroyed me, with the baby you fee here—the wretch murdered my brother in that clofet—at this hour three years fince, he murdered him.—I furvived him twenty days and nights—fo long you will fee me—try to efcape my fate!'

" A dead cold paufe enfued; I remained with my eyes fixed on thefe fearful fhapes

fhapes—they flowly, flowly melted into air!

" Gradually the palpitations of my heart, the tremor of my fpirits fubfided. I flept; and when I awoke in the morning, I afked myfelf whether I had not dreamed all that feemed to have paffed; but the circumftances that had before occurred left me no doubt as to the reality of what I had feen. I remembered that for twenty days the image of the murdered Gertrude was to prefent itfelf.—Good God! if formerly I had been told that I fhould be haunted by a fpeftre, and fear it lefs than the fight of fome exifting beings around me, how fhould I have fhrunk from a deftiny which it would have appeared impoffible to fuftain!

M 4   " I did,

" I did, however, endure it; the next night, the next, and for many fucceeding nights, the perturbed fpirit of the murdered Gertrude, regularly at the hour of twelve, prefented itfelf at the foot of my bed; but, inftead of repeating all it had at firft faid, it only uttered in a moaning and hollow voice,

' Efcape from a fate like mine!'

I now hardly ever flept before the fhape appeared—expeftation of it kept me awake. After it had faded away, I continued to attempt arguing myfelf into a refolution again to fpeak; and if I at any time obtained repofe, it was broken and interrupted. I ftarted at every noife of the wind, as it howled or fighed through the old cafements of my room, and, at length, hardly obtained, in

in the four-and-twenty hours, one quarter of an hour's forgetfulnefs. Want of fleep difturbed my head and ftomach. Of the food that was brought me every day, I fcarce ate half an ounce in the courfe of it. I became emaciated—my eyes were fometimes heavy, fometimes wild, and I believe my reafon was not unfrequently wandering. In thefe intervals I reproached the wretched Pegham; I told her of her crimes, and of her mafter's; I tore up with fupernatural force the tapeftry on the floor—pointed to the blood, and fhriekingly proclaimed that I knew who had fhed that blood, and to whom it belonged. Such conduft gave Mrs. Pegham a good excufe to treat me as a lunatic; but in thefe fits of raving and defperation I fpoke fo much that fhe knew to be true—I afferted

ſerted ſo much that was already ſuſ-
pected, that ſhe dared not ſuffer even
her moſt confidential ſervant to approach
me; and began, no doubt, to hope that
I ſhould ſoon be out of the way of be-
traying the horrors of this den of in-
famy.

" Gertrude every night at the ſame
hour returned, and always repeated once
in a ſepulchral and tremulous tone—

‹ Eſcape from a fate like mine !'

Eighteen of the twenty days on which I
expected theſe nocturnal viſits had now
paſſed, when, without knowing why I
again felt courage to ſpeak to the apparition, I could only ſay—

‹ How eſcape?'

When

When the ſhade, waving its hand, pointed to the door—I ſtarted inſtinctively,
and haſtened to the door of my room;
it ſlowly opened before me, though I
heard Mrs. Pegham carefully lock and
bar it without every night. The ſpectre
glided before me—I followed. It led me
down to a ſort of vault adjoining to that
where I had been confined. I ſaw the
earth riſe a little above the ſurface, as if
there had there been a human body buried.
The pale funereal light, emanating from
the ſilvery and miſt-like ſhade of my diſ-
embodied conductreſs, ſhewed me this:
then the form becoming more indiſtinct,
ſeemed to creep, wavering before me, till
I beheld myſelf, as I had done before,
in the open air. I found the great gate
of the wood-yard open. I paſſed it, and
was at length out of the deteſted habitation;

tion; but ſo weak, and in ſuch dread
leſt I ſhould meet either of the wretches
I had fled from, that when I had got
about half way through the lane leading
to the fields beyond the village, I could
go no farther, but ſat down on a ſmall
hillock, and tried to recover my breath
and recollection. I knew nobody in
the country likely to receive or protect
me; yet ſuddenly I remembered the
rector of the pariſh, whoſe houſe I had
happened to remark the only time I had
ever walked out, becauſe it was ſomewhat ſuperior to the ſurrounding cottages. The road was ſo flat and ſtraight,
that I thought I could hardly miſs it,
and I acquired courage to venture.
How I obtained ſtrength I know not.
The night was wet and ſtormy, and at
intervals very dark; but as the guſts of
wind

wind drove away the clouds, I ſaw the
ſtars —I felt ſomething like hope—I
truſted in Providence, and at length I
reached the aſylum I ſought; but when
I was at length under the window in the
orchard of the good clergyman I was ſo
exhauſted, that I deſpaired of making myſelf heard.—What followed after I was
received into his houſe is already known."

It is hardly neceſſary to ſay, that the
old-faſhioned language of this narrative
has been conſiderably moderniſed and
cleared for the preſs.

It may be agreeable to ſome readers
to hear that Eleanor was reſtored to her
family; and after her firſt huſband deſtroyed himſelf, (as he did in Lincoln
jail to eſcape being hanged for murder,
of

of which he was convicted with his affociate), fhe was married to Mr. Auberry,
who having been, on her union with
Grimfhaw, difmiffed by her father, becaufe he fufpected his attachment to
her, was afterwards taken into his bufinefs. Eleanor always retained a dejected caft of mind, and her conftitution was much injured; but in the
tendernefs of the hufband of her choice,
and the affectionate regret of her family,
fhe endeavoured to lofe the deep impreffion made on her mind by thefe
melancholy and fupernatural adventures.

END OF THE FIRST VOLUME

AZEMIA:

A DESCRIPTIVE AND SENTIMENTAL

NOVEL.

INTERSPERSED WITH PIECES OF POETRY.

By JACQUETTA AGNETA MARIANA JENKS,

OF BELLEGROVE PRIORY IN WALES.

DEDICATED TO

THE RIGHT HONORABLE LADY HARRIET MARLOW.

TO WHICH ARE ADDED,

CRITICISMS ANTICIPATED.

IN TWO VOLUMES.

VOL. II.

No flimfy gauze and frippery fcenes I wrote,
With patches here and there like Jofeph's coat.
CHURCHILL.

London:

PRINTED BY AND FOR
SAMPSON LOW, NO. 7, BERWICK STREET, SOHO.

1797.

AZEMIA.

CHAPTER I.

He is a man, take him for all in all,
We ne'er fhall look upon his like again.
SHAKESPEARE.

" YET fo faid Timothy Twaddle—
that good, faithful, excellent old fervant,
Timothy Twaddle, told me that fhe
loved."

VOL. II.　　　B　　　Such

Such was the foliloquy of the Rev. Solomon Sheeppen, meditating on Azemia's difappearance, as he *galloped ventre à terre* between Royfton and London. A turnpike gate fuddenly intercepted his dangerous career; but fuch was the agitation of his mind (for which a flying leap has often proved a fpecific), that he was on the point of taking it—when the turnpike man, Walter Waglock, who was fettling a point about a difputed three-pence half-penny (with Jack Jerkin, a poft-boy at the Angel at Royfton), ftepped forward, for he took Mr. Sheeppen for a highwayman; when fuddenly recollecting him, for he had known him ever fince he was an under graduate, he faid,

" Good

" Good lack! why, what is the matter with you, Reverend Sir?—Leap over fuch a turnpike-gate as this here?—Why, Lord! it would go nigh to break your neck."

Sheeppen now perceiving Waglock, faid in a faint voice, " Take your money, Mafter Walter, and let me pafs: I have not a moment to lofe." He fpoke in a voice of extreme fenfibility.

The turnpike man would probably have been affected even to tears had he heard him, but he was prevented by the extreme jingling of the Newmarket waggon that moment approaching. Sheeppen ftruck, however, his horfe, and purfued his journey, in a difpofition of mind hard to be defcribed, to-

B 2 wards

wards Enfield;—then gently galloping, and more tardily trotting, through Edmonton, he paffed the ever-memorable fign of the Bell, where he gave a fentimental figh to the gayer adventures of John Gilpin, envying his celebrity, while he regretted the days that were gone, when the involuntary excurfion to Ware of the juftly-celebrated linendraper could enwreathe his cheeks with a fmile.

" It is not fo *now*," faid he: " Love, unhappy love, has obfcured all my profpects, and blighted the bloomy bloffoms of benevolent beatitude. In vain for me now would be all the luxuriant lufcioufnefs of lavifh nature. Though the fun fhould diffufe its moft *fplendid* glories over the *grateful* bofom

bofom of the *humid* earth, and the *moift-eyed* moon fhould melt in her *mellifluous* meridian: though *wild* geefe, or even wild *ducks*, teal, and widgeon, fhould glide glittering over the gay and *gauzy* water, *begemmed* with lilies, and reflecting the weeping willow whifpering over its waving way: though eafterlings, or even coots and dabchicks, fhould fweep its lucid furface with their enamelled pinions; and though dulcet mufic of mountain breezes, and hollow founds of falling cafcades, fhould unite to whifper delicate dreams of dawning delight!—all! all would be in vain!—Even the diftant profpect of Winchmore Hill, hiding its *blue* head in the fevering clouds that float in feathery feftoons—the citizens in their whifkeys—the lower ranks in their plea-

B 3 fure

fure carts — even directors and rich merchants in their handfome coaches, *bounding* and *frifking* along thefe well-kept roads, that lead the amufed eye towards Newington and Kingfland on one fide; on the other, diverging towards Clapton, Homerton, and Hackney: the intermingling notes of woodland melody, from the flower-befprinkled hedge-rows; all prefenting a picture, exquifitely fublime, yet foothe not the fad foul of Solomon Sheeppen! Alas! *he* feels that nothing *can* foothe it, or betray it a moment from the contemplation of the graces of Azemia: fhe has indeed

" Murdered fleep."

Thus faying, he turned his horfe to the left, determining, though he knew not why,

why, to take the Hackney road to London; but when he reached the Mermaid (celebrated in political annals for Middlefex meetings), he felt himfelf fo entirely overcome by a fenfe of his loft happinefs, that he was compelled to enter, and call for a difh of poached eggs.

While he waited for this refrefhment, he took up, in that carelefs way one does at an inn, a newfpaper that lay on the window feat: it was the Sun— a paper remarkable for difinterefted candour and ungarbled fimplicity of narrative, as well as for the elegant purity of its Englifh, and the admirable accuracy of its tranflations from that language become *fo* deteftable from the *exifting circumftances* of the nation

B 4

tion which fpeaks it, that it is *toafted againft* by fome of the moft *manly* and *unblemifhed* characters of *modern old England.*

He gazed moft lackadaifically upon it, " unknowing what he fought," till the poetry, always fo taftefully felected, attracted his attention: that which immediately prefented itfelf was a Sonnet—it was of the melancholy caft—it was pathetic — it was touching—it was appropriate—and it vibrated for a moment on all the ftrings and fources of fympathetic fenfibility, as Mr. Sheeppen read thus:

SONNET

TO DARKNESS.

Oh! Darknefs! hide me with thine ebon ray *,
And let thy brown fhade o'er my bofom drop,
Guard my fad bofom from the torch of day,
And bid thy chills my hurrying pulfes ftop;
While in thy glimmering gloom I gladly wrap
My temples, and attune the foul-fad lay!
Reclining on the meadow's breathing crop
Of bos-befriending † flower-befprinkled hay;

---

* A *ray* of darknefs is a new image; at leaft I recollect only two modern poets who ufe it. It gives me an idea fo perfectly obfcure, that I perfuade myfelf it is what Milton means by darknefs vifible.

† " Bos-befriending." The Italian fcholar will know how to appreciate this expreffive compound epithet. It is hardly neceffary to explain it, even to female readers.

Or 'neath the verdant fhade of cyprefs ftop,
To hear fweet Philomel falute the May.
Come, gentle Darknefs, in thy veil of jet
Enwreathe me, votary of the moift-eyed mufe!
So in thy raven robe I may forget
Pearlina *! and drink deep oblivious dews.

The congeniality of the fentiment re-
conciled our clerical wanderer for once,
to what he had, on fo many occafions,
and particularly in his difputes with
Iphaniffa, defcribed as the fenfelefs
fuavity of fentimental fimplicity, or the
piping plaintivenefs of parading pathos.
Befides, this being a legitimate fonnet,

* Pearlina is a name derived from pearls, appli-
cably applied as a comparative and an emendative
either to the fkin or the teeth of the Fair. The
Italians have feveral names derived from gems; as
Diamantina—Opalina, for a capricious beauty, &c.

and

and upon the Italian model, it was,
he owned, a fhade, a degree better and
more claffical than the poetic baftards
obtruded upon the public tafte, " even
to fatiety." Scarce had he finifhed this
internal critique, when roufing himfelf
from the weak indulgence of the ener-
vating paffion of love, he ate his eggs
with an appetite worthy of a curate who
has ferved five churches; then called
for fome more newfpapers to amufe his
mind from the fad fubjeét of his contemplations, while he digefted them.
All his love-enwoven thoughts, and
even the bright image of Azemia, faded
from his recolleétion as he read the following animated Ode in another of the
conftellation of *Suns* that were brought
to him, and recognized the elegant and
fpirited hand of his long-efteemed

B 6   friend,

friend, and fome time fellow ftudent,
Mr. Paridel Puffwell, now an Under
Secretary of State.

ODE, PANEGYRICAL AND LYRICAL.
TO THE TUNE OF HOSIER'S GHOST.

YE, who places hold, or penfions,
    And as much as ye can get,
Come, and hear the praifing mention
    I fhall make of Mifter Pitt.

All he does is grand and daring,
    All he fays is right and fit;
Never let us then be fparing
    In the praife of Mifter Pitt.

Who, like him, can prate down reafon*,
    Who fo well on taxes hit?
Who deteét a plot of treafon
    Half fo well as Mifter Pitt?

* Not reafon according to the vulgar acceptation
of the word, but falfe reafoning founded on democratic data, which is of courfe no reafon at all. The
word occurs here merely for the *rhythm*.

He's

He's the man to make thefe nations
    Own their millions of debit—
Well incurr'd, as prove orations
    Duly made by Mifter Pitt.

That he's prov'd a great financier,
    'Tis as true as holy writ;
He's a *rate* and *duty fancier*,
    Heaven-born tax-man—Mifter Pitt.

Oppofition try to hurt him,
    Only in his place to fit;
Let *us* not, my friends, defert him,
    Stick ye clofe to Mr. Pitt.

* Certain mechanics fome years ago formed
themfelves into inoffenfive affociations, called Fanciers' clubs: fome were pigeon fanciers, fome felt
emulation about the feathered properties of canary
birds. Happy times! happy men! when *fedition
fancying* was unknown, and no man dreaded the
Mum Aéts. Much are fuch employments to be recommended.——*Note by Mr. Reeve.*

He

He the multitude is humbling,
   Britons that doth well befit:
Swinish crowds, who minds your grumbling?
   Bow the knee to Mifter Pitt.

Tho' abroad our men are dying,
   Why fhould he his projects quit?
What are orphans, widows, crying,
   To our fteady Mifter Pitt?

His is fortitude of mind, Sir:
   That remark do not omit;
He by Heaven was defign'd, Sir,
   To humble England——Glorious Pitt!

You ne'er fee him love a wench, Sir,
   Driving curricle and tit;
He attends the Treafury-bench, Sir,
   Sober, honeft, Mifter Pitt.

What cares he for Fox's raving,
   Or for Sherry's cauftic wit?
Still the *nation* he keep's fhaving,
   Pretty clofe too——Mifter Pitt!

Two

Two thirds of that nation ftarving,
   Now of meat ne'er tafte a bit;
For his friends he ftill is carving,
   This great ftatefman—Mifter Pitt.

Mifter Pitt has elocution
   Greater far than John De Witt*;
Give up then our Conftitution,
   As advifes Mifter Pitt.

He *out-herods* Oppofition,
   Heedlefs he of every fkit†;
For the ftate a rare phyfician,
   To bleed and fweat, is Mifter Pitt.

Britons once were *too* victorious,
   And they love it too much yet;
Humility is far more glorious,
   As 'tis taught by Mifter Pitt.

---

* A Dutchman, whofe intentions were miftaken, and who fuffered unjuftly from popular prejudice.

† A cant word for the paltry effufions of party malice, exhibited at elections, &c.

Lo!

Lo! frefh millions he will raife, Sir,
   Tho' we don't advance a whit;
Give him then imperial praife, Sir,
   Viva viva Mifter Pitt!

Praife him, all ye Treafury Genii!
   That he's wrong, Oh! ne'er admit;
Fear not Fox's honeft keen-eye,
   While ye ftick to Mifter Pitt.

Laud him, Bifhops, Deans, and Prebends,
   All by infpiration lit;
Praife him, blue and crimfon ribands,
   Knights! bepraife your patron Pitt.

Stretch your throats, ye fat Contractors,
   He employs your pot and fpit;
Laugh at impotent detractors,
   Envying you and Mifter Pitt.

New-made Lords fhall join the fong, Sirs,
   Nor will Rofe or Steele forget
To declaim, or right or wrong, Sirs,
   In the praife of Mifter Pitt.

Oh!

Oh! berhyme him, courtly writers!
   Nares and Gifford, men of wit;
Pye, and all ye ode-inditers,
   Strike your lyres to Mifter Pitt!

Learn, each *Jacobin* Reviewer,
   Analytical or Crit.;
Learn from *Britifh* Critics, truer,
   To appreciate Mifter Pitt.

So a chorus fhall arife, Sir,
   That the welkin's brows fhall hit;
Britons' joyous *grateful* cries, Sir,
   Shall be heard thro' earth and fkies, Sir,
And the univerfe furprife, Sir,
   In honour of the heaven-born Pitt*.

Struck with the truth and elevated fentiments of this admirable piece of poetry,

* In fome *low* Jacobin prints, which impertinently copied this *adulatory* ode, another verfe was foifted

in,

18 AZEMIA.

poetry, Mr. Sheeppen (himſelf truly
miniſterial from principle and con-
viction, and having been bred among
the ſuccefsfully *booing* candidates for
mitres, &c.) mounted his horſe, and
animated with the genuine love of the
good things of his country, he determined to wait on Dr. Prettyman, Biſhop
of Lincoln, the very next day, to ſolicit
a living in his gift, not far from Bugden;
once more began galloping; and ſoon,

in, worthy of the vulgar and dirty preſs it iſſued
from—I print it merely to ſhew that it is ſurrepti-
tious—it follows in thoſe diſcreditable papers,
verſe 15.

> Chatham's blood he is belying,
> Teaching Britons to ſubmit;
> But, perhaps the D—— flying
> Might *produce* our Miſter Pitt.

without

AZEMIA. 19

without any farther accident, either from
Cupid or any other markſman, found
himſelf at his lodgings in Suffolk Street,
near the Middleſex Hoſpital.

CHAP.

20 AZEMIA.

CHAP. II.

> Yet when thy *ait* to my enraptur'd eyes,
> In all its blazes of bright glory riſe:
> When with enchanting, novelty you charm,
> With *error* pleaſe us, and with *truth* alarm;
> With awe and wonder I obſerve thy plan,
> And own that Freedom was not made for Man.

" BIRDS and beaſts have all of them
a method *whereby* to comprehend the mutual ſympathy of amorous emotion,
ſomehow—But even kings* and princes
of

* Not all kings and princes; for the kings of
Congo and Dahemy, nations of celebrity in Africa, are
barbarous

AZEMIA. 21

of the human race are obliged to call
in the aſſiſtance of ſcholarſhip in ſome
degree; which is *ſo comical,* in order to
know the tongue, and dialect, and con-
ceits, look you, and notions, and the
like (as my countryman Fluellen would
ſay), of the Fair, whom they would ad-
dreſs, before they can woo her.

" Now it has always ſtruck me, that is
to be lamented, conſidering the admirably brilliant things which our princes
and kings, *in good time,* would ſay
of their own accord in their native
tongues, as our Princes of Wales uſed
to do before the time of Edward the

barbarous enough to elect *their* wives from among
their own ſubjects; whereas, if they ſent for them, as
ours do, beyond ſea, they muſt be ſure to acquire the
ſcholarſhip in queſtion.

Firſt,

firſt, *as I remember.*—And though Balzac terms the ſtudies of foreign languages, the heavy luggage of antiquity, and Locke adviſes us to fill the mind with reflections; yet I ſtill think the art of raiſing aſparagus, as I ſaw it practiſed in 1788*, by one Pierre Le Choux, a gardener near Paſſy, a village in the vicinity of Paris, is preferable to the common mode adopted in our gardens: but Shakeſpeare, when he ſpeaks of Biron, in Love's Labour Loſt, deſcribes a truly faſcinating converſer: and the conſummate idler, who is determined to make too frequent a uſe of the favourite figure Aphæneſis, may amuſe himſelf by figura-

* Juſt on the eve of the dreadful revolution. It is a fact, that not a ſingle ſprout of this uſeful diuretic vegetable has ſince grown in that polluted atmoſphere.

tive

tive expreſſions, as I once ſaw in the *great deſort,* an Arab called " Mahyla Aſhog."

So ſpoke a lady at Mrs. Blandford's *converſazione*—A lady whoſe general knowledge does honour to human nature and to her ſex, and, above all, to the mountains where ſhe was fed by the nine Muſes (whoſe names ſhe would tell in a moment, but which I cannot ſtay to recollect, for my heroine waits for me)—which Muſes undoubtedly nouriſhed her with eclogue-iac, milk mingled with Hyblean honey. So ſpoke ſhe— and the learned, the lively, the acute all liſtened, for *her* converſe was indeed faſcinating; but at the moment ſhe named Mahyla Aſhog, Azemia ſtarted up, caught her hands, and burſt into tears.

" What

" What is the matter, my dear?" ſaid Mrs. Blandford, alarmed.

" Oh! Madam," cried Azemia in *ſpeechleſs* agony—" that Aſhog!—he was a ſervant of my father's, and I have heard my grandmother ſay"——" And what then?" ſaid Mr. Gallſtone, an old gentleman, who had not yet ſpoken — " Come, come, my pretty dear, let us not hear tales of thy grandmother.— Madam," reſumed he, turning ſternly towards Mrs. Blandford, " this young thing's head is filled with agglomerated carnoſities, generated by novels and romances.—Let her get a good cookery book if ſhe *will* read, and learn how to make the moſt proportionate puddings, and to boil them with the moſt attention to the adheſive qualities of the

oviparous

oviparous and lacteal ingredients. " Sir," continued he, addreſſing himſelf to Sir Baptiſt Bamboozle, who ſat by, " Sir, great abilities are not requiſite for cooks, yet man has been juſtly defined as a cooking animal.—I think Mrs. Glaſſe the firſt woman among them; imagination is not required in any part of the culinary ſcience—yet Hannah had great imagination. Sir, when I was at Pembroke College, I taſted a pot of marmalade of her manufacture, and its conſiſtence and ſuavity ſet her very high in my opinion."

To this all the company aſſented; but poor Azemia, who underſtood not one word of it, felt extremely diſtreſſed: ſhe would have given worlds, had ſhe poſſeſſed them, to have ſpoken to Mrs. Albuzzi,

Albuzzi, the lady who had named (as having feen) this Mahyla Afhog. But while Mr. Gallftone ftaid there was no paufe in the converfation—loud, fonorous, and fententious, all he faid was attended to with eagernefs, and affented to with complacency. At length, having a dofe of rhubarb and jalap to take that night, of which he failed not to inform Mrs. Albuzzi, he ftalked away, and the converfation became more general.

While Dr. Profe was telling a very long ftory about Lord and Lady Laudanum, Azemia approached Mrs. Albuzzi, and, trembling as before the very meridian fun of female information, ventured to afk her to give fome farther anecdotes of Afhog.

" Oh,"

" Oh," cried the lady, " all I faid was merely *typical*: in fa&, though I might have feen this perfon, and my imagination is fo lively that I almoft could fancy I did—as Louis the Ninth, you remember, faid to his Almoner— while, in our days, liberty claims a more pofitive fignification, and feems to imply an original grant, a femi-barbarous, femi-focial ftate, like that of the Tartar nations, who live by rapine and fubfift in wandering hordes, " their hand againft every man, and every man's hand againft them," as was *promifed*, you know, my dear, to your progenitor Ifhmael."

Azemia, now totally difcouraged, was going to the other end of the room, leaving this very erudite lady to con-

tinue her admirable, though fomewhat defultory animadverfions in men and things; when fhe was arrefted in her courfe by a group of gentlemen and ladies furrounding a languifhing fair one, who with head reclined, and doing *her poffible* to raife a blufh—fat, or rather leaned, on a fopha in a moft becoming attitude, and looked down, as, in compliance with the entreaties of her friends, fhe repeated flow, yet fweet, in a *penfive* voice, the following

ELEGIAC SONNET

TO A MOPSTICK.

Straight remnant, of the fpiry birchen bough,
    That o'er the ftreamlet wont perchance to quake
Thy many twinkling leaves, and, bending low,
    Beheld thy white rind dancing on the lake—

How doth thy prefent ftate, poor ftick! awake
    My pathos—for, alas! even ftript as thou
May be my beating breaft, if e'er forfake
    Philifto this poor heart; and break his vow.

So mufing on I fare, with many a figh,
    And meditating then on times long paft,
To thee, lorn pole! I look with tearful eye,
    As all befide the floor-foil'd pail thou'rt caft,
And my fad thoughts, while I behold thee twirl'd,
Turn on the twiftings of this troublous world *.

While thefe things were paffing in Margaret - Street, Cavendifh - Square, where Mrs. Blandford had taken a houfe for three months, Mr. Sheeppen little thought how near fhe was to him; but, indeed, had he been aware of it,

* The reader of tafte cannot but recollect the very moral and affecting meditation on a broomftick, which perhaps fuggefted this idea to the *fair author.*

as he was now in search of preferment, he muſt have checked the ebullitions of his paſſion, as Mrs. Albuzzi * would ſay, "*ſomehow;*" for a Clergyman of the Church of England to marry a Mahomedan, would be "*ſo comical,* I think;" for (would ſhe probably add), " cranes and wild geeſe obey a leader, and rejeƈt not ſubordination, which is paid to *him* who has the longeſt genealogy †."

* Let not faſtidious critics objeƈt to this ſecond mention of Mrs. Albuzzi. There is in her manner and her writings a continual corruſcation of catching lights, which irradiate every prominent point of intelleƈt, and ſuddenly enable us to ſeize on a chain, a link, a concatenation of ideas, which we never ſhould perceive if left to ourſelves.

† Vide Britiſh Synonymy, and other admirable works.

CHAP.

CHAP. III.

Laugh then at any but at fools or foes,
Theſe you may anger, but you mend not thoſe:
Laugh at *your friends*; and if your friends are ſore,
So much the better—you may laugh the more.

POPE.

AZEMIA, now every day improving, became infinitely dear to Mrs. Blandford. There was to the obſerving and reflecting mind of that excellent lady ſomething particularly intereſting in marking the development of the human intelleƈt, which, till its ſeventeenth ſummer,

C 4   mer,

mer, had been in a ſtate of infantine ignorance, and on which the light of knowledge had burſt at once.

Inſenſibly the attention ſhewn to her fair protegée induced Mrs. Blandford, though on very different motives from thoſe which had actuated Miſs Ironſide, to conquer that diſlike to public places, and more general ſociety, which had originated in diſappointment and ſorrow. Azemia ſoon became an objeƈt of admiration, as the beautiful Turkiſh girl; and on her account, rather than on that of her own ſuperior intelligence, Mrs. Blandford found her company ſought by almoſt all the literary, and ſome few of the faſhionable world.

Among

Among thoſe who moſt earneſtly ſolicited her acquaintance was Mrs. Quackly, the widow of an eminent phyſician, who lived on a very handſome jointure in a very handſome houſe in Soho Square, where ſhe made a point of receiving all thoſe who were eminent in the world, whether for literary acquirements or any other notoriety. Here the actor had an opportunity of ſtudying his author—and the muſical performer aſſociated with the affluent amateur—the mineralogiſt and the botaniſt might compare their diſcoveries; and the projeƈtor explain his ſchemes for the benefit of the world, to the idle man of faſhion (who was received only becauſe his *name* was flattering to the vanity of Mrs. Quackly), and who cared not if that

C 5   world

world held nothing but the objects immediately gratifying to himself.

Here, with an infinite variety of odd perfonages, were fome who feemed fallen among them, hardly knowing how, by a ftrange perverfenefs of deftiny; and of thefe *Mr. Hillary* was foon diftinguifhed by Mrs. Blandford. His perfon was (though large, and rather what is called heavy) remarkably handfome: he had a countenance fo attractive, and a voice and manner fo fafcinating, to thofe whom he thought it worth his while to pleafe, that it was impoffible to be on one's guard againft the feduction of his converfation. Mrs. Blandford was the firft to be fenfible of its charm: there was a fort of reluctant gaiety about him which feemed to be the effect of philofophy combating dif-
appointment,

appointment, that fuited her feelings particularly; and after meeting him frequently at Mrs. Quackly's, fhe had given him a general invitation to her own houfe, where he often vifited, paying her much of that attention which is at any age flattering, and often fhewing her in confidence fpecimens of thofe poetical talents which began to make fome noife in *the world*.

He was one day prefent when Mrs. Albuzzi was difcourfing on the various meanings of the words folly, fatuity, ideotifm; and faying, that the flexibility of temper, which is ufually called weaknefs, may be driven very eafily to ideotifm: "As," faid the *lively lady*, "I once faw a rich trader prefent a conjuring chemift with a hundred pounds,

only

only for telling him, that if he would grind his cochineal finer, it would go farther; and a lad, paft fifteen years old, perfuaded to *burn his fiddle*, becaufe," faid his playmates, "there is a new difcovery now, that fiddle-afhes fell for a crown an ounce—as there is nothing elfe found out fo certain a cure for the dropfy. We call this," continued fhe, "the power of making *fools* of the *people*; and truly do we call it fo, when mankind are willing to be duped between *delufion* and *collufion* fo far, that they are contented to bury themfelves chin deep in earth . . . . . ."

"Enough, enough, dear Madam," interrupted Mr. Hillary, "you fay very juftly; but never, oh! never confine your remarks in this manner to *retail*

tail inftances, when you may give a wholefale and fublime example of a whole nation. We fee before our eyes a wife and provident people made fuch fools of by this *delufion* and *collufion*, that they have burnt their fiddle, fiddle-ftick, cafe, and all, and are contented to bury themfelves chin deep in debt, from which it is impoffible they can ever emerge—at the fuggeftion of a State Charlatan, who, though regularly bred, and adhering to what is falfely called regular practice, has fo miftaken the *cafe*, that by dabbling in preventives, for which there was no occafion, he has brought on conftipations and ruptures that muft utterly deftroy the conftitution."

The lady's eyes flafhed fire as indignantly fhe looked at her old acquaintance:

ance: fcorn and anger mingled on her
brow, while fhe exclaimed, "And it
is thus, *in good time*, that perfons who
have degraded and debafed themfelves
by their profligacy, and diffipated their
fortunes, have recourfe to *levelling*
fchemes, *I think*; fo that *their* apoftacy
really *frights* one. *Such* a man we all
agree to loath, *I believe*, and, with one
confent, deteft his conduct, while we
abhor his principles."

Mrs. Blandford, who had no idea of
the violent party paffions that boiled in
the bofom of Mrs. Albuzzi, faw her
with fo much diflike thus give way to
them, that fhe was very glad when fhe
rofe and flounced away; while the
gentlemanly calmnefs of Mr. Hillary
interefted her ftill more in his favour.
He

He feemed unwilling to dwell on the
foibles of Mrs. Albuzzi, while he fpoke
highly of her abilities; "which really,"
faid he, "are very uncommon, though
rendered fometimes difadvantageous, and
even ridiculous, by vanity and affectation. But when we remember how *few*
of the people who talk about knowledge
know any thing, let us allow this extraordinary woman to infult us a little with
her violent pretenfions. Think, my
dear Madam, how much more general
her knowledge is, and how much more
cultivation her mind has received, than
the men who pafs for fcholars, or fine
writers. She would make, for example,
much better verfes than the Duke, poor
man! who has been flattered into fancying it is neceffary for Mæcenas to fhew
he can practife the art he patronifes;
and

and fo makes charades, and writes pro-
logues without even the leaft ray of
poetry, and with almoft as little common
fenfe. And then there's Blow-up, the
ci-devant dealer in combuftibles, who
has for thefe twenty or thirty years fatigued the ears of play-going people
with his miferable, vulgar, and fenfelefs
flippancies, by way of epilogues, which
he really thinks are fuperior to thofe of
Garrick and Sheridan, and loves to an-
nounce to the public, as 'coming from
his pen,' at the earneft entreaty of the
author of the comedy. Then there is
poor Jerrygum, a fentimental writer,
who pipes out moft pathetic pieces of
imaginary mifery, and fings them to his
own harp, for all the world like Scriblerus, when he incontinently fnatched
his *little Lyra*, and in extreme difhabille
went

went forth into the balcony to ftill the
indecent contention of two Dames de
la Halle of thofe days, who were fcold-
ing in the ftreet:—only inftead of being
fans culottes, or *fans* any other appen-
dage of a Catholic Chriftian, he fits
with all imaginable pathos in a pair of
inexpreffibles '*couleur de rofe.*' Then
only recollect our acquaintance Fitz-
Jumbling, who has written in verfe a
folio hiftory of Rome, fomething in this
ftyle:

Reader! in this fhort fketch 'twould not befeem us
To fay too much of Romulus or Remus;
Nor to extend the long hiftoric page,
With telling of their birth and parentage;
Or how from wolves they got their education,
Which made them founders of the Roman nation.

" My

" My good friend," exclaimed Mrs. Blandford, " tell me, I befeech you, what could induce you to repeat fuch ftuff?"

" Nay," anfwered Mr. Hillary, " let me rather afk what could induce any man to write fuch."—And again,

" Next let me fing of Numa, called Pompilius;
  Who, like our own good King—was very bilious;
  Yet, we muft own, did not amifs behave—
  His minifter, a lady in a cave,
  Who taught him to arrange his ftate affairs
  Better than thofe that creep up the back * ftairs.

" Then what do you think of the fwarm of ephemeron writers, who, though a

* Vide Junius, &c.

little

little crufhed and chilled by the ridicule that has been thrown on them, now and then venture forth on trembling tender wing—to fing of hermits living in rocks, nobody knows where or why; who tell ftories, and give advice to damfels, coming from nobody knows whence, nobody knows for what; or things beginning with

' All in a caftle on a hill,
    A baron did abide;
  And there, alas! againft her will,
    Young Emma was his bride.'

And fuch ftuff about Sir Ederhead, and Sir Gawine, which they fancy are old Englifh ftories, or at leaft very like them."

" Nay,

" Nay, now," cried Mrs. Blandford, " you are a great deal too fevere. Think, my good friend, that there are innumerable young and fimple folk who love poefy, but who cannot relifh any thing they are obliged to read twice over; and that as there is light fummer-reading for them in the way of novels and tender tales, fo there is a demand for fuch eafily-digefted pieces of poetry as may not overload their delicate intellects. For my part, I own I am ftill child enough, or woman enough if you will, to like fome eafy verfe that fooths my ear, without giving me much trouble to think whether it be fenfe or no —one hears *fo* much very good fenfe that is *fo* tirefome!"

" Mrs.

" Mrs. Albuzzi herfelf," replied Hillary, " could not have given us a more feminine aphorifm, for the fake of being contradicted. I know you have a better tafte. For example, you are delighted with fome of the leffer poems—where he forgets his fatirical talents, and fheaths his claws—of a certain wicked bard yclept Peter Pindar?"

" Undoubtedly."

" The next time I have the honour of waiting on you I will bring you a flight thing of that fort, written by a friend of mine."

" Pray do," faid Mrs. Blandford; " and in the mean time, if incomprehenfible fublimity, and wild extravagance of

paffion,

paffion, be your delight, I am fure you
will be in raptures with an Ode, which
I made Azemia cut out this morning
from a newfpaper. Perhaps you may
know," added fhe, cafting a fly look at
Mr. Hillary, " the fair authorefs, as
well as the dangerous *votary of Apollo*,
to whom it is obliquely addreffed,
though called an

ODE TO SENTIMENT.

What art thou, Sentiment, unkind,
That thus within the ruby-tinctured wave
Of lovers' hearts doft love to lave
Thy fangs, that rend the poet's trembling mind
With rapturous, oh! and danger-breathing thrills?
Dwell'ft thou on rugged rocks, or high-topp'd hills,
Or art thou to the verdant vales confin'd?
I fee thee floating o'er the primrofe ground,
Thy brows with garlands of mimofa bound

And

And myrtle-mingling leaves!
Quivering at thy approach, my tear-ftain'd lids
Are *oped*, as cruel genius bids,
And quick my palpitating bofom heaves!
My fenfes trill!
By mazy rill *,
That feems all form'd of lovers' tears,
The poet of the living lyre appears!
He ftrikes with dulcet hand the chords,
Singing fighs and wounding words;
And featters from his pictur'd harp
Spiry † flames and arrows fharp.
Above, below,
They feem to go;
Where threaded finews feem to ftart,
Charged with each—a lover's heart!

---

* Nothing can be more truly appropriate, or more
affectingly beautiful, than the image of a rivulet of
lovers' tears. How unlike the puerile and profaic
images of moft modern poetry!

† The lovers of poetry will inftantly recollect this
daring imitation, and certainly *improvement* on the
fublimity of Gray.

And

And deeply drink my heart's beft—Oh!
His beamy eyes of fky-ey blue,
Like fapphires in their caves of moffy hue,
Or vernal hyacynths of azure true,
Baptiz'd by Zephyr's hands in flower-extracted dew.
He comes!—Oh! filence with thy ermine glove,
Hufh every found—but that of him I love;
With fandals of the thiftle's * crown,
That feathery floats along the down,
Ye balmy-breathing breezes, move †,

---

* The idea of fandals for filence, formed of the
down of the thiftle, has in it an originality—a tendernefs which I never expect to fee equalled. Cobweb contemplation only emulates this interefting
image. Methinks I fee Contemplation thus veiled,
and the fpiders refpecting her folemn mufing. Then
the tranfition to the luxurious *lyre*, over which *tender wifhes* are *enwreathed with new-blown rofes*,
gives an image to the mind which it parts with reluctantly.

† Ye balmy winds, *beneath my body blow.*

This line is reckoned the moft beautiful of Pope's:
in my opinion this of Matilda's equals it.

Hufh!

Hufh every found but *his voice* whom I love,
And oh! be *cobweb Contemplation* wove
O'er his luxurious lyre,
To notes of foft defire,
That never tire!
Be wreaths of tender thoughts and wandering
          wifhes thrown,
Mix'd with unfaded rofes newly blown!
His trembling ardors he infufes,
Extract from the melting mufes;
And fofter far,
Than from the reed-woven jar
Florentine oil in pearly-dropping oozes.
Oh! his wild notes entrance my foul,
Yet ah! my tranfports to controul,
* Iron Remembrance comes; and copper Care,

And

---

* Iron Remembrance, is fine: it conveys ideas
of " the iron that entereth the foul," but which the
foul devours in filence; while copper *Care* makes us
at once fee fomething avowed and before the world,
as family cares ought to be. Then *fteely* Sorrow fuc-
ceeds; *fharp*, yet falutary, and the epithet is doubly

And Sorrow's fteely form, *upon my foul,*
Roufes the *red Remorfe*;
Ah ! cruel curfe
My paffion fades,
Duty pervades
My every fenfe; my bofom's Lord appears *,
Prudence *nears,*
† Eyes and ears,
Your bofom's Lord obey !
Hufh'd be your murmurs, heart too tender !
Thou to luxuriant Love muft *not* furrender—

---

appropriate : while *red* Remorfe finifhes the beautiful picture. The reader fees at once that Remorfe
could not poffibly be of any other colour.

     * The tender Dame to meet her Lord prepares,
     And Strephon, fighing, flips down the back ftairs.

Thefe lines, perhaps, of Lady Mary Wortley
Montague, might have occurred to the fair au-
thorefs (where fhe fpeaks fo feelingly of her bofom's
Lord), as well as to the *Bard* fhe addreffes.

† There is both moral and pathos in the fair
Lyrift's commanding her *eyes* and *ears* to *obey* in
future *her bofom's Lord*—who, it is to be hoped,
will henceforward " fit lightly on his throne," as
our immortal poet has it.

Let

Let Della Crufca thee feduce no more ;
But to thy conjugal affection true,
Fly for ever from the view
Of eyes, like *fpring-born* Periwinkle's, blue * !
They fade like ftars away ;
While I, deep fighing, fay,
What is pleafure, what is May ?
Love o'er my couch has ftrewn each fweet,
Love has figh'd, trembling at my feet :
He has indeed,
But o'er the mead
He flies ; and Senfibility doth linger †
Only with cruel, quivering finger,
To fay—Henceforth Matilda fhuns
Crufca, and all his wildernefs of funs.

---

     * The *novelty* of comparing blue eyes to the
fpring-born Periwinkle, muft, as well as its fimplicity, charm every true lover of the mufes.

     † Senfibility lingering to direct the poetefs to
fhun the wildernefs of funs, is fingularly happy.
It appears by fome other verfes in the delectable
newfpaper correfpondence, that, in obedience to Senfibility, fhe took fhelter in *Young Grove's fhade.*

D 2   Mrs.

Mrs. Blandford now ceafed reading—
when, to her utter aftonifhment, Mr.
Hillary, without the leaft apparent caufe,
or provocation, took up his hat, and,
glancing his eyes at Azemia with an
expreffion nobody underftood, went
down ftairs, and out of the houfe, without fpeaking one word.

CHAP.

CHAP. III.

The droning fages drop the drowfy ftrain,
Then think, and fpeak, and fpeak and think again.
COWPER.

BEFORE Mrs. Blandford had recovered of her furprife, Dr. Profe entered—though it was rather at an unufual
hour, and all the reft of the company
had departed.

" How are you, my dear Madam?"
faid the Doctor, in his ufual lively way.

" I am pretty well, Doctor, I thank
you," anfwered Mrs. Blandford.

D 3   " And

" And you, my sweet young lady,"
added Dr. Profe, turning to Azemia,
" how do you find yourself this evening ?"

Azemia answered, that she was well.

" We have been a little surprised,
though, my dear Sir," cried Mrs. Blandford.

" Pray, my good Madam, with what ?"
enquired the Doctor.

" With Mr. Hillary," said Mrs.
Blandford.

" He *is* apt," answered the Doctor,
looking significantly under his brows,
" to surprise people."

" So I have often heard; but I cannot say I ever saw any symptoms of it
before."

" Lady Canter knows otherwise,"
said he.

" So

" So I have heard," replied Mrs.
Blandford.

" He is a very odd man," observed
the Doctor.

" But can be very agreeable if he
pleases," answered she.

" I never happened to meet him in
one of his agreeable moods, I suppose,"
said the Doctor.

" Possibly not," said Mrs. Blandford;
" but I assure you, my dear Doctor, if you
had happened to have come in this evening while Mrs. Albuzzi was here . . . . "

" I never do," interrupted the Doctor, " come knowingly to any place
where she is likely to be found."

" Indeed !" exclaimed the lady.

" Indeed," replied the Doctor.

" I wonder at that, though, my good
Sir; for I should imagine, that from

D 4　　　　your

your having visited the same countries,
and being both literary, you must have
a number of ideas in common, that . . ."

" I hope not," answered Doctor
Profe, " for I am sure I should say
nothing about my ideas if they had any
similitude to hers; and besides, my dear
Madam, with such volubility of speech
as that woman has, what chance in the
world should I have of being heard?"

" Of *finishing* a story, if you were
lucky enough to *begin* it, to be sure,
dear Doctor, you would have but little
chance; but then, perhaps . . . . ."

Nobody can tell how long this dialogue, with so sprightly a companion
as the Doctor, might have continued,
if a violent thundering at the door had
not startled them both, and a woman

of

of fashion, but lately known to Mrs.
Blandford, but an old acquaintance of
Dr. Profe's, had not hastened into the
room.

" I am come," said Lady Clara
Clangor, " to take my leave of you,
Mrs. Blandford. And, dear Doctor
Profe, what commands have you for
Italy? I am going directly—How de-
lightful—is it not? There is nothing I
do so abhor, as this England of ours.
Dandy is gone on before us—You know
Dandy—every body knows him. — Is
not he an entertaining creature? We
are to overtake him at Hamburgh—the
dear wretch is to wait for us. Oh! my
God—*il me tarde bien*, not to have set
out already. Well, but, my dear Doctor
Profe, tell me, what do you think of

D 5　　　　public

public affairs? Do you know, some horrid fellows have been telling me that the odious filthy wretches will get the better at laſt!—Oh! my God, if they ſhould—but 'tis impoſſible.—What ſhall *we* be about if they do?—Oh! my good Profe, how *could* you ever ſpeak in their favour? — Do you know, it was vaſtly ridiculous; and you have no idea how every creature, whoſe opinion is worth having, hates a demmy, as we call them. But tell me, Doctor, what do you think of things?"

"My dear Lady Clara," began the Doctor (ſlowly and ſolemnly he ſpoke), "my dear Lady, there are people whom people of rank love to have conſtantly with them, for the purpoſe of applauding whatever they do or ſay; whoſe buſineſs it is to prevent diſagreeable truths

truths from reaching the ears of their patrons, and contribute to make them as vain, weak, ignorant, and capricious, as they themſelves are abject, ſelfiſh, and paraſitical. — Now, my excellent lady, you muſt allow . . . . . ."

"Oh! my God, Doctor!" exclaimed the Lady, "I will allow any thing upon earth rather than that you ſhould make me a long ſpeech. I dare ſay your opinions are delightful, only that it will take ſo much time to hear them, that it is quite impoſſible for me to ſtay—for I am going to Lady Mary Macmidling's aſſembly, and from thence to the Ducheſs's—and then Scarabée and Squirl, and Jack Swindurn, go home to ſupper with me.— By the bye, Jack is at this moment waiting for me in the coach; and ſo, my dear Doctor, to ſhew you I don't mean

to ſavage you, and how vaſtly delightful I think your converſation, I will take you with me if you are going towards St. James's."

The Doctor, whether in hopes of obtaining an opportunity of concluding the oration, or for ſome other reaſon, accepted this gracious invitation; and Azemia was delighted to find herſelf quietly at ſupper with her benefactreſs.

"Well, my love," ſaid Mrs. Blandford, "and what do you think of our viſitors of this evening?"

"Ah, Madam!" replied Azemia, timidly, "I am but a very incompetent judge—but to be ſure Doctor Profe . . ."

"Is not amuſing, I allow—but I aſſure you he is one of the firſt men we have

have as to information. Then there was, you know, Mrs. Chiverly, who is accounted ſo accompliſhed a woman, and is ſo well connected; and has a ſort of aſſociation of people of talents about her, in what ſhe calls 'a little quiet way.'—I obſerved ſhe talked to you ſome time."

"Yes," anſwered Azemia, "ſhe told me a vaſt deal about her family connections; and how Siſter Such-a-one lived at a great caſtle in Yorkſhire, and Siſter Such-a-one was married to Sir Peter Pliable, who had a place at court; and ſhe aſked me if I did not think England a great deal better than my own country. I told her no; that I diſliked it very much, for, except you, and one or two other ladies, the women here

here did nothing but find fault with one another, and tear each other's characters to pieces; whereas in my native country they defired only to amufe each other, and were happy to fit and embroider, or fing together. She feemed to fmile at my fimplicity and ignorance, and told me it was altogether unbecoming in a Turk, but that fhe hoped I was by this time a Chriftian, and I fhould foon learn better. She added, that when once it was afcertained to her (which fhe had yet no opportunity of afking you), that I was baptized, fhe would fubfcribe half-a-guinea with all her heart; and fo would Sifter Such-a-one, and Sifter Such-a-one, and Mrs. Such-a-one, and dear good Mrs. Quibus, the excellent patronefs of all that

that was good and gentle—all, fhe faid, would fubfcribe to the book fhe fhould open for me."

" To the book!" exclaimed Mrs. Blandford, " what could fhe poffibly mean?"

" Indeed," replied Azemia, " that is more than I know. I did not underftand all fhe faid to me—in truth, but very little of it; but I thought fhe feemed to intend me fome kindnefs that fhe fuppofed I wanted."

" You fhall never want any thing, my dear Azemia," cried Mrs. Blandford, " while I live; and Mrs. Chiverly may fpare herfelf the parade of exercifing benevolence, which is never likely to be put to the trial." She then tenderly embraced her beautiful ward, and wiped away the tears that were in her eyes,

eyes, thinking it ufelefs to mortify the unconfcious girl, by telling her that Mrs. Chiverly was one of thofe perfons at once oftentatious and narrow-minded, who love money fo extremely, that they dare not ufe it, and yet are fond of appearing full of fenfibility and charity towards thofe whom they degrade under pretence of affifting, by reprefenting them as objects of benevolence among their great friends. Of fuch there are numbers to be met with, who gratify two paltry paffions at once, and, rifing higher in their own eftimation by the compact, affure themfelves they are the very beft people in the world, and quite *amiable.*

CHAP. IV.

Like *as* they were defign'd to eat, to drink,
To talk, and (every now and then) to *think.*
CHURCHILL.

" MASTER!" cried Bat Bowling to Charles Arnold, as they *wound* down Caftle-rigg, " I am fure I faw two Excifemen of Whitehaven among the trees there; they know, an pleafe your honour, that we are comed from fea, and I warrant they will ftop and fearch us; what fhall I do with the Ingine fchawl, and the two Barcelona handkerchiefs?

chiefs? I lay my life we fhall be put into limbo, and made no more account on than a mufty bifcuit."

The moon (which, in all the moft celebrated novels lately publifhed, fhines every night in the moft accommodating manner in the world) had given this alarming information to honeft Bat, Charles Arnold's fea fervant, while he himfelf had long been fixed in contemplation of that beautiful planet, as it hung in filver radiance over the tall fells among which he was wandering.

"Oh!" beauteous Azemia," cried he, fighing, " where art thou? what has been thy deftiny durin; the almoft twelve months of our cruel feparation!"

Thus

Thus loft in a reverie, Bat was under the neceffity of fpeaking again.— " Prithee, mafter," cried he, "don't get into them there brown ftudies. I tell you we be fcented by a couple of damned rafcally Excifemen, or Cuftomhoufe Officers, or fuch like; and the upfhot will be fome hell of a job or another."

Charles Arnold rode on.

The folemn fcene through which he was travelling reminded him forcibly of thofe where he had paffed the laft three months—the image of Azemia following him whitherfoever he went.

" It was thus," faid he, ftill regardlefs of his fervant, who every now and then

then ventured an admonitory fentence; " it was thus that by thy light, fweet and mild planet, I found under thy quiet beams, among the rocks of Seldzfberg, a fhort refpite from what are called my duties.—Yes! wild northern region, where I have in a boat paffed whole nights in gliding through your labyrinth of rocks—I have envied the fifher, who earns his fubfiftence among them; and J have thought, vain thought! which it will never be in my power to realize, how happy I fhould be in one of the boarded huts that are perched on thofe fantaftic fummits, if Azemia, my charming Azemia, was within it. There! there! would be *my* Paradife!

" Quiet retreats of uncultivated nature, how diftinctly ye return upon my memory!

mory! Would I could retire for ever to your wild folitudes from fcenes of dirt and darknefs—of obfcenity and ignorance, in which I now pafs the greateft part of my time, for no reafon that can poffibly be given, unlefs it be to enforce, as a mere machine, the operation of the

Ratio ultima Regum;

which decides that men are animals, born only to contrive how to annoy and deftroy each other. How can any thinking being believe it? Yet how many other things do we profefs to believe as abfurd; which fo far from believing, we never think about at all! I remember that, till lately, I fhould have ftared at any man, perhaps have infulted him, who had told me that I was a miferable filly

filly fellow to allow myfelf to be fhut up in a floating dungeon, fometimes under the command of a capricious or unfeeling man, for lefs money than I could earn with the faw or the fpade, while breathing the frefh air of Heaven, and gazing on the green bofom of the earth :—and yet fuch is the life to which my mother, I thank her, has condemned me; and which I have been taught to think an honourable profeffion, and one that will produce a great quantity of glory to me."

" An pleafe your honour," faid Bat, who could not get the Cuftom-houfe Officers out of his head; " an pleafe your honour, I've a heard how this here Gert Britton of ourn is the freeeft of all the countries upon yearth, and that there is no let or hindrunce to a man's doing as he wull in no fhape whatever.—Now, thinks

thinks I, fometimes to myfelf, why how can that be — when there's ever fo much money taken from a man, whether he likes or no; and then if he does but go for to buy ever fo little a matter of counterband goods, whip! he's in prifon! Now, for my part, I can't think, as I fays to myfelf, where'd be the harm of our trading with folks of other nations, without all that there. I can't fay as I likes your forrinners—I knows one Eng-lifhman, with beef and pudding in his belly, as the fong fays, can beat ten Frenchmen: and I dares for to fay they always will on the feas, which is our own eilemint all the world over. But then when it pleafes his Majefty, God blefs him, to give us peace, why I fees no why or wherefore, for not enjoying all the good things of both countries, and

and all countries beyond fea; for if they want what we can fpare, why not fend it them, and take in change what they can fpare, and we want, without all this racket of counterband and duties? Now that's my notion of trade, and I do think it would be better.—What cheap brandy we fhould have in that cafe!"

" Your laft argument is a convincing one," replied Charles Arnold, laughing, and roufed from his reverie by this cha-racteriftic remark of his man's; " and in general, friend Bat, thy notions are not bad ones. But, if there were no duties there would be no revenue to pay fol-diers, and fuch honeft fellows as we are, who you muft allow *do* alfo deferve to be paid, becaufe foldiers only are not fufficient to defend an ifland, as this is where we live."

" Aye,

" Aye, aye, mafter, that's as true as the day. Tis *we* that are all in all to old England; and I'll be bould for to fay, that there's ne'r a true-born Englifhman, gentle or fimple, that would not be free to pay us with a good will."

" I believe it, indeed, my good fel-low; and therefore you muft not mur-mur, you know, at duties, and cuftoms, and taxes, that are applied to fo excel-len a purpofe."

" Aye, Sir; but I have heard tell as how there be a power of people, who are neither foldiers nor failors, nor does no yearthly thing for their pay, but ride about in coaches, and dreft in gold-laced cloaths, and have defperate fine houfes, and all manner of good things to eat and drink; and thefe people are paid, they fay, for all this, by the hard labour of poor folks that all helps to contribute rates and taxes; and at the fame time they defpifes them, and tramples upon them, and calls 'em fwine and hogs, and the like of that. Now to be fure, your honour, if fo be as that *is* the cafe, why one can't but think it a little hardifh, that fome folks fhould have a great deal of money paid um for doing nothing but living on the fruits of the yearth, while others agin fhould work early and late to raife thofe very fruits of the yearth, and yet not be allowed enough to keep body and foul together. I got a book put into my hand t'other day, which was wrot, I believe, by fome Juftis of Peace up at London;

and

and it faid, Sir, as how poor folks had no bifnefs to think; that it was a bad thing, and ferved only to make them lofe their time: but I don't underftand that—What! has not a poor man got a foul as well as a rich man?—I am fure our Chaplain have told me he have often and often. Well—and if he *has* a foul, what is a foul but what one thinks with? And if another, becaufe he is rich, and I am poor, goes for to take away my power of thinking, why, what is it but making me not a man any longer, but a brute, like unto his horfe, and his dog, only for the fake of ufing me worfe than he would ufe them? for, to fpeak the truth, the horfes and the dogs of lords and gentry are a great deal better off than their poor neighbours very often."

E 2   " I did

" I did not think, Bat," faid Arnold, " that you had been fo able a metaphyfician."

" No, Sir," replied Bat, with great fimplicity, " I don't pretend for to be able to be a phyfician—but I can fee plain enough, that the reafon why that there Juftis of Peace, or placeman, up at London, as wrote them there books, would not have poor folks *think*:—it's for fear they fhould find out there's no occafion for fuch folks as them; and befides, Sir, let poor folks think ever fo much, they would not be difcontented if they had enough to have comfortable cloathing and wholefome food, and a houfe over their heads; for, if they thought ever fo long, they would know that it's quite an unpoffible thing for all men to

be

be rich and high alike; but fome muft work more than others, and fome muft be learned men to govern the others, and direct their work for the beft, but not make them flaves; and, therefore, the poor would not be angry at not being rich, fince it has pleafed God to make different degrees of every thing; only the poor that work for thofe that have no need to work for themfelves, ought to have the common comforts of life, which to be fure, Sir, a poor man cannot get now if he tries ever fo."

" You fpeak like an oracle, Bat; and if I were not as tired as I am I would anfwer you, and give you my notion of the fubjects you have been talking of— though, I affure you, we who by courtefy are called *gentlemen* are very often fo

E 3   brought

brought up, that the *quality we think with* is no more exercifed than that of thofe honeſt fellows, who are never taught any thing but that they muſt labour for a mere exiſtence. But I'm glad you have got over your fear of Cuſtom-houfe Officers. And now, Bat, do *you* think as hard as you can on your fide, and till we get to the next town, which cannot be far off, I believe, and I will think on mine; and perhaps between us both we may make fome notable difcoveries in politics or philofophy."

" Ah! Sir, Sir," exclaimed Bat, fhaking his head, " I knows what you ſtodies—I'm much out in my reckoning if you ben't a thinking of your fweetheart more than of talking politics—or about Philofophers—and fuch; but,

but, howfumdever, Sir, fince you defire me to hold my tongue, to be fure I knows my duty better than to interrupt you."

The maſter and man were ſtill among the fells; the moon had now funk behind the moſt diſtant of their fummits, but her declining light ſtill irradiated the deep blue expanfe, and had given place to myriads of ſtars, on which the eyes of Arnold were fixed.—The arch of indiſtinĉt brilliance, called the milky way, feemed juſt above his head.—" What art thou," faid he, " thou beauteous path of congregated fires, about which fo many fables have been imagined?—What is thy diſtance from this filly world of ours, where we ridiculoufly think of fo much confe-

quence our paltry pleafures and puerile pains—this very filly world, which is perhaps of no more relative weight in the great fcheme of the univerfe than one of your fmalleſt fpangles of ethereal fire?—And you, ye planets, is this fomething denominated a foul, which my uninformed companion has juſt called the power of thinking, attached to this frail feeble body? or has it a diſtinĉt exiſtence, which, when the miferable turmoil of this ant-hill I now creep upon ſhall be over, will poſſefs feparate confcioufnefs, and be in a ſtate to inveſtigate your orbs, and range among fyſtems, of which the wifeſt of us now underſtand nothing?"

Thus fallen from his aërial journey in that confeſſion we are all compelled

to make, that we cannot long keep above the atmofphere of this our planet, Arnold returned to the contemplation of what was to him the *moſt celeſtial* among its earthly inhabitants, Azemia.

CHAP. V.

═══════

Soft tremors, trembling terrors, cyprefs glooms,
Lovers and fpectres wandering in the tombs!

═══════

WHILE Charles Arnold purfues his journey towards London—

Chewing the cud of fweet and bitter fancy,

and encouraging that hope which ftill revives in the youthful bofom, however chilled by fear, or repreffed by dif-appointment, we will *almoft*, in the words of a noble and elegant fenti-mental

mental authorefs *, relate (though it will form a comparifon, perhaps, but little to our advantage, when contrafted with our own plain and homely ftyle) an in-cident that happened to Azemia, who was now once more with her bene-factrefs in the country, and accom-panying her on a vifit. We are happy that the facts are fo well affi-milated, that we can avail ourfelves of words, fo much more *elegant* than any *we* could have chofen in the de-fcriptive and pathetic united. We muft premife, however, that a young Irifh nobleman had been *very particular* to-wards our beauteous heroine for fome days; and Azemia, who had found the image of Charles Arnold return upon her memory with new attractions among

* The elegant Lady H....

E 6   thefe

thefe fweet folitudes, was uneafy at his notice, and very glad when fhe heard one evening that he was to go the next day. The next day, as he did not ap-pear, fhe concluded he *was* gone, and *tranquillized* her fpirits about it till to-wards evening, when—Lord Scud-about had not been named—a circum-ftance occurred that confirmed Azemia in her hopes that he was no longer a gueft at Luxmore Caftle. This flattering conjecture, in fome meafure, reftored her tranquillity: they were in the li-brary, and a falver of macaroons, queen cakes, and bifcuits, with orgeat and lemonade, was brought round, and found very acceptable. Lady Dorothy Dawdle began to amufe herfelf by looking over fome capital caricatures, though her ladyfhip was rather furprifed to

to find fome of them in fuch a place, becaufe they were exaggerated reprefen-tations of fome very great perfonages, in fituations highly derogatory to their exalted dignity and *ferene* confequence. Mrs. Blandford was examining a whole-length picture of the *late* Emprefs *of all* the Ruffias, which covered one fide of the room : and Azemia, having nothing to do, looked *fearfully* around it; for fhe conceited that Lord Scudabout, who (unlike the generality of his coun-trymen) was of diminutive ftature, might be hid in one of the lower receffes of the mahogany bookcafes, and jump out upon her all of a fudden: however, *difcovering* no traces of him, fhe re-joiced at *difcerning* none, and, advancing towards a glafs door, which was thrown open to admit the fragrance of various fweet

fweet flowers that in luxuriant perfume
furrounded it, fhe was ftrongly tempted
to ftray upon the *verdant* lawn. All was
calm—the breezy air breathed odoriferous gales:—her feet with involuntary
motion led her to a walk, where, as
much as fhe had dared, fhe had thought
of Charles Arnold. The *meeting* beech
formed a canopy above, the *blufhing*,
rofe, and the *twining** woodbine, in wild
profufion, bent their blooming branches
to fcatter beneath her fteps their fuave
fcents. Juft as fhe entered the grove
fhe caft her fine eyes towards the apartment once inhabited by the young

* We need not point out to the tender fufceptibility
of refined *elegance*, how this *meeting*, *blufhing*, and
twining fcene is calculated to foften the heart of a
juvenile female, indulging reveries on the dear youth
of her bofom.

nobleman

nobleman in queftion: the pink lute-
ftring curtains waved through the open
window.—Azemia was a little alarmed,
but fhe proceeded.

The plaintive *Philomela** had com-
menced her evening melody in dulcet
trills.—With flow and penfive air the
beauteous Azemia moved: each feat,
each fhrub, recalled fome dear idea to
her mind; for here glowed the ama-
ranthus; there was reclined the " love
lies a-bleeding," which particularly af-
feted her; and here blufhed the *gay*

* Philomela, always fo much in requeft with the
poets, has lately been preffed into the fervice of the
Novelift to *a degree*; certainly beyond what the facts
of natural hiftory authorife: but when the fun and
moon are alfo in continual requifition, fhall not a
bird obey the witchery?

carnation,

carnation, the ruby-tintured pink, and
the fomniferous poppy, emulative of the
evening fky, and facred to the dull God
of dormitorial and fedative happinefs.

Wrapt in this fad but foothing contemplation, as in a peliffe, fhe advanced
till it grew late, and a wheelbarrow, left
there by the careleffnefs of the under
gardener, obftruted an opening path
apparently defigned to lead to fome
place (as moft paths do, except in novels); its winding turns ferpentined im-
perceptibly up an eafy afcent: fhe was
roufed from her reverie by finding herfelf at the top of the hill, where, contrary to all expetation, fhe beheld a
maufoleum of *black* marble, which put
her extremely in mind of a mofque or a
minaret in her own country. (The ideas
of

of thefe two things were not very diftint
in her mind.) She did not greatly enjoy the difcovery, for it was now almoft
dark; and though the moon could not
choofe but rife on one fide, the fun had
entirely funk on the other.

Azemia, however, entered the gloomy
building—fhe knew not why—(We
know not neither, unlefs, becaufe fhe
was guided by fome *invifible impulfe*;
and becaufe it is now neceffary in novels for all the heroines to go into
black marble maufoleums and grey-
ftone ruins whenever they meet with
them.)—However, Azemia approached;
—the door ftood a-jar: the gloom of
the furrounding evergreens, particularly the cypreffes, caft a folemn fhade
upon the occafion; and an owl from a
neighbouring

neighbouring ivy bufh hooted audibly, and cried, " Tee-whit!" which Azemia had heard from Mrs. Blandford's old houfekeeper was always a bad fign. She ftopped—fhe fhuddered—fhe was infpired with a fecret terror!—fhe felt herfelf irrefiftibly impelled as by an invifible hand to penetrate this drear abode. The noife fhe made in entering alarmed her: the door grated on its rufty hinges; the owl again cried, "Tee-whit!"—and the wind howl'd—All ferved to increafe thefe fepulchral horrors of this lugubrious refidence of mouldering-mortality.

Azemia trembled, as fearfully, fhe beheld the dome; for the moon now opportunely coming from behind a cloud, threw a feeble light through the long

long cafements of painted glafs. Azemia fancied herfelf Juliet in the vault of the Capulets—(for, unlike other foreigners, fhe underftood Shakefpeare to a miracle)—and again fhe fhuddered: a door was half open on the right hand; fhe pufhed it gently, and found it led from the maufoleum into the chapel. She entered the aifle—fomething white appeared at the farther end; the rays of the moon fell directly upon it, and it feemed to move.—Suddenly the great bell in the turret tolled, and Azemia was overcome with horrible dread, and unable to retreat. The tolling ceafed, but fhe heard the tread of feet: fhe became immovable; fhe uttered a faint fcream—a *form* appeared.—*It* perceived her fears—*it* flew to fupport her in *its* arms—it funk

funk with her on the black marble pavement (on which her *white* drapery gracefully floated); and nobody can tell how this terrific fcene might have ended, if Mrs. Blandford, alarmed at the abfence of Azemia, had not moft fortunately arrived at that moment in fearch of her, attended by a footman with a candle and lantern, who found Lord Scudabout fupporting Azemia, yet laughing exceffively at the fear he had put her into. Mrs. Blandford feverely reproving him, he ran to the ftables, mounted his horfe, and galloped back to his companions at Lord Oddberry's, from whom he had fuddenly efcaped to execute this frolic, as if he had forefeen Azemia's evening excurfion.

Mrs. Blandford foon foothed to peace the agitated bofom of her fair ward; and Lady Dorothy Dawdle, who prefided as miftrefs of this hofpitable manfion, declared that Lord Scudabout fhould never enter it again, and that fhe would the next day go with her ponies to the Marchionefs, his mother, who lived about ten miles off, and complain of the indecorous behaviour he had been guilty of.

CHAP. VI.

―――

" Why do the Swinish Multitude repine?"
Quoth fat, 'Squire Gobble, in full swill and cram,
" Rascals!—do they expect like us to dine?
" As to their wanting, that is all a sham."—
From the Dundas MS. collection.

―――

MRS. Blandford, with her fair *protegée*, now went on a short visit to the house of Lady Dorothy Dawdle's son by her first husband.

It is necessary for *us* to give an account of this gentleman and lady.

Colonel

Colonel Brusque, then, born of a military family, and inheriting a handsome fortune, had been brought up to serve (as they call it) his country; that is, he had entered at thirteen into the Guards, and had a very military air, a fine round red chubby face, a decisive manner, a great contempt for the people, and a firm persuasion that a gentleman was an animal, whose highest pretensions ought to be to strut about in a red coat, and enforce, if it were necessary, the orders of his superiors. He seldom read any thing but the Army List, or the Court Calendar, and internally had a great contempt for every sort of knowledge, which was not comprised in those two useful publications. But his wife and her mother, Lady Dorothy, were of the order of women of science;

ence; and Colonel Brusque, who was glad of every opportunity of relieving the insipidity of living alone with the one, and whose interest made it requisite for him to please the other, had given into their system of collecting occasionally all sorts of people; and as they gave excellent dinners, and lived at an easy distance from town, it is inconceivable what a variety of persons might be found at their villa, between Easter and Whitsuntide especially.— Here then various acquisitions of taste and information might be made: here every branch of knowledge was constantly progressive, among professors or proficients in every art or science that gives convenience or lends lustre to social life.—Here (to arrange them with due accuracy) were to be seen,

Aëronauts

Aëronauts and Architects, Actors and Archbishops, Alarmists and Auctioneers, Attorneys; Astronomers and Archdeacons, Accoucheurs and Aides-des-Camp, Antiquarians, and Associators and Agents.

Borough-jobbers, Bishops and Biographers; Booksellers, Botanists, Baronets, and Blacklegs; Barons, Brewers, Bankers, and Butts*.

Critics, Counts, and Calculators; Chymists, Counsellors, Captains (led) and Contractors; Curates (rarely) Clerks, Canal-makers and Ciceroni, Convey-

* A Butt is one of the most necessary animals in a great house. The same useful being, under other names, may be found in other parts of this list.

ancers, Cabinet-makers and Cabinet-ministers.

Divines (dignified), Doctors, Demonstrators, Dukes, Duchesses, and Dancing-masters, (but no Democrats.)

Engineers, Earls, Essayists, Election-men and Electors, Ensigns, Encyclopedists, Enclosure-schemers, Electricians, Esquires.

Financiers, Flower-fanciers, Fellows of the Royal and Antiquarian Societies, Fidlers, Flute-players and Faro-players.

Germans, Geographers, Genealogists, Graziers, Gamesters, Generals, Gazette-writers, and Grooms of the Stole; Gardeners and Guinea-traders, Gaugers

Gaugers and Gunpowder-makers, Heralds, Housebuilders and Histrionic Heroes, Historians, and Hautbois-players and Harpers.

Jews, Jewellers, Improvers, Italians, Jerkers*, Jobbers, and Informers.

Knights of the Garter, Bath, Thistle, and St. Patrick; Knights Banneret, Naval and Civil; and Clerks of the Kitchen and King's Friends.

Lawyers, Loungers, Ladies, Laureats, Liverymen, and Lord Lieutenants and Loan-jobbers.

* A Jerker is something under Government; probably a very *useful* personage with a very large salary.

F 2   Musicians,

Musicians, Magnetisers, Match-makers, Middlesex Justices, Maroon-hunters, and Marquisses; Metaphysicians, Methodists, and Mineralogists; Majors, and Maids of Honour.

Nabobs, News-writers, Novel-makers, Nova-Scotia Baronets, and Necessary Women.

Orthographers, Officers, Opticians, Optimists, and Old Women.

Pickle-sellers, Philosophers, Pensioners, Pursuers of the Picturesque, Players, Priests, Peers, Parasites, Party-pamphleteers, Provosts, Principals, Picture-dealers, Projectors, Physicians, Purveyors, and Poets!

Quacks and Quietists.

Reviewers,

Reviewers, *Rat-catchers*, Remembrancers, Recorders, Rhetoriticians, Raja-hunters, and Reevites and Runners (to the Treasury.)

Spies, Solicitors, Salesmen, Statesmen, Secretaries, Serjeants at Law, and Stock-brokers.

Troubadours*, Thunder-makers, Tourists, Theologists, Trinitarians, and Templars and Toad-eaters.

* Troubadours, Wandering Bards, who, in the days of Chivalry, wandered from castle to castle, and were sumptuously entertained, while they repaid their good cheer by entertaining the Lord and his guests with songs and *stories*. Something of the same sort may be perceived now in the retainers of some great houses.

F 3   Under-

Underwriters, Undertakers*, Un-
derftrappers, and Under-graduates.

Vifcounts, Viol-de-Gambo Perform-
ers, Verdurers, Vintners.

Waiters, Wits, Wanderers, Won-
derers, Word-catchers, &c. &c. &c.

To defcribe half the accumulated
talent that was every day collected in
revolving groups compofed of characters fo various, and generally fo
ufeful, would be difficult; I feel, indeed, that it would exceed my powers,

* Not buryers of the dead : the gentlemen here
meant are defcribed in Comedies of about feventy
years ago.

even

even though I fhould have the refolution to extend this, my firft attempt, till
it fwelled into five very large volumes;
and were I fure that, when I had done,
my gentle readers would have the refolution to read them all : I will confine
myfelf, therefore, to a dialogue or two
explanatory and illuftrative.

The Lady of Colonel Brufque was
not only a perfonage of high mental
pretenfions, but alfo of very illuftrious
rank; and fhe never feemed entirely
able to forget that Lady Arfinoe Arrogant had married a Commoner, though
he was a man of family not very much
inferior to her own. The Arrogant
blood, however, (in fpite of the elegant
refinement of her mind, and a *tint* of

F 4.　　Metho-

Methodifm, which teaches perfect humility) continually reminded her, at
the head of this magnificent and well-
furnifhed table, that Lady Arfinoe was
deplacée.

One day (to ufe the ftyle, brief
and fimple, of an admirable novelift,
whom I am proud to imitate), the following converfation took place at it :

The company were Colonel and
Lady Arfinoe Brufque, Lord and Lady
Limberham, Sir Frederick Fanfaron,
Doctor Didapper, a Divine; Mr. Climbup, a young man of great promife in
the Treafury ; Sir Marmaduke Manchet,
formerly a Paftry-cook in the city, remarkable for the moft excellents puffs,
but

but lately knighted on having carried
up an addrefs in favour of this neceffary
and glorious war; Mr. Muftyflour, a
Commiffary of Stores, who had acquired
a princely fortune in its courfe; together with fome men of inferior note :
Lady Dorothy Dawdle and feveral other
ladies, among whom were Mrs. Blandford and Azemia.

Politics are a difagreeable fubject,
only when they may occafion difcuffions
wherein inferior people and *vulgars*,
who may happen to be admitted to the
tables of the Great, may raife the indignation of " *les Gens comme il faut*,"
by hazarding their abfurd and ill-found-
ed notions. At this table it was accounted certain that every body thought

F 5　　alike,

alike, and that all would join in the juſt and elaborate panegyric which Dr. Didapper began in favour of our heaven born Miniſter; who, as he praiſed the turtle, had not only, he ſaid, by wiſe and vigorous meaſures, imported a more conſiderable quantity of that admirable oviparous *Amphiſbea* than at any former period, but had exported a number of nefarious villains to cultivate the European arts in the Southern hemiſphere, and learn to hunt kangaroos, than any former Premier had ever done. He added, that probably the kangaroo itſelf might ſoon become an article of Britiſh luxury.

" Your obſervation is juſt, Sir," ſaid an eloquent Member of the Iriſh Houſe of

of Commons; " and I am free to confeſs, that, whether I look forward to the paſt, or turn my eyes back on the future, I am utterly loſt in admiration at the magnitude of the indeſcribable genius of this great Premier. He embraces, Sir, with a keenneſs of arm, and a ſtrength of eye that is every way wonderful, a reach of idea beyond the optics of vulgar nerves; and 'tis impoſſible to forbear to obſerve, that, while he diſcourages all trifling and inſignificant levelling, he is himſelf a leveller upon a moſt grand ſcale, for he makes the rich poor; and though indeed I have not heard of his making many poor rich, yet, ſomehow or other, I am perſuaded in my own mind, as I will be glad to explain . . . . . "

F 6 " My

" My dear Mr. *Fitz-Solanum**," ſaid Colonel Bruſque, " your faculties of ratiocination are admirable; but allow me, on the firſt bluſh of the buſineſs, to remark that . . . . . Lady Limberham, you have not taſted this fricandeau— give me leave to recommend it to your Ladyſhip; I aſſure you it is made after a receipt I got at Vienna."

" Colonel!" cried Sir Marmaduke Manchet, who always ſeemed to evade culinary converſation; " Colonel! where do you get your Madeira?—I think it

* Not Solomon, as ſome, through error, might read. Solanum is the Night-ſhade—the Potatoe is of this genus; and Mr. Fitz-Solanum might probably *ſpring* from ſome Mileſian family of great antiquity, cultivators of that admirable and nutritive vegetable.

admirable;

admirable; perhaps the very beſt I have taſted ſince the mayoralty of my friend Sir Anthony Armadillo, who, you know, traded largely to the Weſt Indies, and always ſent *his* Madeira there twice."

"' Faith," cried Mr. *Fitz-Solanum*, " I ſeldom get any good Madeira. I had ſome, it is true, about ſix months ago—the very beſt I ever drank; but the ſhip it was in was taken by a curſed Republican privateer—the devil fetch thoſe free-booting ſons of b——s!"

" As to what you ſay in regard to the poor," ſaid Mr. Climbup to Mrs. Blandford, who had been talking to him in a low voice, " really, Madam, it ſeems to me as if your exceſſive and acute ſenſibility, senfibility, which, pardon me, the ladies are a *leetle* too apt to indulge, has occafioned you to fee this matter through a falfe medium: for, after all, now, really—what have thefe eternal grumblers to complain of?"

" Of exceffive poverty, Sir."

" My dear, dear Mrs. Blandford— the poverty of the poor!—to hear a woman of underftanding talk fo! Good Madam, how can you feparate a poor man from his poverty? Thefe hewers of wood, and drawers of water, would you have them wear filk and velvet, or drink Champaigne and Madeira?"

" By no means," replied Mrs. Blandford, mildly; " but I would have the labourer,

bourer, as was the cafe fince I was old enough to make obfervations, able to carry fome food befides bread into the field where he toils all day, which, I believe, is feldom or never the cafe now. I am told, Sir, that the poor man, in his daily work, is barely fupplied with bread; his family often compelled to live on bran mixed up with greafe, and their drink only water. Now, as you, and every advocate for the prefent order of things and the worthy gentlemen who order them, have invariably perfifted in afferting that England never was fo profperous as at this moment, notwith-ftanding the juft and neceffary war, I wifh to have it explained to *me* (who, as a woman, cannot be fuppofed, you know, to be able deeply to make thefe enquiries), how it happens, that while the

the rich are better, the poor are worfe off than they were twenty years fince? and why, if our trade and manufactures are fo flourifhing, and our refources ftill fo immenfe, it happens, that our gazettes are full of bankrupts, our jails full of debtors; that our feelings are continually fhocked by public executions, and that our poor are literally perifhing with hunger in their wretched cottages? Rouffeau, it is true, fays, that the poor are the immediate children of the rich. He is eccentric and chimerical, I know, but the facts I have ftated I know *are* facts—I do know, for I fee it every day before my eyes, that the diftrefs of the middling and lower ranks has increafed, is increafing, and certainly ought to be diminifhed."

" Impoffible,

" Impoffible, my good Madam—the thing is impoffible.—(Give me leave to drink a glafs of wine with you, Mifs Mincer; which do you choofe?)—I fay, Madam, that, in the exifting circum-ftances, it appears clearly to me, who am in the Treafury, the natural refort of all thofe fort of things——(Lord Limberham, fhall I fend you any jelly?— Give me leave to help you, Sir Frederic? —A tartlet, Mifs Hickumbottom?)— fort of things—happen to know a little of all that, that . . . . on the face of— (a little of that Blanc Mange),—it is impoffible to arrange things otherwife than they are."

" Lord! Mr. Climbup," drawled Lady Arfinoe, " by what chance have you begun fuch converfation as you have chofen for dinner?

dinner?—For goodnefs' fake, don't make
one fick with talking of fuch naufeous
fubjects! Sir Frederic Fanfaron, you
were at the Opera on Saturday. *Can
you tell me who that exceffive odd-looking perfon was with Lady Aviary?*"

" Oh, true! I know perfectly whom
your Ladyfhip means, but her defigna-
tion is beyond me. The Lady Bob-
kinfes were quizzing her paft compute:
I believe I afked Jack Biddycoop, but,
'faith, I've forgot what he faid; I dare
fay we fhall fee her at Lady Buckray's
mafquerade. Your Ladyfhip will be
there?"

" Yes, I fuppofe, one muft endure
it," replied the Lady with the moft decided apathy, " for an hour or fo; but
I fhall

I fhall make my efcape as foon as I
can. I fufpect that dear woman, who,
to be fure, has a moft unwearied way of
driving all her friends wild in pure ci-
vility, will have an affemblage of all
the queereft animals fhe can mufter, and
that Noah's ark, or Exeter Change, will
be nothing to her collection of odd fifh
and unheard-of fowl."

Sir Frederic now whifpered the lady,
who nodded, and cried umph; and, as
the deffert was foon after finifhed, and
the ladies had taken their wine,
the party broke up. The next day
Mrs. Blandford left a houfe in which
the fociety fo little fuited her; but was
very much furprifed to receive, on
reaching her own houfe in Hertfordfhire, which was eleven miles diftant
from

from Colonel Brufque's, and about twice
the diftance from Lady Buckray's, a card
of invitation to her Ladyfhip's mafqued
ball for herfelf and Azemia. With this
lady Mrs. Blandford had been acquainted from her infancy: they were
fchool fellows, and had lived, for the
firft fifteen years of their lives, much
gether—when one had married an Irifh
Peer, and the other a Country Gentleman. Their friendfhip now languifhed
on the part of the woman of fafhion,
who ftill, however, nodded and fmiled
whenever fhe faw her old friend, and
occafionally lamented how forry fhe
was that they did not meet more
frequently; declared how little pleafure
there was in her ftation of life;
how fatiguing it was to go to Court;
and how happy fhe fhould be if ever
her

her Lord's avocations permitted them
to retire fnugly into the country to
focial and domeftic happinefs, where
fhe could fee her old friends in a quiet
comfortable way.

Mrs. Blandford, to whom neither the
moft brilliant nor the fnuggeft of thefe
affociations could afford any pleafure,
never feemed to doubt the fincerity of thefe
profeffions, becaufe fhe cared nothing
whether they were fincere or no; nor did
fhe ever appear to refent an eftrange-
ment which did not at all affect her.
She was, however, little difpofed to attend a mafquerade; an entertainment
for which, though fhe did not think it
much more dangerous to young people
than others, fhe had no predilection.
She therefore fent an excufe; but was
the

the next day furprifed by a vifit from
Lady Buckray herfelf, who fo earneftly
preffed, and even infifted on Mrs.
Blandford's obliging her, that, rather
than appear to refent her former coolnefs, fhe agreed to be prefent with
Azemia at this fête, and that they would
ftay the night; Lady Buckray affuring
her that fhe need not encounter the
fatigue of returning, as there were beds
at her fervice. Mrs. Blandford, however, in affenting, could not but re-
colleft what had paffed at the table of
Colonel Brufque, nor help fufpeéting
that fhe was among the odd fifh, and
unheard-of fowl, hinted at by Lady
Arfinoe.

CHAP.

CHAP. VII.

 ═══

" I do beguile the thing I am."
SHAKESPEARE.

 ───

" And painted Flattery hides her ferpent train in
flowers."
GRAY.

 ═══

NOVEL-writers are accuftomed to
amufe their readers with mafquerades,
as well as with ghofts. Following then
one or other of our two moft celebrated writers (Fielding and Madame
D'Arblay), I am ftrongly tempted to
try

try my fkill in the arduous tafk of defcribing, at full length, the adventures
of the mafquerade: but my modefty
conquers my ambition. Repreffed,
therefore, by that humility which I
hope will be deemed graceful by the
beft judges, I will confine myfelf to a
defcription taken from a diurnal print,
the proprietor of which was prefent,
and which is fo admirably done, that I
fhould defpair of making my account,
were I to attempt it, at once fo com-
prehenfive and fo brilliant.—*Allons
donc!*

" On Tuefday laft the grand mafquerade and fête, fo long in prepara-
tion, and fo much the objeé of ex-
peétation in the firft circles, was given
at the Right Honourable the Countefs
of

of B——s——, at her delightful villa of
Laurel Lodge. The fuper elegant and
tafteful decorations were highly creditable to the care and contrivance of
Signor Babinetto, who conduéted them,
as well as to the exquifite tafte, and
beautiful fancy, of the fair and noble
direétrefs of this magnificent entertainment. The great faloon was hung with
rofe-coloured fatin, feftooned above
with a drapery of filver crape, bordered
with foils of various colours, and knot-
ted up at intervals with wreaths of the
fineft artificial flowers, mingled with
gold and filver taffels. The leffer faloon was fitted up to reprefent the hall
of Jonquils, as it is defcribed in one of
the fairy tales from the admirable pen
of Madame La Comteffe D'Anois;
but, elegant as it was, the great drawing-

room exceeded it. This fuperb room opens on the fouthern lawn by a pair of very large folding-doors of the fineft crown glafs: the beauty of the internal arrangements of this room may be imagined, by our readers of tafte, when we inform them that, on each fide, were placed reprefentations of various trees, fo admirably done, that they conveyed a complete idea of " the Fathers of the Foreft." In fhort, it admirably prefented the Enchanted Wood of Taffo; and at a given time, when much of the company was collected into that apartment, a mafque reprefenting Rinaldo, a perfon of high diftinction, entered, ftruck thefe maffy repofitories, and, lo! from each ftarted an angelic nymph, who were, we are affured, fixteen of the moft celebrated beauties in fuperior life.

Their

Their lovely hair flowed gracefully on their fhoulders, crowned with myrtle; their drapery was the lighteft and moft tranfparent: in a word, they were the forms embodied that had glowed in the luxurious, the florid imagination of the Italian poet. Thefe ladies, joined by an adequate number of the moft interefting mafques in the room, immediately compofed a d ance previoufly ftudied for that purpofe, and which was foon increafed, till it ftruck into a country dance; and the joyous company danced from the great drawing-room quite out upon the lawn, on each fide of which there were ranged, parallel to the artificial trees above-mentioned, orange and myrtle, and other odoriferous exotics—garlands of coloured lamps being fufpended from one

G 2

to

to the other. This vifta of radiance was clofed by a ftatue of Minerva, crowning the buft of our heaven-born Minifter, as the political faviour of Britain: it was furrounded by *tranfparent* paintings, or rather deceptions, of very ingenious contrivance. One reprefented Political Rhetoric in the act of making

The worfer feem the better reafon;

and the other Prudence, inftigated by Fear, putting a padlock on the lips of Common Senfe; who, not being able to fpeak, feemed to exprefs the pain of this enforced filence by menacing contortions, which the company feemed to confider as a mighty good joke.

The

The rareft delicacies of this and every other country were prepared as a rinfrefco, under a fuperb tent of white tiffany, lined with fky-coloured farcenet, placed near this group of emblematic figures: it confifted of ices, jellies, conferves, fruits of all forts and feafons; cold meats of every defcription; poultry and game:—earth, air, and water had been ranfacked to contribute to this moft elegant *fête!*—After the *goûté*, a band of mufic was called from the adjacent woods, who played the air dear to the heart of every true Briton,

" God fave the King,"

and a full chorus repeated it three times three. After which, the whole concluded by an afs-race: the laft who came in to poffefs, as prize, a cap, with a figure of

G 3

Moria

Moria upon it in coloured foil, which
was won, with eafe, by the Honourable
Thomas Titmoufe. After another flight
refrefhment with liqueurs, the company
departed highly gratified by their entertainment, and the fuavity and complacency of their amiable hoftefs.

A mafquerade generally produces a
great variety of adventures, and almoft
as generally an elopement, or an *enleve-*
ment of the heroine: in the prefent inftance, however, I choofe it fhould be
otherwife. Nothing is fo enchanting
as novelty—from its name it muft, of
courfe, be the foul of a novel; and
therefore to give this, at leaft in one
inftance, I beg leave to relate, that
Azemia, though dazzled by the fplen-
dours of " the furrounding fcenery,"
                                                    was

was rather diftreffed by the figures that
peopled it. The hideous mafks that on
every fide met her eyes, on which were
all the deformities that could render difgufting

            " The human face divine."

fometimes aftonifhed, but oftener terrified her. From the flippant pertnefs of
fome of the women, from the infolent
familiarity of many of the men, fhe
fhrunk in difmay; and turning from
thefe, fhe met only among the very fine
people, mawkifh fatiety, or cold indifference; for they were of thofe, who,
while they languidly attempted to fhew
that they were amufed, betrayed the
melancholy truth that they were tired
to death.

                    G 4

One figure among this motley group,
however, particularly attached himfelf
to her: he was clad in a drefs that he
meant fhould imitate that of an ancient
Britifh bard; and on his head he wore
a wreath of oak, and he had put leaf
gold on fome of the leaves, left it
fhould fail to be confpicuous. He bore
a fmall harp in his hand, on which he
fometimes ftruck chords that founded to
the ear like harmony; at others he
played very ill fome of the vileft and
moft unmeaning trafh that ever iffued
from the brain of

    " Maudlin Poetefs, or rhyming Peer!"

This man chofe to follow Azemia
wherever fhe went with the moft ful-
fome flattery, till at length fhe was com-
                                                    pelled

pelled to quit the young ladies, with
whofe party fhe had been trying to
amufe herfelf, and feek Mrs. Blandford, whom fhe found fitting alone
in an alcove of the garden, fomewhat remote from the company; where,
though fhe forbore to fay fo when our
heroine joined her, fhe had been contemplating the ftrange and capricious
difpofition of the things of this world.—
" Here," faid fhe, " are a fet of people
got together to try to be happy—the
leaft nicely dreffed, the leaft expenfive
among them, probably pays for his or
her night's diverfion twice as much as
would keep for a week a man, his wife,
and three or four children, in the neceffaries of life.—The lady of the houfe,
who fo elegantly entertains her guefts,
will probably find the amount of her
            G 5   tafteful

tafteful hofpitality debit her in a fum that would have been a handfome, nay, a great portion, a century and a half ago, for the eldeft daughter of her illuftrious houfe; and yet all this is in a country which they fay is ruined, and which really is fo, if one may judge by the apparent condition of more than two thirds of the people. How many induftrious perfons, who have laboured all day, fhrink fupperlefs to their hard beds, trying to forget in fleep the faintnefs of hunger! How many mothers by the light of this clear fummer moon fhining through their fcanty, and perhaps broken, cafements, gaze on their fleeping children with aching hearts, uncertain if, with the coming day, they fhall be able to find for thefe unconfcious fharers of their poverty that fubfiftence,

fubfiftence, which half the expenditure of one of thefe gay individuals that are now glancing about before me, would have amply fupplied, not for one only, but for many days!"

Such were the contemplations of Mrs. Blandford; but fuch contemplations were totally unneceffary on the Levant, and Azemia had not been long enough in England to have learned to make them, nor did her protectrefs wifh that fhe fhould.

All Azemia's wifhes at prefent, therefore, went to the fhaking off her importunate new acquaintance, who had infifted upon being allowed to be called her bard; fung fongs, fuch as they were, in her praife; and quoted com-

mon-

mon-place fpeeches with a vehemence of voice and manner that had very much diftreffed her.

When they joined Mrs. Blandford, his adulation took a more quiet and more fentimental turn: he walked with her, acquiefced in every thing fhe faid, praifed her fentiments, and extolled her tafte to the fkies. At length, he prevailed on the two ladies to fuffer him to attend them to the fideboard, where in a manner, *tout patelin*, which, as Mrs. Blandford did not know the man, fhe was not upon her guard againft, he begged leave to toaft with them the friend moft efteemed by both the ladies. Mrs. Blandford, half laughing at the obfolete vulgarity of the propofal, agreed, however, to humour it, for the

the abfurd *fanfaron* fort of manner of the bard with his harp amufed her.— She gave, therefore, a celebrated orator, in whofe praife the fon of Apollo very eloquently held forth; and then turning to Azemia with an odd fort of fmirk on his face, he gently entreated her to favour him with hers.

Mrs. Blandford having explained to her what was defired, becaufe fhe had only imperfectly comprehended it, Azemia in the fimplicity of her heart, and becaufe fhe in truth liked nobody better, gave Charles Arnold.

Our bard now affected to be ftruck with the greateft pleafure and furprife: he repeated rapturoufly the name of Charles Arnold, at the fame time declaring,

claring, that he was the beloved companion of his childhood (though Azemia, who now faw his face, could not imagine how that could be), and the cherifhed friend of his youth. He then, foliciting the ladies to fit with him on an artificial bank, covered with green velvet to imitate mofs, under one of the beautiful orange-trees on the lawn, fpoke thus—having introduced his *eloge* by an harangue in praife of humanity and fenfibility:

" My invaluable friend Arnold has always been the moft tender-hearted of human beings. I have attended to the dawn of his being—I remember when we both rode hobby-horfes together, (though I was a little his fenior, I ftill, as indeed I have always done fince, loved

loved a canter on that amiable contrivance); I fay that in our infantine fports I watched the progrefs of the facred fpring of Pity's heavenly dew, which has fince fpouted forth a fountain of living water—(even fuch as fprang from the rock at the call of Mofes)—and who, like him, was always fo full of " the milk of human kindnefs!" Was a lamb to be domefticated—to him it was given; and not its own woolly mama could nurfe the firftling better (except in the article of lacteal nourifhment, which was happily fupplied by fkim milk.)—Was a calf to be hobbed— to him, to my beloved Charles, was delegated the tender tafk of hobbation; and through his fifts (little fifts they were then) was imbibed the nourifhment of the lowing orphan. Io herfelf hardly

hardly made a more dulcet nurfe. Was a brood of young turkeys to be reared— it was he—he himfelf, my foft-hearted friend, that gave each of the plaintive neftlings an exhilarating pepper-corn: it was he who fed them with chopped eggs, and mingled clivers with their fnowy curd!

" Was a chicken neglected, pecked, ill-treated by its mother—my dear Charles wrapped it in flannel, put it in a fmall bafket, and endeavoured by fufpenfion near the fire's genial warmth to fupply the animal heat of its unnatural parent!

" Had that parent the pip—he forgot her inhumanity, and thought only of her diftrefs: he opened the oil-containing bag

bag with his beft knife—he cured, he releafed her.

" Never, dear friend! fhall I forget his tendernefs—his fenfibility towards a gudgeon—he had caught it. The innocent pifcatory fufferer looked piteoufly up in his face; ftruck with the pathetic appeal, he obferved to me— ' My Courtney,' faid he, ' this fated fifh may have friends—may have connections in this limpid ftream: nay, he may even have fome amiable, fome filver-fpotted maiden gudgeon waiting his arrival, under the roots of that willow!—An oyfter, *we know*, may be in love, and a gudgeon, of courfe liable, be more diftractedly enamoured in proportion to his fuperiority of fufceptibility;—but while I expatiate my prey expires.'

expires.'—So faying, he releafed the unoffending fifh—it glided away, and in that moment, what muft have been his generous feelings? Amiable youth! my heart glows with participating fympathy—Humanity marked him for her own, and he has honoured her adoption.''

The oddity of this oration extremely amufed Mrs. Blandford, who was not without a tafte for humour and fingularity of character. The converfation, however, of the *foi-difant* bard, (whofe name, out of mafquerade, was Perkly,) was of that defcription, which, though it entertains even by its abfurdity for a few hours, varies afterwards, and not unfrequently makes the lifteners repent the attention they at firft gave, if it
seems

feems to occafion repeated claims for the fame exertion of complaifance.

Mrs. Blandford, therefore, gave no encouragement to Mr. Perkly, when he faid with great apparent delight, that he was now on a fummer tour among his friends, and that he was fo fortunate as to be going the next day the fame way, as that which led towards her refidence in Hertfordfhire, and would fet out at the fame day and fame hour, in order to have the fupreme felicity of efcorting her and Azemia on their way.

The next day came, and a fatigued and heavy-eyed party of the guefts affembled at an elegant breakfaft, where, after the delights of the preceding evening had been difcuffed, the converfation

tion would have languifhed, had not fome of the company, and particularly Mr. Perkly, produced fundry efforts of their mufes in the forms of rebufes and charades—happy and fortunate refources againft thofe awkward fufpenfions of ideas which fometimes occur in the very beft fociety.

To accommodate fuch of my readers who may occafionally be bored with the blank and comfortlefs fenfation of having nothing to fay (when they have no mafquerade to talk of and no entertaining novel, like this, to recommend to their auditors)—I here fet down from memory fome of thefe interefting *jeux d'efprit*.

CHARADE, BY VISCOUNT ••••••.

My firft is rude, ftormy, and windy,
  My fecond, foft tender and blue :
O Celia ! if you were but kind, eh !
  How bleft might the whole be with you!

ANOTHER, BY MR. PERKLY,

More remarkable for the propriety of the fentiment than for harmony of numbers.

My firft I cannot name to ears polite,
My fecond was my character laft night :
When we adopt my whole, and ceafe to fight,
I hope, with all my heart, things will come right.

An odd-looking man, with a black cropped head, and rather a ftern countenance, who had long fat filent, and fomewhat fulky, then defired the attention of the company to a new one of his
which,

which, notwithftanding an angry look from the lady of the houfe, he pro-duced, and which was to this effect:

> If I *could* do my firft,
> I would foon from his ftation
> My fecond difplace
> For the good of the nation
> And then in my tout
> I would make an oration.

Either the Countefs was a remarkable good gueffer at charades, or had heard this before. However that was, fhe arofe in apparent difpleafure; and fay-ing her ponies were waiting to take her an airing round the park, thofe who were returning to their refpective homes that morning took leave, and the com-pany difperfed.

CHAP.

CHAP. VIII.

> If every juft Man, that now pines with want,
> Had but a feemly and fufficient fhare
> Of that which lewdly pamper'd luxury
> Now heaps upon fome few with vaft excefs!
>
> MILTON.

MRS. Blandford and Azemia now fet forth to return home, not in the car-riage of the former, for it had been left in London to be new lined and painted; it was an hack poft-chaife that con-veyed Azemia and her maternal friend, while Mr. Perkly, who was, he faid, going

going the fame way, ambled by their fide on a pony.

They had proceeded about half way, when the poftillion ftopped fuddenly, and, difmounting in a great hurry, went to the hind wheel of the carriage, and prefently, with marks of concern, in-formed the ladies that the linch pin was loft, and there was danger of their being overturned if they did not get out. Mr. Perkly, riding up at the fame time, defired leave to hand them out into a neighbouring cottage which appeared under a group of tall elms and walnut trees, about fifty paces farther, where the road receded, forming a fort of green, behind which rofe a woody hill. The look of the place was inviting, it would have made a fweet landfcape; and

and Mrs. Blandford willingly agreed to fit down on a bench at the door, till fome remedy could be found for the defect in the vehicle. They approach-ed; but the fun, as it was now about two o'clock, was very oppreffive, and as the trees threw their fhade on the other fide the hedge, Mrs. Blandford pulled the ftring of the latch, and, fol-lowed by Azemia, entered the cottage.

She was furprifed to fee only a very old woman, quite paralytic, and very deaf, who held in her feeble arms a new-born infant, while a little creature, not two years old, was hanging on her gown, and expreffing, as well as it could, its want of food, which the poor old woman was apparently preparing for it, over a few embers, in an earthen pot.

Mrs. Blandford, whofe appearance
and queftions feemed to make little impreffion on this half-fenfelefs being,
learned, with fome difficulty, that fhe
was the mother of a poor woman, who
had the day before been delivered of
the little infant, her eighth child : the
father, fhe faid, was out at work four
miles off—the eldeft boy only at fervice. The fecond was gone to tell the
doctor, who lived fix miles off, that his
mother was very ill, and to get her
fome doctor's ftuff: the eldeft girl was
fent to beg fome linen of a charitable
lady, but fhe lived at a great houfe ftill
farther diftant. The fecond girl was
nurfing her mother, and her third and
fourth fifters, who were both fick in the
fame room, with what the old woman
termed a *defpert* bad faver, and the
                                    mother

mother herfelf, fhe faid, had tafted nothing that day but a little tay; for that,
till James comed back, they had not a
bit of bread in the houfe.

Affected by this account, and the
extreme poverty which every thing
within this abode exhibited, Mrs. Blandford defired to fee the poor woman;
and taking in her arms the new-born
infant, which its infirm grandmother
feemed incapable of carrying fafely, fhe
followed her trembling fteps up a fteep
ftair to a room, where a fpectacle of
ficknefs and want prefented itfelf that
wrung her heart.

The mother, pale and faint for want
of neceffary nourifhment, and on a
wretched bed, was half raifed from it,
            H 2   furveying

furveying one of her children, a girl of
five years old, who feemed to be in
extremity; while in a corner of the
room, on a few rags, lay another girl
about feven. Mrs. Blandford prefently
perceived that the complaint of the
children was a low fever, the effect of
bad nourifhment; and that the mother,
between the anxiety of her mind and
the weaknefs of her fituation, would too
probably perifh. Her pallid countenance, her funken eyes and parched lips
were evidences too ftrong of her fufferings; and Mrs. Blandford, always active
in benevolence, was eager to give this
fad group immediate relief.

This, however, was by no means eafy.
This lone cottage was the only one
within three or four miles, and the
                                    neareft

neareft were not likely to fupply any
of the articles neceffary for thefe poor
objects: it was fo far to the town, that
before any meffenger could be fent and
return, the evils fhe wifhed to remove
might become irremediable. What was
to be done? In fuch a cafe, all confideration for her perfonal convenience
was forgotten by this excellent woman—
fhe endeavoured to comfort the languid
fufferer with affurances of fpeedy relief;
then, haftening down, fhe went to the
place where Mr. Perkly and her fervant
were affifting the poftillion to remedy the
defect of the wheel, which, it appeared,
was of more ferious confequence than
they had at firft imagined, inafmuch as
the wheel itfelf was broke. Mrs. Blandford now defired the poftillion to mount
            H 3   one

one of the horſes, and haſten to a neighbouring town.   The man grumbled, and
demurred.   Mrs. Blandford, however,
inſiſted; and though Mr. Perkly obſerved that it would be better to ſend
her own ſervant, yet, as he was mounted
on a favourite old horſe, ſhe refuſed to
alter her intentions, and, after a long
argument, in which Perkly gave his
opinion with more freedom than Mrs.
Blandford thought his acquaintance with
her authoriſed, the poſtillion departed;
and Perkly, who ſeemed to think this
delay an inconvenience to himſelf, was
very coolly told by Mrs. Blandford,
who was already tired of his poor attempts at wit, and his hypocritical parade of ſentiment, that there was not the
leaſt neceſſity for her to reſtrain him,
and

and that he had much better go his own
way, ſince it was very uncertain how
long ſhe might ſtay.

Mr. Perkly, who had reaſons of his
own for wiſhing to keep that ſhare of
Mrs. Blandford's favour which he imagined he had obtained, now began to
change his tone; and the good lady, who
could not imagine what motive he could
have for his uncommon attention, which
he paid principally to her (for of Azemia he took little notice), was for once,
notwithſtanding her natural intelligence,
and the judgment ſhe had acquired in a
long intercourſe with the world, induced to believe that he really found
pleaſure in her converſation.

Willing, therefore, to make it as in-
ſtructive as pleaſurable, ſhe began, as
they all ſat together on the bench near
the cottage door, waiting the return of
the poſtillion, to enter into a diſquiſition
on the various conditions of men in a
ſtate of civilized ſociety.   This was begun by Mr. Perkly's ſaying—" You
ſeem much intereſted, Madam, for theſe
poor people."—" Should I not be deſ-
titute of feeling, were I otherwiſe?"
ſaid Mrs. Blandford.   " Can I do otherwiſe than conſider them as beings formed
with the ſame feelings, and liable to the
ſame neceſſities as I am?   And can I,
after having been lately in a ſcene of ſuch
luxurious profuſion, help being ſhocked
to think, that, while a perſon like our
hoſteſs of laſt night can, for a few hours
amuſement,

amuſement, expend a ſum that would
make many families happy for years,
there is, within a few miles of her
ſplendid abode, a poor induſtrious group,
a father and mother, an aged grandmother, and ſo many children, who are
actually liable to periſh for want of the
mere neceſſaries of exiſtence?"

" But, my dear Madam," cried Mr.
Perkly, eagerly.

" And, my dear Sir," interrupted Mrs.
Blandford, " I know every thing you
would ſay.   The common-place, and,
pardon me if I ſay, the unfeeling ob-
jections that have a thouſand times been
made, and a thouſand times incontrovertibly anſwered—I mean to the me-

lioration of the condition of the lower ranks in this country."

" Good God!" exclaimed Mr. Perkly, " is it poffible that a woman of your fenfe—of your underftanding, can, for a moment, allow yourfelf to be fo mifled by the nonfenfical clamour of the multitude, as to imagine that a plan could ever fucceed that went to univerfal equalization?"

" No, Sir," faid Mrs. Blandford coolly, " I do *not* join in that clamour. I know, and fo does every body of common fenfe, that equality, according to the fenfe you affect to annex to it, cannot exift: but there ought to be equal laws for all men."

" And

" And *are* there not?" cried Perkly, eagerly. " Is there a country under Heaven where law is fo equally dealt as it is in ours? Is there not juftice to be had for every body?"

" Juftice!" anfwered Mrs. Blandford. " Oh! mockery of terms! You may as well fay to the wretched pauper who befeeches in the ftreet your charity to relieve his hunger—' Friend, why are you hungry? There is a tavern open on the oppofite fide of the way, where you may eat your fill.'—Would not this be a barbarous infult to the poor mendicant's diftrefs?—Yet it is precifely thus people talk who urge to the oppreffed in common life the excellence, the equality of the Englifh law.—' It is very excellent, I dare fay,' might the

H 6　　　　fufferer

fufferer reply, ' but I have no means of buying it; for, whatever it can do for me, I muft pay fo high, that, if peradventure I get relieved from the oppreffion I complain of, I fhall be as much impoverifhed as I am now.'— No, never talk, my good Sir, of the equality of our laws, while a Chancery-fuit is ranked as an evil of as great magnitude as a fire, an inundation, a defcent of the enemy, or an earthquake; and really as to the ruin they produce, I fee but little difference—what difference there is, is rather againft a Chancery-fuit: the invafion, inundation, earthquake, may render a family houfelefs and defolate at once; a Chancery-fuit keeps them in lingering mifery for years, and leaves them beggars at laft."

" Well,

" Well, well," faid Mr. Perkly, who felt, though he determined not to own it, that he had hitherto the worft of the argument; " well, well, but . . . . that . . . a . . that . . . a . . is not . . . a . . my meaning. No, no—I mean, dear Madam, *that* equality of property, or, as we fay, the Agrarian Law, about which fo much nonfenfe has been talked."

" I do not know," anfwered Mrs. Blandford, " that it might always be fuch abfolute nonfenfe, however impracticable it is in the prefent ftate of fociety. That it is impracticable, I believe: if any twelve mechanics, for example, of nearly as can be, in fuch numbers, the fame age, intellects, and information, as well as the fame bodily powers, were each to have a certain portion of land affigned

affigned them, with inftruments of huf-
bandry to work, and grain to fow their
fields, you would fee that fome would
be ignorant, fome idle, fome, perhaps,
unfortunate and unfufpecting; fo that,
before two years had paffed, the faga-
cious, the induftrious, the fortunate, the
cunning, would have poffeffed themfelves of their neighbour's property;
and thefe would have two, three, or
more fhares, while the idle and diffipated would be entirely bereft of theirs,
and then, of courfe, there muft be an
end to the equality with which they fet
out."

" Such men then," faid Mr. Perkly,
" would be impoverifhed through their
own folly."

" Moft

" Moft of them, undoubtedly."

" And yet," cried he, exultingly,
" you feel a great deal of pity for the
poor; and feem to think that thofe who
have great affluence are never to enjoy
themfelves in any elegant amufement,
becaufe there may happen to be poor
people in the world?"

" Not fo," replied Mrs. Blandford;
" it would be requiring of human creatures virtuous felf-denial, which I cannot
expect in civilized, or perhaps any
other fociety. All I mean is, that when
the thinking mind is fhocked by fuch
ftriking difparity as between the fcene
I was in laft night, and what I now
witnefs paffing in this houfe, it is very
apt to advert to the great nations where
fuch

fuch fymptoms were the forerunners of
dreadful convulfions. It is a difeafe
which we know from repeated experience is fatal: I would prevent its being
fo here; I would not have the rich live
much worfe than they do, but I would
have the poor fupported a great deal
better."

" I don't fee that they want any
thing," faid Mr. Perkly, carelefsly, " or
if they do, 'tis only becaufe they are
drunken, or idle."

" Would to God," exclaimed Mrs.
Blandford, " that you, Sir, who have,
as you fay, no wife or family, were
compelled to live, for one month only,
on the fum that, during that fpace, fupplies the labouring owner of this cabin,
his

his wife, mother, and feven or eight
children, with all the means of life!
Believe me, good Sir, you would find
yourfelf moft terribly ftraitened; and
you would then, perhaps, own, that the
poor are not quite fo well off as they
ought to be in a country of whofe profperity thofe that live on the fat of the
land fo feduloufly endeavour to convince us."

Mr. Perkly ftared, and fhook his ears
at this, as if he was not quite eafy at
hearing even the remoteft hint of fuch
an experiment.

The meffenger foon after returned
with the fupplies directed by the benevolence of Mrs. Blandford, who gave
another

another hour to feeing them difpofed of for the comfort and relief of the poor family. She then renewed her journey with a grumbling poftillion, and one tired horfe, Mr. Perkly looking fome-times as if he repented of his having thus volunteered in the fervice of one whofe feeling, or affectation of feeling, made his gallantry tedious and trouble-fome; for, not content with having fupplied the poor family with necef-faries, Mrs. Blandford flopped at the next town, where fhe hired a nurfe to attend on the fick woman, and engaged an apothecary to vifit her and the chil-dren. Before all this could be completed, the night was advanced when they ar-rived at Mrs. Blandford's home—Perkly feemed to wifh to be invited to ftay; but, wearied by his attempts at wit, and difgufted

difgufted by the many proofs fhe had feen of real infenfibility, under the af-fectation of refined fentimentality, Mrs. Blandford made no pretence of wifhing his prefence. Having ftrutted about therefore a quarter of an hour, and affected to admire her houfe and gar-den, he departed, as he faid, for the abode of a friend, about four miles nearer London, who had given him a preffing invitation to ftay fome time; while Mrs. Blandford, fatigued with her excurfion, was confoled for her loft time by the confideration that fhe had, in confequence of it, found an oppor-tunity effectually to relieve a diftreffed family.—Azemia, extremely glad to find herfelf once more in the comfortable home of her benefactrefs, formed no other

other wifh than that they might, during the reft of the fummer, have no in-vitation, or at leaft accept of none to leave it.

As to a mafquerade, fhe befought Mrs. Blandford, while they breakfafted the next morning, never to take her to another.—" It is," faid fhe in her broken Englifh, " fuch a melancholy fight to fee fuch a number of people making fimpletons of themfelves by way of trying at fomething extraordinary, which, after all, feems to amufe none of them. I could not help being quite forry to look at fome of them dreffed up fo little like reafonable beings, and fqueaking nonfenfe, with fuch deformed mafks on, that they feemed to try both in

in their minds and perfons to libel hu-man nature."

Sagacious reader!—and Oh! more formidable critic! do not here fhut the book, and exclaim that fuch reflections are not in character, and never were made by a girl of feventeen, and a ftranger.—Confider whether, if they are not natural, they are juft, and remem-ber that the heroine of a novel is a pri-vileged perfon, who is to do and en-dure what never was done or fuffered in real life. She may faft four or five days, or as long as Elizabeth Canning: fhe may ride over hills, through woods, and round lakes, nights and days, and be no worfe at the end of her journey, than if fhe had taken an airing to

to Kenſington with her grandmother;
and ſhe may make reflections worthy
of a Lord Chancellor, or an Archbiſhop, though it is well known that
in actual life beautiful young ladies
very ſeldom reflect at all.

CHAP.

CHAP. IX.

So Pluto ſeized on Proſerpine.

IT was two months after this time, and
ſummer was gradually fading into autumn, when Mrs. Blandford was ſuddenly ſummoned to London to meet an
old friend, who, after a long reſidence
in the Weſt Indies, had returned to
England in ſo bad a ſtate of health, that
ſhe was unable to leave London, as ſhe
was deſired to do, for Bath; and finding herſelf daily become worſe, ſhe
deſired

deſired to ſee her oldeſt and beſt friend,
and to give her ſome directions about
her family, before ſhe became too ill to
execute theſe taſks of duty and prudence.—Mrs. Blandford loſt not a moment in obeying the ſummons—it was
likely that ſhe ſhould be abſent only a
few days; and as Azemia wiſhed rather
to remain, unleſs ſhe could be uſeful,
and Mrs. Blandford was unwilling to
take her, it was agreed that ſhe ſhould
be left in the country.

Mrs. Blandford then departed; and
Azemia, who now found the advantage
of the reſources ſhe had acquired,
taſted reading well enough to amuſe
herſelf many hours: then, the evening
being remarkably cloſe and warm, ſhe
ſtrolled towards a ſmall lawn that partly
ſurrounded

ſurrounded the houſe, but had hardly
proceeded many paces before a ſervant
from the houſe, following her, informed
her Mr. Perkly was come, and deſired
to ſpeak to her. Azemia diſliked this
man at all times, but particularly diſliked to ſee him in the abſence of Mrs.
Blandford: ſhe was not, however, well
enough acquainted with the numerous
ways there are of eſcaping importunate
viſitors, and therefore returned, though
reluctantly, into the houſe, where Perkly
had viſited three or four times ſince
their meeting at Lady Buckray's, though
Mrs. Blandford had been very far from
giving him encouragement—Azemia
now thought him more importunate and
diſagreeable than ever; he aſked a thouſand queſtions, ſuch as the name of the
lady to whom Mrs. Blandford was gone,

the ſtreet where ſhe lived, how long the
viſit was likely to be, and many other
interrogatories, which, though ſhe always thought him impertinent, now
ſeemed more ſo than ever.

Azemia at length took courage to
tell him, that as Mrs. Blandford was
abſent, ſhe could not aſk him to ſtay;
and, with great ſatisfaction, ſhe ſaw him
depart.

The next morning ſhe went out to
attend on ſome India pheaſants, for
which a ſmall wooded corner of the
garden had been netted off; when ſhe
was ſurpriſed by a note from Mrs.
Blandford, written, as it ſeemed, in great
diſtreſs of mind. It was to inform her
that her friend was worſe, and that, as
ſhe

ſhe was herſelf unwell, ſhe could not
diſpenſe with the attendance of her dear
Azemia; and begging that ſhe would
therefore ſet out for London immediately in her friend's poſt-chaiſe, which
was ſent for her. Azemia flew into the
houſe, forgot all her diſlike to going to
London; and calling the houſemaid to
aſſiſt her in packing a few neceſſaries,
(for Mrs. Blandford's own maid had
accompanied her miſtreſs) ſhe was ready
in a few moments; and, with a mind
ill at eaſe on account of the indiſpo-
ſition of her beloved benefactreſs, got
into the handſome poſt-chaiſe that
waited, and, attended by a creditable
ſervant in livery on horſeback who had
come with it, began her journey.

I 2   The

The day was exceſſively warm, and
their progreſs ſlow: Azemia began to
think it extremely tedious. The chaiſe
ſtopped at a little alehouſe by the road-
ſide to refreſh the horſes, and Azemia
ventured to enquire of the ſervant how
far they yet had to London. The man
aſſured her they would ſoon arrive
there; adding, as a reaſon for the time
they had taken, that, to avoid ſome
ſandy and hilly road, the poſtillion had
come round an eaſier way, which beſides
gave them the advantage of getting into
London by a quarter of the town nearer
to Mrs. Anderton's houſe, by which
means they would avoid going over the
ſtones for above a mile.

Azemia ſuppoſed all this perfectly
true; yet a ſenſe of the great difference
of

of the time taken up in this and her
former journey ſoon recurred to her
again, as ſlowly they travelled on in
very ſhaking roads. The ſun was now
ſunk; it became dark; and Azemia,
who had never till then had much idea
of fear, began to feel uncomfortable
when ſhe reflected that ſhe was alone
in a very lonely, and, as it now ſeemed,
in a ſort of wild and woody country;
for ſhe obſerved by the twilight that
the carriage had left the road and en-
cloſed lanes, and was driven over graſs
among thickets of trees: ſhe thought
it neceſſary to ſpeak again; for, by all
ſhe recollected of the approach to the
metropolis, nothing could be more unlike it than the place where they then
were. It was ſome time before the
poſtillion heard; and when, at laſt, he
I 3   ſtopped,

174 AZEMIA.

stopped, he answered somewhat sullenly, that it would not be long before they got to the place where they were going to. Azemia, still more terrified, as well by the man's rude answer as by observing they were going into a darker part of the forest by a narrow road, desired to speak with the other servant. The postillion answered, in a yet more surly way, that he was gone on before. Azemia then asked whither?—and if he was gone to London?—The fellow made no answer.

Impenetrable darkness now fell around, and the road appeared to be so bad, that the chaise was likely every moment to be overturned: at length, however, after being for about half an hour shaken among ruts that threatened dislocated

AZEMIA. 175

dislocated limbs, the motion of the carriage became easier; she saw lights move about in a house before her, gates were opened, and she was soon at the door, where the servant who had attended her from Mrs. Blandford's opened the door of the chaise, and desired her to alight.—" Oh! pray," exclaimed she, " tell me why I am brought hither?— This is not London?—Mrs. Blandford cannot be here?"

No answer was returned: Azemia was led into a large handsome room; a female servant appeared—and, speaking loud, as if because she was a foreigner she could not hear, said that the lady she belonged to would be there to-morrow; that in the mean-time she must eat her supper, and go to bed. The

I 4

176 AZEMIA.

The woman spoke to Azemia exactly as she would to a child of ten years old, and seemed to assume an authority which added to the alarm she had already conceived—fears of she knew not what. She spoke as well as she could to the woman; but her apprehension occasioned her to express herself with more difficulty than usual, and the only answer she obtained was— " Ah! well, well; there, there—I don't understand you. I warrant you ben't much hurt in being brought to such a house as this here. Come, Miss, no whimpering!—What!—I wonders what you have to complain on indeed!"

Azemia, finding her remonstrance of no use, remained quiet; the woman went away, and the fair young prisoner began

AZEMIA. 177

began to explore the precincts to which she was confined. —The room wherein she was left opened by a large mahogany door into another still larger—it seemed to be magnificently furnished with large pictures; it was carpeted, and the curtains were of the richest damask, with gilt cornices. The candle Azemia held in her hand cast but a feeble light around so large an apartment; the doubtful obscurity dismayed her, and she returned, with light steps, to the room she had left, where a female servant, a sort of housekeeper, whom she had before seen, appeared, laid a cloth on a small table, and made signs to Azemia to seat herself, and to eat of the jellies, pastry, and fruit, with which it was covered.

I 5 Without

Without any diſtinct notion of the cauſes ſhe might have for perſonal alarm, the greateſt uneaſineſs Azemia felt was on account of Mrs. Blandford. Why ſhould ſhe have written to her as ſhe did? or if, as ſhe began to ſuppoſe, there was any deception in it, for what purpoſe, and by whom, could ſhe have been thus drawn away from the protection of Mrs. Blandford? and what muſt her beloved benefactreſs think when ſhe learned that ſhe was gone!

Theſe reflections, and the vague fears that tormented her, kept her waking the whole night on the bed of down to which ſhe had been conducted. At the dawn of day, which ſhe watched through the gilt window-ſhutters and chintz curtains of her room, ſhe aroſe, and

and opened them. She ſaw that the houſe on that ſide was ſituated in a large and beautiful garden: a gravel walk, bordered with variety of flowering ſhrubs and foreſt trees, led round an extenſive lawn to a canal edged with weeping willow, and winding away till it was loſt among plantations apparently of conſiderable extent. Azemia, having dreſſed herſelf, intended to go down ſtairs and walk in the pleaſant grounds ſhe ſaw before her: but, on attempting to leave her room, ſhe found the door locked; and in a few moments afterwards ſhe was amazed and alarmed by the appearance of Miſs Sally!—a perſon who was almoſt expelled from her recollection, but who now, diſagreeably enough, was recalled to it. Her chubby white face ſeemed

I 6 ſwelled

ſwelled with malignant triumph: ſhe addreſſed herſelf to Azemia with a ſneering reproach for her eſcape, and treated her like a creature over whom ſhe had obtained a right and might to diſpoſe of as ſhe pleaſed. Her manner was enough to overcome the ſpirits of the innocent girl, who, recollecting all that Mrs. Blandford had endeavoured to impreſs upon her mind as to the former conduct of this woman and of her firſt captor, was ſtruck with dread of their preſent deſigns, and burſt into tears.—Miſs Sally, without feeling or pity, continued to exclaim on her ingratitude and her folly: ſhe added— " However, Miſs, you are now come back to thoſe you belong to; you are far enough from the impertinent meddling old woman who choſe to keep you

you from your right friends; and *they* will take care, I aſſure you, that you ſhall not ſet out on your travels again in a hurry."

Azemia, weeping bitterly, enquired if ſhe might not be permitted to walk in the garden.—" Yes, yes, you ſhall walk, never fear; but you'll have no opportunity here to walk away. Come, no whimpering—you'll ſpoil your pretty eyes, Miſs: I adviſe you to make yourſelf eaſy, or, I aſſure you, it will be worſe for you."

To prevent my readers forming various conjectures as to the preſent ſituation of *our* heroine, they are to know, that, at the maſquerade, a certain celebrated

lebrated Political Orator and Writer had appeared as Peter the Hermit, while, among other Crusaders and chivalrous Knights assembled round him, was the noble Duke mentioned in the first part of these memoirs, who forbore to unmask the whole night, and whose presence was known only to the lady of the house. He no sooner beheld Azemia, and discovered that she was the lovely Turk once an inmate of his house, than he felt the most unconquerable wish to get her again in his power. Mr. Perkly had long been one of his accommodating friends: he immediately received instructions to make an acquaintance with Mrs. Blandford, and what had followed was by his contrivance. Azemia being a person belonging

longing to nobody, and kept, as was supposed, by Mrs. Blandford through charity, it was believed that none would think it worth while to enquire about her; or, if they did, that none possessed any right to reclaim her.

CHAP.

CHAP. X.

━━━━━

From bad to worse too oft the Sufferer falls,
  Yet let no Sufferer for that cause despair:
Good out of evil, Destiny oft calls—
  Which we see not—Alas! how blind we are!
                                ANONYMOUS.

━━━━━

THE amazement and consternation of Mrs. Blandford, when she returned to her own house, are not to be described. She made, in vain, every enquiry in her power of her servants, and then every attempt to trace her unfortunate ward, but all in vain: no person could give

give any account of the chaise, or its attendants; and, in fact, it had been driven a cross road, for near twenty miles, to the forest on which this villa of the Duke's was situated, though it was not much more than that distance from London.

While Mrs. Blandford was tormented with the most uneasy conjectures as to the fate of poor Azemia, which increased in proportion as time went on, the noble owner of her prison thought proper to visit his beautiful prisoner.

Azemia, who had for some days ceased to regard the occasional insults of Miss Sally, and was for the greatest part of her time left at liberty to walk

in

in the plantations, or amufe herfelf as
fhe chofe, and who faw no perfon appear to alarm her, was become more
tranquil; and, not knowing the pre-
cautions that had been taken to elude
all fearch, flattered herfelf that Mrs.
Blandford would foon difcover her, and
that fhe fhould once more be reftored
to her protection. Her difpofition was
naturally cheerful and fanguine; and her
imagination was uninfluenced by fuch
reading as tells of

" Moving accidents by flood or field;"

fhewing how damfels have been fpirited
off, and fhut up by fundry evil-difpofed
gentlemen—a circumftance which is
hardly omitted in any novel fince the
confinement of Pamela at Mr. B—'s
houfe

houfe in Lincolnfhire, and the *enleve-
ment* of Mifs Byron by Sir Hargrave
Pollexfen.

Of all thofe hiftories, and of thofe
of modern romances, wherein ladies are
carried per force into caftles, and fcud
about woods by moonlight to efcape,
Azemia was happily ignorant; fo that
ideal grievances added but little, for
fome time, to the real one of being feparated from Mrs. Blandford, and occafionally compelled to endure the impertinence of Mifs Sally.

But when the venerable nobleman
arrived, and, confidering her as ignorant
even of the language he ufed, furveyed
her as he would a beautiful animal,
then with a moft ridiculous, yet difgufting

ing expreffion of admiration, approached and took her hand, Azemia became
immediately confcious of the fate to
which fhe was condemned, and, acquiring
at once courage to repel the infults
which fhe thought it would be too probable he might offer, told him in a
calmer tone than could be expected,
that fhe infifted on being releafed; that
no perfon had any right to detain her;
and that fhe would inform Mrs. Blandford that he confined her contrary to
her inclination.

The Duke heard her with the fort
of fatisfaction with which one liftens to
an amiable child, who, in its infantine
anger, fhews unexpected marks of
ftrength of mind. He feemed aftonifhed
at the progrefs fhe had made in fpeaking
Englifh;

Englifh; and in a few days, from mere
liking to her beautiful form, he became
fo dotingly fond of her for the energy,
as he called it, of her mind, that he
no longer approached her but with
refpect; and inftead of the bafe intentions he had at firft harboured, he
appeared to be difpofed to end all his
follies by marrying this lovely Afiatic;
and would, perhaps, have done fo, if
on one hand, he had not been pofitively engaged before to Lady Belinda, and to five equally amiable fair
ones; and on the other, if he had not
foon feen, that, while Azemia beheld
him with unconquerable averfion, fhe
was totally unmoved by, though fhe
perfectly underftood, the various advantages of fortune and rank he had
the power of offering her.

After

After ſtaying more than a week, the enamoured antiquity, who fancied him-ſelf more in love than he ever was in his life, returned to London, giving or-ders that Azemia might not be contra-dicted in any thing; that all which could amuſe and engage her might be ſup-plied, and that ſhe might be allowed to walk in the garden whenever ſhe pleaſed—only that care ſhould be taken ſhe went no farther than about the grounds; which was altogether impro-bable, as they were ſurrounded on all ſides either by a wall, or a very high paling, within which was a wide and thick plantation of firs, other evergreens, and large trees; while without, next the foreſt, a deep ditch ran all round be-yond the paling. There was no entrance but by a lodge, where the porter knew how

how to obey the orders that were given him, too well to leave the leaſt doubt of the innocent priſoner's eſcape.

Miſs Sally, fatigued by a cloſe attend-ance as jailoreſs for almoſt three weeks, and occupied by ſome plans of her own, inſenſibly relaxed her vigilance; and a day or two after the Duke's departure Azemia was ſuffered to wander about as ſhe would. She returned regularly at the hours Miſs Sally expected to ſee her; and it was a relief to the latter not to be under the neceſſity of following her.

The doors of her apartment were now no longer locked; and one even-ing after ſhe had taken her ſlight repaſt, and retired to it, ſhe obſerved from the windows that the moon ſhone with un-common

common luſtre: its glancing rays were tremoling on the canal, and among the trees that waved over the lawn. Its che-quered radiance gave a penſive ſweet-neſs to the ſcene, which Azemia deſired to enjoy in the open air.—The ſtairs and paſſages were all carpeted, ſo that her light footſteps were not heard by any one; and ſhe ſoftly unbarred the glaſs door opening on the lawn, which opened afterwards by a ſpring lock, of which ſhe knew the ſecret.

With the feelings of a bird that has regained a momentary liberty, Azemia walked forth; for at all other times, however far ſhe had rambled from the houſe, ſhe always thought herſelf watched. Now ſhe believed ſhe was wholly unobſerved; and the pleaſure that

that ſuppoſition gave her, counteracted every ſenſation of fear at the ſilence and lonelineſs of the ſcene, that ſhe might at another time have felt. Approach-ing the canal, ſhe followed its winding banks, and admired the effect of the moon-beams trembling at intervals among the trees on its ſurface, which was gently curled and agitated by the night breeze, as it ſighed among the woods, that bent and ſwathed as it paſſed them.

Azemia, loſt in a pleaſing ſort of me-lancholy muſing, walked on towards the darker parts of the lawn where the trees cloſed over the broad graſs walk lead-ing round to its extremity. No living creatures ſeemed to be abroad but the hares, which at firſt ſtartled her as they darted acroſs her path, on being difturbed by her approach. There were an infinite number encouraged and protected here by the noble owner of the domain, who would have punifhed a peafant, or petty farmer, more feverely for deftroying one of *them*, than for killing half a dozen parifh children. Having obferved above twenty of thefe innocent animals feeding or fporting among the fhrubs, the fudden fcudding of two or three almoft over her feet no longer alarmed her: fhe even ftepped more lightly, if poffible, not to break in, even in their timid apprehenfions, on the fecurity they appeared to enjoy at this hour of filence, for it was midnight.

Re-affured as to any fears for herfelf by the perfect tranquillity of every object around her, Azemia, without any intention

intention of efcaping (for to efcape feemed impoffible), continued her way. She now entered a darker and narrower wood walk, almoft at the extremity of the plantation. Several cedars, and curious firs feathered down to the ground, had an area cut round them to admit air, while beyond them laurels and holly, privet and phillyrea, formed beneath the high elms and limes a fcreen of impenetrable darknefs; and Azemia could only fee the moon among thefe receffes; in the narrow parts it did not even enlighten the path before her. Suddenly, as flowly fhe purfued her way, fhe was fomewhat ftartled by a fhrill and often repeated cry, not unlike that of a young infant; it feemed almoft clofe to her: but before fhe had time to confider what it might be, three men rufhed out from

K 2 the

the dark thicket, and darted towards the place from whence the cry feemed to proceed. The fight of a human creature feemed to alarm the two laft, who ftopped and evidently meant to impede the paffage of the trembling Azemia; while the third, who had more eagerly purfued his game, ftepped from among the coppice wood in half a moment, exclaiming with an oath—" I've got another, and a devilifh large one!"—He held a hare in his hand; and feeing his companions, who had by this time feized on the half-dead Azemia, he joined in their efforts to carry her out of the grounds; which they prefently effected by means of fome pales they had fo loofened, that they could remove them at their pleafure, and replaced fo as that it could not be difcerned that they were

were loofe. Thefe three depredators of the night had no difficulty in conveying their light and almoft unrefifting burthen acrofs the deep foffé furrounding the grounds; and Azemia was now amidft the pathlefs wildernefs of an extenfive chace, in the power of three ruffians, one of whom was a notorious footpad that had long infefted the roads round London, and had retired among perfons very little better than himfelf, to fubfift with them on poaching and other petty thefts, till the fearch made for him in and about the metropolis, in confequence of a recent robbery and murder, was a little abated: with them he had affociated in fetting fnares for game, and the cry Azemia heard was that of a hare taken in a wire.

K 3 CHAP.

CHAP. XI.

What if our Heroine meet with dire mifchance,
Loft in the mazes of this tangled wood?

READER! if I now chofe, in this my concluding fection, to follow the example of a great mafter, and his ingenious copyift, I might gravely begin a long differtation, and difcourfe admirably and very much to the purpofe as to the probability of what I have juft made my heroine encounter. I will not—no, I pofitively will not take undue advantage

advantage of your impatience to know what becomes of my interefting Azemia. I will recollect how often I have myfelf impatiently turned over, without reading it, a profing digreffion, when I was impatient to learn whether the fair ideal creature, for whom I had fuffered myfelf to be anxious during many chequered pages, was killed or married at their clofe.

Oh! ye amiable and graceful female readers under twenty, who may perchance perufe this my firft effay " in the novel line," as ye wait in your machine till the Nereids in blue flannel at Margate or Brighton fhall wade towards you in your turn; or who may take it up in the parlour window while ye wait for your horfe, or your fociable—(for

K 4   now,

now, alas! the chance a novelift had of being read as your hair was dreffed is at an end)—ye will difpenfe with any argument by which I can prove that my heroine's adventure is extremely probable, if I haften to relieve ye from the pain your fufceptible bofoms muft feel, when ye reflect on the fituation of my fair, young, innocent and beauteous Azemia, in the hands of three ruffians, in the midft of a wild foreft, in the middle of the night, when nothing was fo improbable as her being faved from the horrors that awaited her.—To proceed then:

After the three men had carried her out of the plantations, they began to debate how they fhould difpofe of her for the night; and he who was the moft

moft daring, and of courfe had a fort of afcendancy over the others, infifted upon their helping him to convey her to the lone cottage, where he was himfelf concealed, which was two miles farther in the foreft. To this the others objected: but the fiercer wretch pulled a piftol from his pocket; and knowing they were unarmed, except with hunting poles pointed with iron, he fwore that the firft of them that made any refiftance to what he directed fhould have a brace of balls through his body. Azemia, who, a little recovering, had fallen fenfelefs on hearing this hideous wretch fpeak as he did, was borne between the two fubordinate men, who were only poachers; the other, who was a ruffian of a much more dangerous defcription, following them with his piftol in his hand.

K 5   Several

252

Several crofs roads interfeſted the
foreſt, all of which it was impoſſible to
avoid in going towards the place where
the robber infifted on having his prey
conveyed. They arrived at a broad
green road, where the turf was but little
marked by wheels, and were proceeding acrofs it, when the quick approach
of horfemen ſtartled them.—Confcious
guilt generally creates cowardice. The
youngeſt of the men that bore Azemia
let go his hold, and was prefently loſt
amid the thickeſt wood: the other was
about to confult his own fafety, and
efcape alfo, when he was feized by the
nervous arm of one of the horfemen,
while a piſtol difcharged by the ruffian
was inſtantly anfwered by the firing of a
piſtol by the other man on horfeback;
and then leaping from his horfe, he cut
at

at him with an hanger he wore by his
fide, and, clofing with him, threw him
on the ground—but not till he had himfelf received a ball from another piſtol
in his arm. The fecond poacher had
by this time difappeared; and the ſtranger,
ordering his companion, who was his
fervant, to fecure the fallen robber, ran
to the affiſtance of the female, who was
left lying on the ground, and who was
to all appearance dead.

What were the fenfations of the brave
and fortunate champion of innocence in
diſtrefs, when he faw his Azemia—his
long loſt, his adored Azemia! for know,
gentle reader, that this young hero was
no other than Charles Arnold himfelf.

K 6   It

It would be a vain attempt to defcribe
the fenfations that crowded on the heart
of the gallant young feaman, while he
thus held in his arms the lifelefs form of
her whom he had fought at every interval of recefs from his duty, and never a
moment ceafed to think of with paffionate tendernefs. His firſt apprehenfions were that fhe was dead—his firſt
hopes to bear away the lovely form from
the ruffians, whom he expeſted every
moment to return. He threw himfelf
upon the ground by her—fpoke to her,
chafed her cold hands, and then attempted to raife her; his faithful fervant was ſtill employed in fecuring the
difabled ruffian, who with dreadful exe-
crations ſtruggled to force himfelf from
the grafp of honeſt Bat.

" Tie

" Tie his hands behind him," cried
Arnold, " and haſten to me, or it will be
too late to fave—to recover this lovely
creature." Bat, with difficulty, performed this troublefome office; and then
his maſter mounting his horfe, he lifted
Azemia into his arms; and Bat, having
fecured the piſtols that had been fcattered around this fcene of fudden contention, followed on the other horfe.

Azemia, after a few moments, opened
her eyes, and Arnold, in the gentleſt accents, endeavoured to prevent the ef-
feſts of a too fudden furprife, while he
convinced her, that fhe was not only in
prefent fafety, but proteſted by her
fondeſt, tendereſt friend. Joy was the
momentary fenfation that affeſted the
heart of Azemia; but it was too fudden

den and tumultuous to affift her in re-
gaining her ftrength. She poffeffed only
recolleftion enough to cling round the
neck of her deliverer, while her head
funk on his fhoulder; and in this fituation, after about an hour's journeying,
they arrived at the houfe of the uncle
of Charles Arnold, who lived about
fix miles from the place where he had
fo miraculoufly refcued Azemia from
the probability of a fate a thoufand
times worfe than death.

Arnold, who was always welcome at
his uncle's houfe, and had been ufed to
go thither whenever, arriving from fea,
he had a fhort leave of abfence, made no
fcruple of rapping loudly at the door;
where, however, they waited fome time
before the family were roufed. At length
the

the trufty old houfekeeper looked out
of the window; and hearing the voice
of Arnold, who was a great favourite
with every body in the houfe, fhe
called up the reft of the fervants, and
haftened down herfelf to open the
door.

This good gentlewoman, an ancient
fpinfter, who had been educated rather
above what is ufual in her ftation, was
amazed at feeing her mafter's nephew
appear, bearing between him and his
fervant a young woman, whofe uncommon beauty, notwithftanding the fituation fhe was in, gave the prudent houfekeeper the greateft alarm for the difcretion of her young favourite, Mr.
Arnold.

Arnold,

Arnold, in a hurried voice, and
fomewhat impatiently, anfwered the queftions fhe put to him; then entreating
her not to lofe a moment in talking, but
to attend the young lady to a bed, and
call up one of the maid fervants to affift
in procuring what might be neceffary to
her refrefhment and comfort, he flew
to his uncle, and, awakening him without fcruple, related in a few words
all that had happened—not difguifing
from him, that the young creature he
had fo providentially refcued was the
fame Turkifh beauty who had, about
fourteen months before, made fo deep
an impreffion on his heart, for which,
whenever they had fince met, his uncle
had rallied him without mercy.

Mr.

Mr. Winyard (fo was this worthy man
called) knew Charles Arnold too well
to fuppofe, that, under this ftory, he
concealed one of thofe frolics in which
young men fometimes indulge themfelves; he therefore rang for his houfekeeper, and gave her ftrift orders to
take the utmoft care of the young lady:
then bidding his nephew attend to his
own refrefhment and repofe (for he
looked extremely pale and fatigued), the
good man betook himfelf to recover his
fleep, and poftponed till the next morning the enquiry that fomewhat puzzled
him, by what ftrange chance a young
woman could be found in the middle of
the night in the power of three ruffians,
and in fuch a place.

He

254

He knew nothing of the wound Charles Arnold had received, or he would have been much more difquieted. Our hero was himfelf hardly fenfible of it, while any thing remained to be done in the fervice of Azemia : but as foon as he found her completely reftored to her recollection, and faw that fhe fhed tears of gratitude to heaven, and to him, as the immediate inftrument of her deliverance; and when he afterwards learned from the good houfekeeper that fhe was in bed, had taken fome refrefhment, and feemed quite calm and eafy, he began to feel that fome attention was neceffary to himfelf; he therefore took off his coat, and fummoned his faithful Bat to infpect his wound, which the coldnefs of the night had prevented from bleeding fo exceffively as it would otherwife have done. Bat,

Bat, who was no unfkilful furgeon, having attended as Doctor's fervant in two engagements, declared, after a flight examination, that he felt the bullet very plain on the other fide of the arm, through which it had paffed without touching the bone.—" Cut it out then," cried his mafter; " cut away, my good fellow, and let's have done with it, for I have no time to nurfe it; and if I fend for one of your regular-bred land doctors, they'll make a job of it perhaps."—Bat, with the moft perfect *fangfroid*, did as he was bid. Mrs. Gerkin, the houfekeeper, was then called, who, with a thoufand lack-a-days! and goodneffes, and oh! dears! applied fuch remedies to the wound as her limited knowledge of fuch matters made her believe

believe would the moft readily heal it; and Arnold, whofe life had within a few hours obtained in his eftimation a greater value than he had ever fet on it before, was prudent enough to forbear taking any thing ftronger than a little whey; after which he retired to the bed that was always referved for him, but not to fleep: the ftrange adventure of the night, and the joy of having faved his Azemia, prevented him much more than the pain of his wound from clofing his eyes till day-break; when, overcome with fatigue, he funk into temporary forgetfulnefs, but foon ftarted from it; and as a confufed remembrance of what had paffed recurred to him, he eagerly afked himfelf if it was not all

all a dream, till the pain his arm gave him affured him of its reality, and for doing fo the fevereft pain he could have endured would have been welcome.

CHAP.

CHAP. XII.

――――

" None but the Brave deferve the Fair."

――――

IMPATIENT to enquire after Azemia, on whom he felt that his happinefs more than ever depended, Arnold
was at her door at eight o'clock, and
learned from the woman who had fat by
her bed-fide, that fhe had for fome hours
flept calmly, and had awaked greatly
refrefhed. Made happy by fo favourable an account, Arnold then haftened
                                    to

to his uncle, whom he found already in
his garden. The good man, who had
never felt to excefs, and had long fince
ceafed to feel the paffions that now agitated the bofom of his nephew, was a
good deal difturbed by the vehemence
of his manner, as well as by the extreme
palenefs of his countenance. To make
him eafy as to the latter, Arnold told him
of his wound, affuring him at the fame
time it would not be of the leaft confequence. Mr. Winyard, who loved his
nephew more than any other perfon on
earth, though he had four children of
his own, was greatly alarmed, and infifted upon fending for the beft medical
advice in the neighbourhood. Arnold,
finding all oppofition in vain, confented,
and the more readily, becaufe he thought
it highly neceffary that the ftate of Aze-
                                    mia's

mia's health, after fo great a fhock as
fhe had received the preceding evening, fhould be attended to.

Azemia, however, had already recovered herfelf much more than could
have been expeded. Towards afternoon fhe was able to rife ; and being accommodated with a change of clothes by
the houfekeeper (for Mr. Winyard's
daughter was married, and had left him
fome years), fhe dreffed herfelf ; and her
native, untaught politenefs told her that
fhe could not too foon thank her prefent benefadors, nor inform her firft
benefadrefs of what was become of
her.

A meffage, defiring to fee them, brought
Arnold and his uncle to her. If he had
                                    thought

moft lovely in the drefs of her country,
when he firft faw her in the early bloom
of youthful beauty, fhe ftruck him now
as being even more beautiful and interefting. The ruftic fimplicity of drefs
fhe wore, (that of a grave old fervant),
her palenefs, her languor, and the
words, imperfed yet forcible, in which
fhe attempted to exprefs the grateful
feelings of her heart, were all fo many
charms that ferved to rivet more ftrongly
than ever the fetters that the enamoured
failor had worn from the firft day of
their meeting.

Eager to know by what ftrange accident fhe had been fo accompanied when
he fo fortunately met her in the foreft,
he defired Azemia to explain to him
what had happened to her fince they laft

256

met. Azemia endeavouring to collect
at once English and courage enough to
go through it, though she had herself but
little idea of the real causes that had in-
fluenced her various removals, Arnold
perfectly understood them from her art-
less description of the persons she had
been among. His indignation was particularly excited against the old Captain,
her first captor, who had, he thought, most
basely and ungenerously sold her to
some man of rank, by means of the
woman with whom she had been placed.
Her last escape, however, which he
thought might possibly be from the same
man who had thus at first purchased
her, shocked him still more, and made
him apprehensive for her future safety.
But towards Mrs. Blandford he felt the
liveliest gratitude; and upon Azemia's
mentioning

mentioning how much she wished that
excellent friend to know she was in
safety, Arnold, knowing she would be
perfectly secure in the protection of his
uncle, expressed an eager desire to go to
her himself. But this his uncle absolutely
forbade; for, though the distance across
the country was not more than thirty
miles, his recent wound made even so
short a journey extremely imprudent.

Honest Bat was, however, immediately dispatched, and directed to take
a man or two with him from the nearest
village, to the scene of their combat
with the poachers, and enquire into the
fate of the wretch whom they had left
wounded on the ground.

L 2　　　　No

No traces of him could be found;
and it seemed certain that, being less
severely hurt than they had imagined,
he had found means to loosen his hands,
and escape to some hiding-place amid
the thickets of the forest. Bat therefore, vowing vengeance against this felon
if ever he met with him again, proceeded to the house of Mrs. Blandford
with a letter from Charles Arnold.

That excellent woman had suffered
so much uneasiness during the three
weeks since Azemia had been unac-
countably betrayed from her protection,
that she was now too ill to have left her
home on any occasion less interesting
than that of seeing and having her lovely
ward restored to her.—She now he-
sitated

sitated only till the next day. On account of the danger of travelling late
the road she was to go, she set out
attended by two servants armed, besides
Bat, who, as he led the way through
the forest, pointed, with some degree of
triumph, to that part of it where he and
his master had put to flight and dis-
comfited three stouter men than themselves.

While at Cherbury (which was the
name of Mrs. Winyard's house), Azemia and Arnold waited the return of the
messenger sent to Mrs. Blandford. Arnold, delighted that Azemia could now
understand him, made the best use of
his time to express to her the sentiments he felt for her. Azemia, who
had never seen any human creatures
L 3　　　　that

that fhe loved, fince her refidence in
England, but Mrs. Blandford and Arnold, had no more notion of difguifing
her affection for one of them than for
the other: fhe therefore frankly told
him, that, attached to him both by
choice and by gratitude, fhe defired him
to be affured, that fhe wifhed for no
happier deftiny than to be united to
him according to the laws of his country, and to fhew him, through life, the
gratitude and tendernefs of her heart.

Her ignorance of the modes and
manners of a country where every circumftance differed fo materially from
her own, made her look forward to
their future union without any of thofe
anxieties that clouded the happinefs of
Charles Arnold.

Unfortunately

Unfortunately left dependent on his
mother, he had been but too well convinced, by many preceding inftances,
that his fucceffion to his father's property was not only diftant, but doubtful;
and all his fears as to his mother's intentions were turned into certainties,
when he learned, as he had lately done,
that the good lady had married an Irifh
Lieutenant of Dragoons, whom fhe had
met with at a card party, where he had
arrefted the attention of the company
by relating his dangers and exploits
during the laft campaign.

" She lov'd him for the dangers he had pafs'd;
" And he lov'd her that fhe did pity him."

As fhe did not think it neceffary to
communicate thefe her matrimonial intentions to her fon, he had only heard

L 4 of

of it, by chance, on coming on fhore
for a fortnight's leave of abfence; and
was haftening to confult his uncle on
this unpropitious intelligence, when he
fo happily met Azemia in the moment
of her extreme diftrefs.

What had then paffed drove every
thing out of his head; but now he was
at once under the painful neceffity of
relating to Mr. Wynward what had
happened, and to liften to the exclama-
tions he very warmly, though naturally
enough, uttered, on the folly, the in-
confequence, the cruelty of women.—
" And what," faid Charles Arnold to
himfelf, " what will he think of that
" of men, if I tell him that I intend, when I have not a penny on
earth but the income of a Lieutenant,
and

and about two hundred pounds in prize-
money, to marry Azemia? He will
never hear of it: yet to relinquifh her
I feel to be impoffible.—I dare not,
however, now venture to fpeak of it."

The arrival of Mrs. Blandford was a
comfort to Azemia beyond all fhe had
ever felt; and her benefactrefs, liften-
ing to a detail of all fhe had fuffered,
could never be enough thankful to
Heaven, that had fo miraculoufly directed her firft acquaintance in England
to her refcue in a moment of fuch extreme peril.

It was difficult for the coldeft-hearted
perfon to be long with Charles Arnold
without loving him. The fweetnefs of
his temper moderating the ardour of his

L 5 fpirits,

fpirits and the manly good-nature which marked his character, particularly endeared him to Mrs. Blandford; and after two or three days, when Azemia was fo far recovered as to make her protectrefs fuppofe fhe might undertake the journey home, Arnold at length acquired courage to tell her (what fhe was well aware of before) that he was diftractedly in love with Azemia, and wifhed, notwithftanding the flendernefs, or rather nothingnefs, of his fortune, to marry her.—Obferving that Mrs. Bland-ford liftened to him without any marks of difpleafure, he proceeded with more courage to reprefent that her beauty, her youth, and the fingular and unfor-tunate circumftance of her belonging to nobody, would occafion her to be continually expofed, even under Mrs.
Blandford's

Blandford's protection, to dangers of the fame nature as that fhe had already efcaped: in fhort, he pleaded fo well, and the generous nature of Mrs. Bland-ford fo well difpofed her to admit his arguments, that, after hearing what were his profpects (wherein he related fimply the truth), fhe told him, that though the principal part of her income was for life, fince fhe had now no children, fhe had a fum of about four thoufand pounds in the funds, which it had always been her intention to give to Azemia, fince fhe had no relations who either wanted or deferved it. This, therefore, fhe would immediately fettle upon her; and till preferment in his profeffion, or fome other lucky chance, gave him greater affluence, Azemia fhould continue to live with her, where he alfo fhould

L 6　　　　　always

always find a home whenever he was on fhore.

With a heart overflowing with joy and gratitude, Arnold then flew to his uncle, and eagerly communicated this unexpected profpect of happinefs.—Mr. Winyard, who was delighted with his vifitors, and already confidered Azemia as his daughter, told him, that, though he had three fons and a daughter of his own, they being all provided for, he had, thefe laft two or three years, been laying by a little fund for the nephew he loved.—" I have fcraped together about fifteen hundred pounds, my dear boy," faid he: " I give it you rather before my death than after, that I may be repaid by feeing you enjoy it. Marry the woman you love, be as good a lad

as

as you have hitherto been, and never doubt but you will do well."

Parties being thus agreed, no unne-ceffary delay was created; and in lefs than a month from her fortunate refcue Azemia returned to the houfe of Mrs. Blandford as the wife of Charles Ar-nold.—He was foon obliged to leave her, to return to the duties of his pro-feffion; in which he foon after fo emi-nently fignalized himfelf, that he paffed rapidly through the intermediate fteps, and obtained a fhip.

His frequent abfences were the only circumftances that gave an alloy to the happinefs he enjoyed with Azemia; and while Mrs. Blandford and Mr. Win-yard had the fatisfaction to contemplate,

as

as their own work, the felicity of these
deferving young people, I take leave of
my readers with this agreeable impreffion on their minds, and heartily hope
that many of them have met with fuch
good folks as thefe laft. I cannot fay I
have yet been fo fortunate myfelf; but
if I do not alarm my amiable young
countrymen too much by thus appearing in the character of a writing lady,
I do not defpair of fucceeding fo well
in my literary career as to make a
pretty little addition to my fortune;
with which (if it did not look too much
like advertifing for a hufband), I would
intimate, that I fhould be fuperlatively
bleffed to contribute to the happinefs
of fome tender, yet fenfible youth, who,
could be content with rural felicity in
an elegant cottage in Wales (for Bellegrove,

grove Priory is the inheritance of my
elder brother); which cottage, with the
profits of this work, I propofe to fit
up in the moft elegant ftyle—and
doubt not but, in time, it may humbly
emulate that of the juftly celebrated
Llangollen.

TO

TO THE

REVIEWERS OF ALL THE REVIEWS;

ALL THE MAGAZINES;

AND

ALL THE NEWSPAPERS.

GENTLEMEN,

FROM being in habits of reading for
many years your monthly lucubrations,
to an infirm female relation who formerly lived in the literary world, I have
ever fince I was thirteen been infpired
with the moft ardent ambition to fee myfelf fpoken of favourably in every one
of your pages, replete as they are with
difcriminating

difcriminating knowledge and refined tafte. I know, gentlemen, your chafte impartiality, and am well aware, that you never fuffer either the rank or fituation of an author to influence you: you never give undeferved praife to any work, becaufe you are perfonally acquainted with the writer; or fpeak well of a performance utterly contemptible, becaufe your Review is edited by the publifher of fuch performance. Party, which has fo much effect in this our beloved country, that it fometimes fets the father at enmity with his fon, and divides the brethren of the fame houfe, never, I know, induces any of you to make the fmalleft variation in your rectitude. In a word, gentlemen, as I know nothing fo deftructive to a young author as your difapprobation, fo I feel that your

your commendation is the acme of my afpiring hopes.

As a young artift ftudies with indefatigable perfeverance the moft celebrated models in fculpture or painting; fo I, to avoid the common error of becoming a Mannerift, and to attain the felicity of

" Tranfplanting one by one into my work
" Their feveral beauties, till I fhine like them,"

have ftudied with unwearied attention *all* the moft approved novels of this prefent as well as the paft day. You will not think me a plagiarift, when I declare that I have taken from the immortal Fielding, in one chapter, almoft word for word; and truft I am, at leaft, in that paffage, as *much* like him as *he* was
to

to Cervantes. If I have omitted the incomparable Richardfon, it was becaufe my narrow limits would not allow me to defcribe, with his exquifite minutenefs, the Cedar parlour, and Grandmama's great chair; nor could I, by any means, though my Heroine weeps now and then, continue to bring my Hero to wipe her eyes *with her own handkerchief*, and *bow* upon her hand.

To attain the mafculine force and ftrong colouring of the great Dramatift and Novelift of the prefent day, Mr. Cumberland, was quite beyond my flender attainment; but I have paid a due tribute to his tafte, fagacity, and knowledge of *womankind*. Thrown at a great diftance from the moft engaging models among my own fex, I yet look up with
more

more confidence to attain, at fome future day, a feat on that point of Parnaffus where they hold fuch eminent rank. In this hope I have fometimes affumed the ftately ftep with which the pupils of the Burney fchool follow in *folemn*, yet *inadequate* march, *their inimitable leader*. *This*, however, I have attempted in *ftyle* only. I have not feen enough of the world to fketch even in the way of a fcholar, fuch admirable characters. With lefs diffidence, though ftill with great humility, I have ventured with fhuddering feet into the World of Spirits, in modeft emulation of the foul-petrifying Ratcliffe—but, alas!

" Within that circle none dare walk but fhe."

Even if I *had* ever had the fortune to fee a *real natural ghoft*, I could never
defcribe

defcribe it with half the terrific appa-
ratus that fair Magician can conjure
up in fome dozen or two of pages, interfperfed with convents, arches, pillars,
cyprelfes, and banditti-bearing cliffs,
beetling over yawning and fepulchral
caverns. Her pictures,

" Dark as Pouffin, and as Salvator wild,"

can only be faintly copied;—to rival
them is impofſible.—I own I do *not*
feel quite fo difheartened, when I try at
making fomething like the luminous
page of Mrs. Mary Robinfon: I even
flatter myfelf that I have, in more than
one inflance, caught the *air of probability* fo remarkable in her delectable
hiftories, as well as her glowing defcription and applicable metaphors.

To

To Mrs. Gunning's Novels, and
thofe of her amiable daughter, I owe
all in thefe little volumes that pretends
to draw the characters and manners of
high life. With due humility and trepidation I have feized the mimic pencil: I feel that I cannot wield it with
their happy freedom and felicity—*faut
d'ufage.*

To be infenfible to the univerfal
knowledge of the accomplifhed *Italian
Traveller,* the attractive friend of *the
Leviathan of Literature,* would be to
want tafte enough to value the glory of
my fex. But the extenfive erudition of
that lady, grafping at all that literature
and fcience can give; her elegant defultory gaiety; her elaborate refearch;
her acute remarks; her erudite judgment;

ment; and, above all, her political candour, are as much above *my* praife as
fuperior to *my* attainment.

From the parterres of Mifs Lee,
Mrs. Inchbald, and Mrs. Smith, I have
culled here and there a flower; and I
fhould have enlarged my bouquet with
buds and bloffoms of other very agreeable writers, of whom I could make
(like Mr. Pratt) a very refpectable lift,
if I could have induced my publifher
to have allowed my work to be enlarged to what I intended it, viz. fix
very large volumes. He affured me
that it was too much for a *debut*; that
my head was not yet furnifhed enough
to fupply fo capital a work with ftory,
fcenery, incident, character, dialogue,
reflection, and all the various articles
neceffary

neceffary for an Epic in profe. I do
not, however, defpair (if you, Gentlemen, light me on my way up to the
fummit of Fame) of producing hereafter, *feven very large volumes* thickly
printed, duly interfperfed with pieces of
poetry, fuperior to what I have now
fown with extreme diffidence in the
prefent volumes—Volumes, Gentlemen,
which I offer you as my firft imitative
Effay—And (to finifh this fentence in
the *manner* of the *fweetly, the foftly fufceptible author of the meek and mild novel
of " Julia,")* I have, in this work, like
the mocking-bird of the American wildernefs, caught with emulative ambition the dulcet notes of the harmonious
chorifters around me: the attempt is
exhilarating to the youthful fancy; and
fhe who at once attends to admonition,

and attempts excellence, though she may never equal the delicious *trills* of the Poet's beloved nightingale, may yet soothe the ear of the candid listener; and, if she does not soar into the empyrean with the lark, may at least enliven the hawthorn with the finch, or the orchard with the linnet!

Ah! Gentlemen Reviewers! Critics! by what name soe'er ye love to be invoked, do not crush my ambition in the shell; let it unfold, and, like the little Nautilus, float buoyant on the sea of public favour; be your animating *puffs* extended as well to me as to others of my sister Historians—Suffer me to

" Enjoy the triumph, and partake the gale."

To change the metaphor—do not blight with ungenial gales these efforts of budding

ding genius—drive them not back into their *hybernacle*, by the chilling frosts of Criticisms. If I have faults, ye will tenderly hint at them—if I have *merit*, praise it; but I know you will, all of you, Gentlemen Reviewers by profession! for some of you are my particular friends, others are old acquaintances of my dear Grandmama, (who, good old Lady, used now and then to *do* an article herself, particularly in the British Critic)— To all of you I will send copies of my work.

Besides, ye are so tender-hearted, that ye will consider the tremors, the trembling breathless solicitude of a young beginner.—With what eagerness shall I, after my work is published, run over the list of " *Contents*" on your blue covers!

vers! and when, Oh! moment of trepidation! " Jenks's Azemia" meets my eye, with what impatience shall I tear open the important page on which the fate of my literary life depends!

Suffer me to enjoy, by anticipation, the praises I am sure you will give me.— Seven or eight months, perhaps, may first elapse, and my work may be in a third or fourth edition, before I shall read thus in

THE MONTHLY REVIEW.

" Modern Novelists may be said to possess " their principal share of excellence in an artful " construction of their *fables*. That a happy " combination of story is necessary we do not " attempt to deny, but we think many other " circumstances equally so: thus character is undoubtedly

" undoubtedly one of the first requisites. In this " we know not whether the fair Authoress of " Azemia has not failed. Captain Wapping- " shot is a mere sketch, caricatured on some of " the various Sea Characters ably delineated " by Mr. Cumberland; but, upon the whole, " this young lady's drawing is sufficiently " correct: the sentiments she puts into the " mouths of some of her characters are ap- " propriate and natural;—the poetry inter- " spersed in these little volumes is lively and " agreeable. We are sorry our limits do not " allow us to gratify our readers with a spe- " cimen."

———

Thank ye, Gentlemen, a thousand times: this discriminating, calm praise is just that temperate medium to rear a nursling of the Muses.

Now,

263

246   CRITICISMS ANTICIPATED.

Now, then, ye sterner, but not less
sagacious personages, who oblige the
world with

THE CRITICAL REVIEW.

" We are here presented with the first
" essay of a very young lady, who, it must be
" allowed, gives some proofs of not being
" totally destitute of genius. We disapprove,
" however, of the episode introduced at the
" end of the first volume: such tales are cal-
" culated to impress terror on young minds,
" and multiply, by imaginary evils, the real
" evils of life; whereas the business of the
" Novelist should be to recommend fortitude
" and prudent resolution. We think this
" lady's verse, in many instances, better than
" her prose :—the sentiments she expresses, as
" to the condition of the poor *under existing*
" *circumstances*, do honour to her heart. We
                                        " have

CRITICISMS ANTICIPATED.   247

" have no doubt but that a little more expe-
" rience in writing (which we think she will
" do well to endeavour at acquiring) will
" render this young lady's writing no con-
" temptible addition to the *first* rank of the
" *second class of Modern Novels :*—at present
" we cannot place her higher."

———

Gentlemen, I acknowledge ye have
dealt honourably by me, and I will take
your advice; I will acquire experience
as fast as possible.——Now for

~~~~

THE ANALYTICAL.

To be analysed, and so severely too!
Heavens! here *are* authors who would
almost prefer annihilation—but I am of
M 4   better

248   CRITICISMS ANTICIPATED.

better heart. Perhaps these Gentlemen
may have no objection to ghosts, or rather to the shadows of shades.—*Voyons.*

" This lady, who is, by her own account,
" a novice in the line of Novel-writing, seems
" to possess a small share of that uncommon
" talent for exhibiting, with picturesque
" touches of genius, the vague and horrid
" shapes which imagination bodies forth, that
" has rendered another lady so deservedly ce-
" lebrated. Her mode of telling the story
" of ' another Blue Beard,' reminded us,
" *faintly*, of Mrs. Ratcliffe. The nature of
" the work obliges us to digest improbabili-
" ties, of which there are several striking
" instances in the progress of the story, as well
" as in the before-mentioned episode. We
" cannot help wishing, in regard to the latter,
" that she had accounted for the supernatural
" appearances in the *natural* and *probable* man-
" ner of her justly-celebrated prototype. As it
                                        " is,

CRITICISMS ANTICIPATED.   249

" is, we are obliged to have recourse to an-
" cient legends, relative to *immaterialism*,
" which are *entirely exploded*, and which *we*
" *are sorry to see revived in any book of rational*
" *entertainment.*

" In general we approve of this writer's
" sentiments; of which the following is no
" unfavourable specimen."

Here follows a quotation.——And,
again :

" Of our Author's descriptive powers we
" shall take the scene in volume the first, im-
" mediately after the departure of her lover :
" of the Poetry, the lines from ' the For-
" ficularis to her Love,' are the best."

———

I make my courtesy to you also, Gentlemen, and then, with a sort of tender
                                    confidence,

confidence, as a daughter, or a ward, I addrefs myfelf to *you*, ye *Britifh Critics*—my dear Grandmama's old worthy friends. Methinks I fee ye, venerable arbiters of tafte! I fee ye of both fexes (as my friend, Lady Harriet, fays ye are of each, fome male and fome female, and truly I believe it)—I fee ye, in *deep divan*, fitting with folemnity on my work :—your fecretary takes his pen —a refpectable matron—for with you, as the age of chivalry ftill exifts, it is always " *Places aux Dames*"—I fee her, (her cap a little on one fide by accident, which adds to the fagacity of her countenance) and I hear her dictating thus :—

" We congratulate the Novel-reading world " on the acquifition of the fair Author of this pleafing

" pleafing work, as an amiable labourer in the " vineyard. She is, undoubtedly, a young " lady of the firft promife ; and, if our *illuf-* " *trious Premier* were not fuperior to all com- " parifon, as he is exalted above all praife, " we fhould have a flight degree of envy at his " being honoured with fuch a panegyrift : " but his *eximious* merit deferves that all the " talents of the Britifh nation fhould be united " in loud acclaim."

The venerable Lady here refigns her dictatorfhip to a Reverend Divine.

" If it were poffible to make any objection " to a work, the beauties of which would " 'ftrike us blind to its defects, were they " more numerous, we might *juft hint*, that " Mifs Jenks fhould have been more minute " in her defcription of Azemia's baptifm ; " whether *the fees* for that facred ceremony " were duly paid, *who were the fponfors*, and " in

" in what *parifh* the fair creature, *thus refcued* " *from Mahometifm, was regiftered :* the pow- " ers of our Authorefs would have fhone, in " defcribing *the dinner* given, and the emotions " of the beauteous convert *on that* occafion."

Here the man of the church refigns his place, and is fucceeded by a *Lay Brother*, who holds a comfortable finecure under Government.—This fage Reviewer obferves :

" If we were difpofed to cavil at any thing " in a book where there is fo much right, " and as it ought to be, *we* might hint that " there are *fome* paffages, which the evil dif- " pofed might conftrue into reflections on the " manners of the upper ranks of fociety—a " ftyle which, at this period, fhould by no " means be admitted by any lover of good " order ; nor can *we*, with all our efteem for " Mifs Jenks (with whofe honourable family " we

" we have long been connected), help advifin " her never to make the perfonages of he- " hiftory (even when fpeaking in character " retail common-place, we might almoft fay, " Jacobinical common-place, on the condi- " tion of the poor.—To our certain knowledge " *no ground for any fuch remark does exift*, or " *can exift*, under the prefent *happy, fortunate*, " *flourifhing*, and *glorious ftate of this country*.

" We were extremely amufed with the " Charades, though we could difcover *le mot* " of the *firft* only, which we had indeed before " heard accidentally.—We will not deprive " our readers of the pleafure of gueffing at the " fenfe of this very ingenious effort of elegant " female talent."

THE END.

BOOKS *just published by* SAMPSON LOW,
No. 7, BERWICK STREET, SOHO.

~~~~~

	£	s	d
MARCHMONT, a Novel, by CHAR-LOTTE SMITH, 4 Vols. –	0	16	0
Ditto on Large Paper, in neat Boards	1	0	0
FORESTERS, a Novel, by Mifs GUN-NING, 4 Vols. –	0	12	0
MATILDA AND ELIZABETH, a Novel, by the Authors of HONORIA SOMERVILLE, &c. 4 Vols. –	0	12	0
COLE's LIFE OF HUBERT –	0	5	0
Ditto, Second and Third Parts –	0	1	6
MILISTINA, a Novel, 2 Vols. –	0	6	0
TRAVELS IN NORTH AMERICA	0	3	0
PICTURE; OR, MY OWN CHOICE, a Play – – –	0	1	6
HINTS TO FRESH MEN, from a MEMBER of the UNIVERSITY of CAMBRIDGE, 2d Edit. –	0	1	0
GENTLEMAN's GUIDE IN MO-NEY NEGOCIATIONS, and BANKER'S, MERCHANT'S, and TRADES-MAN'S COUNTING-HOUSE ASSISTANT.	0	1	0
ABBOTT's AUCTION TABLES	0	1	0